Public Relations
Concepts, Practice and Critique

Public Relations
Concepts, Practice and Critique

Jacquie L'Etang

Los Angeles | London | New Delhi
Singapore | Washington DC

First published 2008

Reprinted 2012, 2013

SAGE Publications Ltd
1 Oliver's Yard
55 City Road
London EC1Y 1SP

SAGE Publications Inc.
2455 Teller Road
Thousand Oaks, California 91320

SAGE Publications India Pvt Ltd
B 1/I 1 Mohan Cooperative Industrial Area
Mathura Road
New Delhi 110 044

SAGE Publications Asia-Pacific Pte Ltd
3 Church Street
#10-04 Samsung Hub
Singapore 049483

Library of Congress Control Number Available

British Library Cataloguing in Publication data

A catalogue record for this book is available from the British
Library

ISBN 978-1-4129-3047-5
ISBN 978-1-4129-3048-2 (Pbk)

Typeset by C&M Digitals (P) Ltd, Chennai, India
Printed and bound in Great Britain by CPI Group (UK) Ltd, Croydon, CR0 4YY
Printed on paper from sustainable resources

Dedication

Deek

Do mh' eudail bho chridhe na h–Alba a thug spiorard
ùr, cùrsa ùr, neart ùr dhomh.

Contents

Preface

This book aims to provide a critical introduction to key concepts and issues in public relations, and to convey something of critical thinking processes. My approach was to define key concepts and root disciplines to show how insights derived from multiple perspectives can enlighten public relations (PR) theory and practice. Thus, this text provides a gateway to other disciplines. A key feature of the text is the 'Discipline Boxes' that summarize many of the theoretical roots of PR. I wanted to show different ways of thinking about PR and raise questions for students who will shape the occupation over the next thirty or so years.

I should acknowledge some tensions that I experienced between functionalism and criticism while writing this book. I wanted to write something helpful that would shed light on public relations work, the workplace and organizations. At the same time I was keen to try to encourage readers to see PR from alternative perspectives: from those of the journalist, the senior manager, the social critic, the media sociologist and the social theorist. I also wanted to highlight some of the criticisms of PR and the reasons for them.

Each chapter consists of definitional discussion and a review of key issues, especially focusing on those which are challenging or emerging or simply not given that much attention in most texts. In order to balance and contextualize the conceptual discussion, a number of short vignettes (in Boxes) have been selected either to illustrate points or to provide a focus for the reader's critique. The term 'vignettes' is chosen deliberately, since the term 'case study' has particular methodological requirements not achievable in a text of this type and length. Key concepts are listed alphabetically at the beginning of each chapter and appear emboldened where they are defined. Repeated key concepts are listed in chapters where relevant as a reminder for readers. Throughout the text some terms are italicised for emphasis. Also included are short sections of interview, largely taken from my own primary research, again with the intention to leaven theoretical description. The multi-layered nature of the text is designed to intrigue but also to facilitate re-reading at different levels. Fundamental to the book's approach are a series of reflective questions and exercises to help the reader develop his or her own views and to be aware of their own analytic processes. In this way, it is hoped that the book will develop the skills of reflexivity and critical thinking.

The choice of chapter topics requires some explanation: I chose to explore public relations through what I believe to be some core themes and issues for the field. Thus the book explores concepts of promotional culture, globalization and celebrity, in addition to more predictable topics, such as risk, image and impression management. I was also keen to share some zanier ideas from a variety of disciplines and explore their connection to PR. Where appropriate, I have indicated how some of the great thinkers of our age have reflected upon issues relevant to public relations practice: for example, Habermas, Bourdieu, Chomsky and Foucault. Each chapter also includes a short review of key sources and recommended readings.

Although chapters can be read in any order, the book does have a developmental feel to it. The early chapters start from the basics and the later chapters introduce more complex ideas and open-ended debates. Thus the book can be used at under- or postgraduate levels in a variety of teaching contexts. Less experienced students will appreciate the definitions of concepts and the boxed-out sections of quotes and vignettes, but at a later stage they may return to the book with a more sophisticated understanding, ready to engage with the many critical reflection boxes, questions and exercises that are presented throughout the text.

How did this project come about? During my university career to date I have found that in order to prepare teaching materials I have needed to read contributions from many different disciplines. Increasingly, I have felt that it was educationally important for students to understand original sources because I thought that sometimes concepts were 'lost in translation' or not articulated by some PR authors. Therefore, I wanted to share my own pleasures of intellectual promiscuity! And as someone who has got herself into a reasonable amount of academic trouble asking inconvenient questions, I thought it might be useful for PR practitioners and academics of the future to have access to a text which encouraged their curiosity and rebelliousness to combat the death knells of consensus and apathy.

I was tremendously aware, when writing this book, of the substantial volumes on offer that introduce the public relations student to the field. I see this book as a useful complement to such texts in offering a critical and eclectic view. I have tried to avoid an unduly polemic approach but to provide, nevertheless, a cornucopia of ideas. I was keen to try to write for a different audience and to write in the textbook genre, and I hope that my divergent approach to the topic creates some classroom debate and that students and lecturers alike find the book accessible, engaging, quirky and fun!

The book begins with an introduction to critical thinking and shows how this is relevant to public relations theory and practice. It also introduces a version of the public relations discipline's family tree!

Chapter 2 is the most substantial chapter in the book and covers a breadth of issues, including: basic definitions of public relations and public relations work in practice; public relations processes; public relations as a professionalizing occupation; and the connections between PR, 'psyops' and propaganda. In this chapter I critique public relations evaluation practice; the notion of 'strategy', and dominant interpretations of PR history.

Chapter 3 links the formation of organizational reputation to that of the individual, drawing on psychological, psychoanalytic and impression management sources and making reference to personal image consultancy.

Chapter 4 begins with a brief explanation and critique of the systems metaphor and its use in public relations theory to understand environments, issues and publics. The role of issues management as surveillance is explored in terms of societal implications. The chapter unpacks the concept of risk and the professionalization of risk knowledge and management in relation to PR. Finally, the chapter critically reviews debates on business ethics and corporate social responsibility.

Chapter 5 explains approaches to and definitions of 'public', 'stakeholder', 'public affairs', 'public sphere', 'political communication', 'lobbying' and 'public opinion', and the relevance of these concepts to PR. The work of critical PR academics is highlighted in relation to the process of defining publics and how this affects the relationship between an organization and its publics.

Chapter 6 provides a succinct summary of key media theories and explains their relevance to PR practice. It considers journalism as a professional practice and presents journalism and media studies accounts of PR practice with the intention of contributing to PR students' and practitioners' own self-understanding.

Chapter 7 reviews a challenging field that is subject to the forces of globalization, economics and politics. The main focus is on large-scale health campaigns and the contrast between social change approaches and those based on individual change. Key psychological terms are defined and the limits of psychology to underpin campaigns of persuasion noted.

Chapter 8 reviews managerial thought, highlighting those aspects which relate to public relations. Use is made of critical management theory to show how there is room for more critique within the field of public relations. The chapter includes discussion of management gurus and makes reference to the 'creative industries'.

Chapter 9 explains the field and its development, its relevance to PR and the challenges entailed in trying to analyze organizational thought. A critical post-modern view is presented of organizational culture and a range of issues is discussed, such as emotion and punishment. Finally, there is a critical review of the process of 'communication audit'.

Chapter 10 discusses the cultural model of public relations introduced by critical PR theorists. The chapter considers 'PR in everyday life' and how such an approach might add to the understanding of the role of PR in society and its impact upon the 'lifeworlds' of practitioners and publics. Finally, since celebrity is a feature of promotional culture, there is a brief review of this concept linked to a consideration of public relations as an occupational culture with its own stars and fame academy.

Chapter 11 reviews ideas about globalization and considers its relevance to PR theory and practice. The chapter suggests that PR has benefited from globalization as well as contributing to its development. The chapter includes a discussion of the diplomatic role played by public relations in a globalized world.

Chapter 12 begins with a selective review of the paradigms in the field, highlighting some key contributors to diversity. It lays out the dominant paradigm and explains a variety of different theoretical approaches to thinking about public relations. The chapter complements the first chapter in the book in its promotion of the critical paradigm.

What this book is not

This book does not teach the administrative logistics or *technic* of public relations, although it discusses its *praxis*.

Textbooks are usually seen as presenting standardized knowledge in the field as Magda Pieczka pointed out:

> A textbook is firmly associated with the establishment, in the sense of representing the views central to the field and containing an up-to-date body of knowledge. ... [It] serves as a medium through which the direction of the development of the field is reaffirmed, and also functions as a mechanism for self-perpetuation. (Pieczka, 1996b: 143; 2006c: 347)

I hope this 'textbook' will not only introduce readers to the PR establishment but also to its dis-establishment. Rock on!

Jacquie L'Etang
December 2006

Acknowledgements

Acknowledgements are to the following authors and publishers for permissions:

Pearson Education for their permission to use Figure 2.2.4 'Dance's helical model' on page 16 and Figure 2.4.2 'kite orientation model' on page 23 from their publication *Communication Models for the Study of Mass Communications* by D. McQuail and S. Windahl.

Sage for their permission to use Exhibit 7.1 checklist for Effective Strategic Public Affairs Management on page 99 in 'The Management of Public Affairs in the United Kingdom' by P. Harris in *The Handbook of Public Affairs* (2005) edited by P. Harris and C. Fleisher.

Sage for their permission to adapt Exhibit 3.1 'The circuit of culture showing the interrelationship of the five moments' in Curtin, P. and Gaither, T.K. (2007) *International Public Relations: negotiating culture, identity and power,* London, Sage page 38.

Thomson for their permission to use Exhibit 13.2 in Miller, D. 'The circuit of mass communication' in Miller, D. (1999) 'Mediating science: promotional strategies, media coverage, public belief and decision-making' in Scarlon, E. and Yates, S. (Eds) *Communicating Science: contexts and channels,* London, Routledge.

Lawrence Erlbaum Associates for their permission to use Figure 15.4 on page 291 and Figure 15.3 on page 289 in 'Public Relations Expertise' by M. Pieczka in *Public Relations: Critical Debates and Contemporary Practice* (2006) edited by J. L'Etang and M. Pieczka.

Dr Matt Hibberd, Director of the MSc in Public Relations (online), for his permission to allow me to use some of the materials I have written and developed for that degree, particularly for the Module *Public Health and Scientific Communication*.

Thanks also to Dr Layla Al Saqur, who allowed me to adapt one of the diagrams from her thesis and to refer to her work in social communication campaigns.

Every effort has been made to trace all copyright holders, but if any have been inadvertently overlooked the publishers will be pleased to make the necessary arrangement at the first opportunity.

It has been a lifetime ambition of mine to be published by Sage and I feel very fortunate to have been given that opportunity. I am grateful to the anonymous reviewers of the proposal whose points I have tried to take on board.

My work is the product of the education I've received, the people I've worked with, and my friends from many walks of life with whom I've debated issues bearing on communications in our contemporary world. I owe particular debts to my friends Magda Pieczka and Heike Puchan, with whom I worked very happily for 17 and 10 years respectively. They both shaped my ideas and teaching very greatly and they are therefore silent contributors to this volume (although they can't be held responsible for any weaknesses). In particular, Magda shaped my thinking on systems, public opinion, content analysis, media, professionalization, management gurus and much else besides. To my knowledge she was the first person to refer to PR practitioners as 'discourse workers' (Round table call, Stirling Media Research Institute, 1999) and to articulate the term 'Sociology of public relations' (Pieczka, 2006c: 32). My colleague Derek Hodge read and commented on the manuscript and has also helped me develop my ideas in relation to research and evaluation, media technology and content analysis. My colleague Jairo Lugo helped me greatly in relation to journalism education and media campaigns. I am also grateful to a former colleague, Professor Paul Jeffcutt, who introduced me to organizational symbolism and postmodern approaches to organizational analysis. The exercise at the beginning of Chapter 9 and the Indian fable are based on his teaching, which I observed in the early 1990s. In 2006 I was fortunate to attend a Sports Studies conference at Stirling during which Professor Coalter, Professor of Sports Policy at Stirling University, reviewed programmes of sport in developing countries. His comments on the formulation of objectives were clearly usefully applicable to public relations and I am indebted to his insights.

I am also grateful to my friend Maggie Magor, who bravely took on the task of copy-editing my first manuscript and indexing the work. As a professional media researcher her subject specialist knowledge was an added bonus, and her feedback went way beyond copy-editing. Karen Forrest did a superb job with the diagrams from some spectacularly horrid scribbles.

Further afield, I have learnt much from David McKie, Jordi Xifra, Kay Weaver, Jesper Falkheimer and Julia Jahansoozi. I've been lucky to teach on the MSc in Public Relations at the University of Stirling since 1990 and I've gained many insights from full-time and online students; from our wonderful alumni who keep in touch; and from the doctoral students I've been privileged to supervise and examine. My friend Penny Shone from Citigroup, Singapore, has been invaluable in helping me to understand the intricacies of corporate social responsibility practice as has Katie Meech, and I have learnt a huge amount about management from Andy McGuigan and Fiona Somerville. Matt Hibberd has been a wonderfully positive and supportive colleague over the past few years. For those who have kept me grounded: thanks to Fiona and Robert Somerville, Cathy Freeborn, the Fulton family, and, from Stirling Triathlon Club: Fi Moffat, Catriona Phin, Jenny Cuthill, Sarah Gleave, and Andy McGuigan. Last but not least, an incalculable debt to my fiancé, Deek Mepham, without whom this book would probably never have been written.

Jacquie L'Etang
Stirling Media Research Institute
December 2006

Introduction: Critical Thinking and Interdisciplinary Perspectives

BEFORE YOU READ A SINGLE WORD...

Take a pen and write down your response to the following:

- What should a public relations text do and why?
- What do you want to learn?
- How do you want to change?
- What would you like to change about the world?
- Why are you interested in public relations?

Keep your answers somewhere safe. (You could set them up as a blog.) Do not change them. But do add to them or record any changes in perspective as this happens. This is a form of *research diary* in which you keep reflections and personal observations and record change. Here you are researching and observing yourself!

Key concepts

Assumptions	Functionalism
Critical theory	Interdisciplinary
Critical thinking	Paradigm
Dominant paradigm	Reflexivity

What's this book about and where is it coming from?

This is a textbook with a twist! It aims to achieve two objectives: to introduce key concepts in public relations using a wide range of interdisciplinary sources and to stimulate reflexive and critical thinking which can inform academic and professional work in the field.

The book was inspired by the desire to share some alternative perspectives with student readers and by the ambition to write a text which not only challenged assumptions, but showed how and why it is important for public relations practitioners to do so. Challenging received truths has long been seen as important to public relations practitioners in the workplace. See Box 1.1 for examples.

Box 1.1 Practitioners' perspectives on challenging norms

'Resourceful, direct and prepared to challenge the status quo.' (Peter Brooker, *PRWeek*, 30 June 2006)

'A driving force, not afraid to challenge change.' (James Lundie, *PRWeek*, 30 June 2006)

'Energy, presence, sensibility, a broad orientation, and, most of all, 'guts' is what a practitioner needs to succeed'. (Top head-hunter from the Netherlands) (van Ruler, 2005: 159–173)

'What I look for [when I'm recruiting] is: have they got critical abilities? Have they got a critical mind? Are they persuasive in writing and oral communication? Can they bring people along with them? Thirdly, integrity, and here I look for evidence that they're likely to have personal courage – that is to take their hat off the peg and to stand up and talk for themselves, or get the hell out of it – have they got real courage?' (Interview, senior practitioner, 1998)

'Part of my job here is if there are problems of morale or if people, however senior, are not doing their jobs particularly well, for example if a board director doesn't seem to be communicating and inspiring, then it's up to me to tell the very senior management that I'm not actively happy with this. That's often quite difficult but someone has to do it because organizations are constantly changing organisms and if they don't understand what's driving change, whether it's good or bad – they won't go forward.' (Interview, senior practitioner, 1998)

A key ideal for public relations consultants is that if asked to work on an account of which they did not approve, they should act according to their ethical principles and leave. Why is this so important for public relations? One might suggest that precisely because PR as an occupation has been critiqued by the British media since the 1950s, and apparently has a poor reputation in the UK, it is all the more important for individual practitioners publicly to espouse integrity and appear as authentic and truthful as possible in order to establish trust.

Book aims

By the end of this book readers should be able to:

- describe, discuss and critique theoretical and applied (practical) approaches to public relations at campaign, societal and global levels
- apply the key theoretical concepts that are required to construct and deconstruct public relations practice
- understand the reasons for the emergence and growth of public relations in a variety of cultural contexts
- understand how public relations has emerged as a discipline, its conceptual roots and main paradigms
- apply critical thinking to concepts and cases

Does this book have an agenda?

Yes, this book is written to encourage you to explore diverse perspectives and to reflect critically on your own opinions. This book is also written from a particular point of view: it is critical, and written within the European context from the periphery of Great Britain (Scotland). As with my other articles and books, it has been written partly in response to those from the dominant paradigm. In this book I explain something of that debate and how academics in public relations approach the subject from different perspectives. I write within the critical tradition and this approach is explained later in this opening chapter. As you encounter the various arguments and read other books alongside this one, you should start to develop a sense of your own opinions, where you sit in relation to debates and why.

CHAPTER AIMS

On completion of this chapter you will be able to:

- understand the benefits of 'critical thinking' and be able to apply the concept to texts and case studies
- define critical theory
- understand and explain the concept of 'paradigm'
- notice assumptions that exist in writing and arguments in texts or broadcast media
- explain why critical thinking is important in public relations

Chapter contents

The chapter begins by defining critical thinking and critical theory before explaining how to develop critical thinking skills. This is followed by a short reflection on the nature of public relations as an academic subject and questions that are raised as to its status. The notion of 'paradigm' is then introduced in the context of public relations concepts and research, and subsequently linked to the notion of assumptions that underpin arguments and the ways in which we can uncover these so as to better determine the motivation that lies behind a piece of communication, whether academic, professional or journalistic.

Critical thinking

There are at least two rather different ways of conceiving **critical thinking**. The first is to define such work as emanating from critical theory, which emerged in the 1920s from Western Marxism which highlighted maldistribution of power and sought to change society. Work in this tradition:

- challenges existing assumptions
- analyzes and critiques policy or practice
- alters boundaries of or between fields and thus changes the agenda by introducing new topics or approaches or ways of thinking about a field

Critical theory (**CT**) particularly focuses on power, its distribution and elucidating the structures and processes which limit human potential. Critical theorists tend to write with a view to highlighting unfair practices in order to change society (L'Etang, 2005).

Another way of thinking about critical approaches is in terms of developing intellectual skills to tackle such work. Critical work assesses ideas and arguments, working through the pros and cons. It is critical, but not necessarily negative – better to think of it as the surgeon's rather than the assassin's knife.

But how should one start? Where to begin? In fact a good start is to question our own beliefs and motivations and being clear about our own assumptions and biases. Only then are we in a position to ask:

- Does this author present their view as one of several options, as factual information or as morally right?
- Is the author fair or do they reveal a bias? If they reveal a bias, are they open about this and do they explain their reasoning for this position? (Ruggiero, 1996b: 6)
- How does this relate to my own views – how can I or should I accommodate this new information? (Paul and Elder, 2004: 1)

Developing critical thinking skills for reading and writing

Drawing on Paul and Elder (2004) and Cottrell (2005), it is useful to ask:

- Is the purpose clear?
- What is the scope of the main and subsidiary questions (aim and objectives)?
- What assumptions are made – are they implicit or explicit?
- What sorts of arguments are used and how much evidence is presented with them?
- Are alternative views presented or is a reason stated for their exclusion? (Cottrell, 2005)

Critical thinking analyzes arguments and 'unpicks' concepts. It often looks at 'the other side of the coin' or plays 'devil's advocate' to test an argument. Sometimes it will take a minority or unpopular view, criticizing those in power or exposing unfair practice.

In short, as Cottrell (2005) pointed out, critical thinking demands:

- a healthy scepticism
- patience to work through someone else's argument
- being open-minded
- being cautious with personal emotional responses such as anger, frustration and anxiety
- juggling a range of ideas for purposes of comparison
- supporting arguments with evidence and experiences from 'the real world'.

Interdisciplinary perspectives

You, as a PR student, may have been asked by family or friends: 'How can you study that? It's not a proper subject – why don't you study psychology or sociology?'

Such questions challenge the notion of public relations as a legitimate subject to study. Yet subjects such as psychology and sociology started in the same way, borrowing concepts from other areas to build new disciplines. For example, psychology evolved in the nineteenth century from the disciplines of ethology, physics, statistics and philosophy. And sociology emerged as a 'scientific study of collective human behaviour', the consequence of nineteenth-century philosophers, faced with the massive upheaval of the Industrial Revolution, asking questions about how society evolved (Ruggiero, 1996: 1). Key ideas which emerged to explain developments included: natural progression; survival of the fittest; conflict; and consensus. These assumptions also influence the way that different historians explain the emergence of public relations in various cultures. So in a way, public relations can be seen as a form of sociology even though *sociology of public relations* is a term barely heard. (Pieczka, 2006c: 328–329)

In the 1960s, sociology was seen as a trendy, radical and a rather subversive discipline that suggested particular political allegiances. Now it is established as part of the academic elite and has spawned other sub-disciplines and fields such as *media studies* and *sociology of the professions* (something to which I'll return later). So disciplines emerge and develop and atrophy and die over time according to the current *zeitgeist* and fashions of the day. These processes may be influenced by funding and resources, so it is not just a question of the best ideas lasting, but of national policy and educational politics in funding councils and universities. Those in established disciplines do not want to see resources draining away into newer areas. Academic disciplines operate as a system of hierarchies (a class system in effect). They distinguish themselves partly through the efforts of individual academics who may develop 'guru' status either as 'media dons' or as behind-the-scenes experts, called upon to advise outside bodies such as think tanks or governmental committees. For such work they are rewarded by membership of renowned societies such as the Royal Society of Arts. Academic disciplines are also judged by the production and quality of journals in relation to those in more traditional fields (and there is a distinct pecking order!) and internally to each discipline. There is nothing particularly 'natural' about current relationships between disciplines: they are arbitrary and based on power. Therefore, the relationship between disciplines is both intellectual and political. In inter-disciplinary work, concepts are borrowed and shared between related disciplines to broaden understanding and to develop theory. Disciplines may be seen as families sharing gene pools. Inter-disciplinary work draws on a mixture of sources, for example PR has drawn on psychological concepts (persuasion) and methods, ethical concepts (from moral philosophy), and sociological concepts (power and gender). It is also possible to draw together different disciplines (tourism, religious studies, sports studies) in a creative way to bring about new understandings on all sides. Inter-disciplinary thinking draws upon a wide range of subjects to try to understand a problem. It is central to public relations education and to its practitioners who need to engage with multiple interested parties, perspectives and relationships.

Box 1.2   Academic journals publishing articles on public relations

Specialist journals
Journal of Public Relations Research (www.erlbaum.com/)
International Journal of Strategic Communication (www.erlbaum.com/)
Public Relations Review (www.elsevier.com/)
Corporate Communications: An International Journal (www.emeraldinsight.com/info/journals/ccji/ccij.jsp)

(Continued)

Journal of Communication Management (www.emeraldinsight.com/info/journals/jcom/jcom.jsp)
PRism (praxis.massey.ac.nz/prism_on-line_journal.html)
Non-specialist journals publishing articles on public relations
Media, Culture & Society (msc.sagepub.com)
European Journal of Communication (ejc.sagepub.com)
Australian Journal of Communication (www.anzca.net/)
Asian Journal of Communication (www.tandf.co.uk/journals/titles)
British Journalism Review (www.bjr.org.uk)
Journalism Studies (www.tandf.co.uk/journals/titles)

At present public relations is an emergent discipline with porous boundaries to a range of other disciplines: marketing, management, organization studies, communications, journalism, media studies. All of these have their own journals, paradigms, concepts, theories, 'gurus' – and a sense of what it means to do good work in the field.

Disciplines have boundaries although these are often subject to negotiation and realignment. Throughout this text, key disciplines of importance for public relations are highlighted in 'Discipline boxes' (but nothing to do with punishment!).

It is because public relations cuts across these disciplines that it is important to read beyond public relations books and journals and think more broadly about problems. For example, can we really think properly about 'strategy' without reading some sources in *strategic studies*, the host field? Can we talk about 'persuasion' without reading *psychology* and *political science*? Can we learn about techniques of media relations without studying research into media processes and considering the role of media in society (*sociology of the media* or *media sociology*)? There is a danger that public relations academics and students can be too introspective or 'navelgazing', working convergently within rigid railway grooves rather than wandering freely and creatively in search of useful insights. As Curtin and Gaither pointed out, 'there's much for public relations to learn about itself by stepping outside of comfort zones and its traditional knowledge base, provided largely by Western scholars and global public relations enterprises' (Curtin and Gaither, 2007: 261).

Thinking divergently can help our creativity (a facility much prized in public relations) by forcing the pathways in our brains to work in unusual ways. Working in different areas is challenging, hard but rewarding. Public relations students need to be curious and intellectually brave, not just clever!

Public relations has a potentially complicated family tree and one version of this is depicted in Figure 1.1.

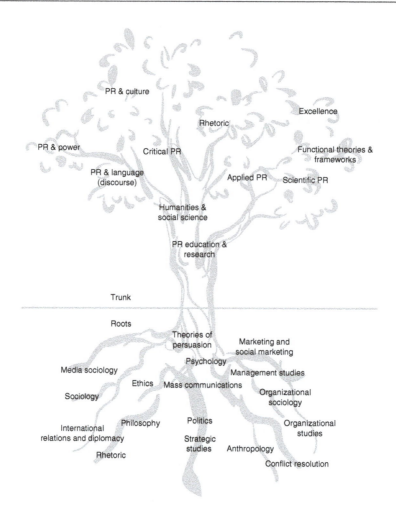

PR & culture

Excellence

Rhetoric

PR & power

Critical PR

Functional theories &
frameworks

PR & language
(discourse)

Applied PR

Scientific PR

Humanities &
social science

PR education &
research

Trunk

Roots

Theories of
persuasion

Marketing and
social marketing

Psychology

Media sociology

Management studies

Ethics   Mass communications

Sociology

Organizational
sociology

International
relations and diplomacy

Philosophy

Politics

Organizational
studies

Strategic
studies

Anthropology

Rhetoric

Conflict resolution

Figure 1.1 PR's family tree

Studying public relations usually means picking up a completely new subject. This can be scary as one needs to adapt to a new discipline's language and conventions, which may be quite different from the subjects in which we have first been educated (either at school or at first degree level). If the first subject degree is communications or marketing, there is less work to be done (though you may have to work harder to challenge your assumptions). But if the first degree is science or maths or engineering, it is much harder – it can take some weeks to adapt from the particular rigour and ways of working in formal science to the apparently (and only apparently) 'wishy-washy' approach in social science. Conversely, those from humanities (languages, history) may find the social science emphasis on spelling out 'methodology' in articles completely unnecessary if not alien. In my own case (I studied for an MSc in Public Relations in 1988/1989) I had a background in history (BA American and English history; MA Commonwealth history) and remember struggling with some management terminology (especially 'models'). While I was used to narrative being presented in a discursive linear fashion, I was unused to breaking down workaday actions into boxes and arrows.

This shows that different disciplines inculcate their own ways of thinking and seeing the world (paradigms) as well as introducing different (not better or worse, just different) points of view. We are therefore comfortable in one intellectual space (the familiar) and out of our comfort zones elsewhere. It is perhaps more positive to think of ways in which we can explore our 'development zone', where we can achieve intellectual growth and broader perspectives by listening to and understanding views that are not our own. This applies as much to public relations practice as is does to academic debate (and life).

What is a paradigm?

A **paradigm** is a worldview that frames and influences our approach to everything we see. It is like a lens which may be tinted light brown or blue. In some ways it is a sense-making tool which enables us to interpret information. Examples of paradigms include vegetarianism, astrology, capitalism, Marxism, fascism, traditional religious systems, new religious movements, sects, feminism, ethnicities, qualitative research paradigm, quantitative research paradigm. A paradigm comprises taken-for-granted values, assumptions and approaches to the world. A paradigm in the academic context will be apparent by reference to the same names or concepts which will be presented as basic knowledge of a field, that does not require to be explained in detail each time or defended.

'The dominant paradigm'

Within a specific discipline the **dominant paradigm** is that which is the most popular or majority approach to the subject. The dominant paradigm in a field comprises the framework and methodologies that guide most research in the field and which are regarded as the most important ideas. Ultimately these ideas become ingrained into a set of formal beliefs about what the discipline stands for. The dominant paradigm is supported by sets of assumptions or taken-for-granted beliefs, which may lead to blinkered thinking. Even if there are different perspectives, they are still likely to refer extensively to the dominant ideas as a reference point or as a starting point for disagreement. Thus alternative paradigms define themselves in relation to the dominant paradigm. The dominant paradigm shapes debates to such an extent that other points of view are drowned out or not heard. What is wrong with this? Well, as Magda Pieczka rather famously remarked in her critique of the use of systems theory and functionalism in public relations:

> Well, what is wrong with the Ten Commandments? Only that they make perfect and profound sense to the converted, but appear problematic to those who operate outside them. ... There is nothing wrong with choosing one [set of] views over another, as long as it is clear that as a result of the choice certain questions do not get asked. These might be questions about power and knowledge or power and language; or they might be questions about the position of the public relations practitioners and researchers, within the scheme of things: is knowledge independent of the one who knows? Could one not see society as organized not around consensus, but struggle. (Pieczka, 1996b: 154, 156; Pieczka, 2006c: 355)

The dominant paradigm has focussed on functional issues such as effectiveness, excellence, methods, evaluation, professionalism, PR roles and status. It has been criticized for its functionalism by a range of non-US scholars (Pieczka, L'Etang, Motion, Leitch, Roper, Weaver, McKie).

Functionalism and PR

Functionalism has been defined as 'any view which analyses something in terms of how it functions, and especially in terms of its causes and effects' (Lacey, 1976: 83). It emerged from research in anthropology and sociology that sought to understand explicit and implicit societal practices, for example a Hopi rain dance may also be seen as a way of promoting social cohesion (Giddens, 1989: 697). Functionalism 'views societies as integrated, harmonious, cohesive "wholes" or "social systems", where all parts ideally function to maintain equilibrium, consensus and social order' (O'Sullivan, 1994: 124).

A functionalist approach focuses on elements such as PR or the media which can assist societies or organizations to function as integrated sub-systems by maintaining equilibrium or consensus (O'Sullivan, 1994: 124). Functionalism appears to have first been linked to PR by German scholars who tried to understand PR as a societal as well as organizational function that could produce consensus, and the following discussion is heavily based on Heike Puchan's excellent review of the German literature (Puchan, 2006). Possibly the first was the German author Albert Oeckl who wrote in his *Handbook of Public Relations*, published in 1964, that, 'The decisive role for public relations is: public relations is two-way communication, it is information flow in both directions, it is dialogue. Hence, it has ... to achieve its threefold task: information, adaptation and integration' (Oeckl, 1976: 305 cited in Puchan, 2006: 117). Likewise, Carl Hundhausen, from the same era, argued that the most important goal for public relations was the achievement of 'harmony' through adaptation (Puchan, 2006: 117). Subsequently, in the 1970s, Professor Franz Ronneberger was one of the first academics to develop a comprehensive society-orientated theoretical approach to public relations arguing that PR negotiates competing interests (Puchan, 2006: 116–117). Together with Professor Manfred Ruhl, Ronneberger developed 'the first comprehensive analysis of public relations within the context of its societal function' (Puchan, 2006: 119). Use of systems theory, on which much of this functionalism was based (see Chapter 4 pp. 71–75 for discussion of systems theory) was also made by Ragnwolf Knorr in 1984, Ulrich Saxer in 1991 and Werner Faulstich and Anna Theis in 1992 (ibid).

Functionalism is an attractive ideology but it does appear to assume a consensual view can emerge and prevail. This raises questions such as: whose views dominate, how, and why? What some might see as 'functional' might be 'dysfunctional' for others. This dualism in itself might stimulate conflict rather than consensus.

This book is written within the *critical paradigm* in public relations, which comprises a small group of scholars mostly outwith the USA. The critical paradigm has partly positioned itself against what its authors have seen as the 'dominant paradigm', which consists of the bulk of the work published making extensive reference to systems theory, 'the four models', 'boundary spanning', and associated terminology. To give one example, many non-US texts present a model of public relations development and typology based on US history and culture as though the American experience can sensibly describe and explain events in non-US settings (L'Etang, 2004: 9–10).

The dominant paradigm in public relations has tried to build theory in a coherent way that is useful (*functional*) for practitioners. While there is nothing wrong with that, there are other ways of exploring and understanding public relations practice. Over the past decade there have been more academics exploring alternative approaches to public relations concerned with language, rhetoric, critique of various types. In Box 1.3 is an example of an open acknowledgement of *paradigm shift* and debate in public relations that appeared in *Public Relations Review* in 2004, edited by two important academics from The New Zealand School, Professor David McKie and Debashish Munshi.

Box 1.3   Paradigm shift in PR?

Call for Papers

Edge-happening maps: paradigm movement for public relations

Recent research suggests that significant trends can be identified early by exploring happenings at peripheral points. This special issue seeks to chart such explorations at the edge. This issue looks to the margins for signs of change, beyond the widely

(Continued)

(Continued)

accepted current theories. As New Zealand educators we exist on an economic, geographical, political, and population perimeter compared with the demographic and disciplinary centres of Europe and the USA.

Accordingly, we particularly welcome contributions from geo-political peripheries and encourage researchers working on, for example, public relations history after the four models, specific historical accounts of regions and nations (which may diverge from the evolution of public relations in the US), untried or underutilized theoretical approaches, research influenced by scientific advances and thought and methodological innovations.

In order to chart diverse 'edge happenings', we invite contributions that may range from distinctive practice-informed theory and theoretically-informed practice, through different kinds of field research and iconoclastic speculation, to unexpected theory, expansive visions, and beyond.

Source: McKie and Munshi, *Public Relations Review*, 30(3) 2004: 243

The 'Call for Papers' shown in Box 1.3 also throws up another important aspect of the dominant paradigm in public relations, which is that it has tended to carry out quantitative rather than qualitative research. The 'Call for Papers' explicitly seeks alternative methods and perspectives which challenge the very nature of knowledge that is put forward by what is perceived as 'the dominant paradigm'.

When alternative ideas about public relations practice and the PR *research agenda* began to be articulated in the mid-1990s, those from the dominant paradigm were forced to defend their views and take account of different interpretations. For example:

> Whenever a theory becomes as ubiquitous as the models of public relations have become, it also becomes the target of criticism by scholars who want to defend or develop competing theories. Therefore it is not surprising that the models have become the target of several critics. ... The misinterpretations of my idea ... suggest that I have not always been successful. (Grunig, 2001: 18, 27)

CRITICAL REFLECTION

Read the quote above and consider:

- What do we learn about the state of the field of PR?
- What do we learn about the author?

Although many academics seek to 'build PR theory' one might wish to question the existence of such. The very term 'PR theory' almost seems to imply there could or should be a single framework. This book suggests that utilizing inter-disciplinary approaches can contribute multiple perspectives to PR, some applied, some conceptual, some normative.

In summary, public relations is a field in which some alternative perspectives are beginning to be explored. This makes it a very exciting time to be studying public relations.

Assumptions, reflexivity and motives

Experts in critical thinking, such as Ruggiero (1996b), Paul and Elder (2004) and Cottrell (2005), highlight the importance of understanding assumptions, reflex-ivity and motives. As they point out, **assumptions** are taken-for-granted beliefs about the way the world is, an idea of the 'natural order', whether it is applied to international relationships, developing or developed countries, economic and political systems, social relationships and class systems. Reflexivity is a self-questioning and transparent form of writing in which the author acknowledges her presence, her interests and experiences. Assumptions are beliefs that seem so obvious that we rarely question them and can scarcely articulate them. Assumptions shape the 'knowledge' we think we have and they shape what we know, how we speak, write and use rhetoric to ensure a comfortable consis-tency. They are interesting for academics and important to public relations practitioners because by digging deeper and seeking what lies behind state-ments we can understand more fully motivations, orientations, values, and therefore put arguments into a broader context. In public relations practice this process can help us to understand better organizational stakeholders, senior management and the media.

In writing, whether it is an academic essay, a piece of journalism or promo-tional writing, the challenge is to be aware of one's assumptions, which are the consequence of life experience and education, and to be transparent about our personal positioning in relation to other writers, thinkers and disciplines. Conventionally, in formal writing, whether academic or organizational, there may be stringent attempts to disguise agendas that may arise from assump-tions and to present argument or opinion as rational, scientific and 'objective'. Why is this? Because contemporary culture is heavily influenced by rational-ism and science. Acknowledging subjectivity is a practice that does indeed occur in social science within the qualitative paradigm, which stresses that all research is value-laden, that 'reality' is socially constructed and interpreted by readers, and where there is an interest seeking out *discourses* that shape our understanding. Such acknowledgement is termed **reflexivity** and has the potential to bestow transparency. These rather philosophical issues show exactly why it is difficult for public relations academics or practitioners to claim that they present 'the' truth. Anne Surma, academic, editor and consultant, eloquently raised some key issues in her book *Public and Professional Writing*:

> Is writing in the public domain inevitably about impersonality and detachment? Are writing subjects to be (always) absent as well as (sometimes) invisible when writing in a professional capacity? And if we aren't able to talk to ourselves when writing as professionals, how do we write to others meaningfully? The above questions challenge a common assumption about the conventions of professional writing. (Surma, 2005: 15)

Surma argues that public relations writing can be peculiarly difficult because the PR practitioner will often have to blend many voices into a fictional person or identity – the organization. For example, annual reports and corporate social responsibility reports are typically contributed to by many sources from within the organization, edited and re-written by the PR department and also include collages of interviews and personal perspectives. Combining and juxtaposing material in this way can pose problems of authenticity and believability in the text – problems that the public relations writer is supposed to overcome. Audiences may be wary of such public writing, as Anne Surma points out: 'It isn't surprising that many readers approach corporate and public texts with a sense of cynicism and distrust. Readers recognize self-serving rhetoric' (Surma, 2005: 3). Public relations practice, especially in entry-level jobs, consists of a great deal of writing and editing, often of texts for media consumption. It can be easy to assume that texts are read at 'face' value. But, as Surma's argument makes clear, there are many possible 'faces' and many possible motives behind them. Likewise, there are multiple 'readings' or interpretations of any one text, each of which depends on the worldview (paradigm), assumptions, beliefs and motivations of the reader or editor.

Techniques for identifying assumptions

What questions should be asked about a piece of academic or professional (workplace) writing? Here are some suggestions:

- What does this author say about themselves? What is included or excluded? Are they written out of the book entirely?
- Is it possible to identify (for example) political allegiances? How are these made apparent? Openly? Or do they emerge subtly? Can one read between the lines?
- How satisfied is the author with the status quo?

Exercise

Apply the questions above to Box 1.3.

Apply critical thinking now!

Taking on board the suggested strategies of thought, read back over this opening chapter and also the preface. How successful have I been in explaining my approach? Have I, as author, been sufficiently reflexive? How legitimate does the approach taken in this chapter seem, and why?

In conclusion

This chapter has reviewed some key ideas about critical thinking and its importance for public relations, both academically and in practice. It has introduced the notion of paradigm and the importance for all who study public relations being self-aware of their assumptions and approach to public relations ideas and practice.

REVIEW

Return to the questions asked of you at the beginning of the chapter and consider:

- What do you think now about the questions?
- Did the chapter work for you and if not, why not?
- Has it changed anything about the way you think? If so, what, and were you persuaded or did you make up your own mind?

Again, write down your responses and keep your log, blog or diary to hand.

RECOMMENDED READING

An excellent book on critical thinking is Cottrell (2005). There is also a very useful pocket guide (Paul and Elder, 2004) produced by the Foundation for Critical Thinking (www.criticalthinking.org). The first public relations book which contained 'critical' in its title was Heath and Toth (1992). This classic was a landmark work which I found immensely inspiring. It opened a lot of doors for me, and helped me to think about public relations as a rhetorical practice. Through reading this book and engaging with its arguments and perspectives, I began to develop my own personal take on public relations.

Public Relations: Defining the Discipline and the Practice

2

BEFORE YOU READ A SINGLE WORD...

- What do you think public relations is?
- Where have you drawn your ideas from?
- If you are thinking of pursuing a career in public relations, explain why.

Key concepts

Evaluation	Public
Linearity	Public opinion
Othering	Public relations
Professionalism	Public sphere
Propaganda	Strategic PR
Psyops	System of knowledge

Introduction

This chapter will give you a good understanding of the function and purpose of public relations, the key processes that are utilized in practising public relations and a broader understanding of the public relations occupation in society. The chapter combines **functional** and **critical** approaches (Table 2.1).

Table 2.1   Functional and critical approaches in public relations: key questions

Functional questions	Critical questions
• How can I measure media content? • How can I evaluate this PR campaign? • Which psychological models could be used to structure a persuasive campaign?	• Does PR impede or assist democracy? • Is public relations another term for propaganda? • Is public relations a profession?

CHAPTER AIMS

On completion of this chapter you should be able to:

- understand aspects of the diverse nature of PR work and the complex role of PR in society
- understand the connection between the study of PR and the discipline of communications
- describe key PR processes and language used in practice to describe PR work
- critique a 'checklist' approach to PR
- apply key principles to PR evaluation
- debate the connections between PR and propaganda and issues that arise from this for the PR discipline and practice
- describe various possible reasons for the evolution of PR in a variety of cultural contexts
- describe how sociology can help us to understand the PR occupation more fully.

Public relations: its purpose, role and scope

If we think about the term 'public relations', we can understand a great deal about the activity by analyzing the term and pursuing a number of readings. On the one hand, it clearly suggests ongoing relationships that are open to view – they are 'public'. Alternatively, **public** may suggest a particular group or 'the general public' or **public opinion** – and the latter term in particular suggests that the practice of PR is partly linked to notions of democratic process and broader political arrangements. It implies the importance of the majority view and notions of consensus and dissensus. There is also the concept of **the public sphere** as a space where rational discussion among citizens can take place in resolving opinion about the current issues of the day. The terms 'public', 'public opinion' and 'public sphere' are discussed in more detail in Chapter 5.

Then there is the term specific to public relations, that of *publics* – this is clearly derived from the analytical work of the sociologist Park in the early twentieth century in his work distinguishing certain types of group from crowds or masses (Park, 1972). The term 'public' focuses our attention on specific groups within society who have interests in particular issues or with particular organizations. The term 'publics' is sometimes used interchangeably with that of audiences – however, the latter term implies a more passive and possibly less powerful group.

To take a more pragmatic and descriptive approach:

Public relations involves the communication and exchange of ideas to facilitate change. American PR author Banks remarked, 'Public relations literally is born and immersed in controversy – no need for change, no need for PR' (Banks, 1995: ix). Change entails the expression of opinions and discussions of ideas and policy options. Organizations need specialists to perform that function and to interface between the organization and those groups with which it has or would like to have relationships. Public relations entails the analysis of organizational actions which may impact on relationships or reputation.

However, PR is not 'customer care' or simply 'promotion' of the organizational view. It also entails anticipating the analysis of new and emerging issues that may affect an organization, not just a set of communication techniques. It is about clarity and intellectual honesty based on evidence, not sucking up to people or being likeable or liked (though that may help in any job!).

In basic descriptive functional terms, public relations involves the communication and exchange of ideas either in response to, or to facilitate change. It entails argument and case-making. It is thus intrinsically connected to policy initiatives, their promotion and responses to these by organizational actors and their representatives. Most communication is achieved through the use of various technologies (telephone, e-mail, internet, SMS), some is mediated by *public media*, and some is direct face-to-face communication (meetings, press conferences). It also requires the facilitation of individual *intra-personal communication* (reflection and reflexive thinking). Thus public relations involves *interpersonal communication*, *intra-group communication* (within groups), *intergroup communication* (between groups) and *mass communication*. But public relations practitioners need not only to understand communication processes but the social and organizational context in which communication takes place. Thus public relations work takes into account a very wide range of factors, some of which are relational, some of which are organizational and some of which are environmental, encompassing local, national and international issues and contexts.

Public relations exists in all sectors at many different levels. See Box 2.1 on public relations work and Box 2.2 on jobs in public relations.

Box 2.1   Public relations work

- **Ideological PR: promoting democracy in Iraq**
  Consultancy Bell Pottinger won a £2.3 million contract to promote democracy in Iraq (*PRWeek*, 11 March 2004)

- **Sports tourism**
  The England cricket team's 'Barmy Army' supporters' organization recruited a PR agency to promote its tours and establish a press office (*PRWeek*, 21 July 2006)

- **Fashion PR**
  Modus Publicity re-launched Selfridges, throwing a party which involved 'a transvestite in the cooking department doing cookery demonstrations with oil and chains, and a feminist poet in the beauty department strapped to a lipstick' (*PRWeek*, 15 September 2006)

- **Promotion of science … intra-governmental lobbying**
  The UK National Endowment for Science Technology and the Arts (NESTA), an organization created by the British government, aimed to 'improve the climate for innovation across the UK' and to influence government policy, especially the Department of Trade and Industry (DTI) and the Treasury with regard to the improvement of science teaching in schools (*PRWeek*, 9 June 2006)

- **Behavioural change: car safety**
  Liverpool City Council used a consultancy to raise awareness of the dangers of overcrowding in cars and drink and drug driving (*PRWeek*, 17 December 2006)

- **Consumerism vs religion**
  Lobby group Deregulate sought a PR agency to help it completely deregulate Sunday trading whereas their opponent, the Lord's Day Observance Society, planned to use in-house expertise and was confident it could mobilize pubic support (*PRWeek*, 16 June 2006 and 23 June 2006)

Box 2.2   Job opportunities in public relations: definitions, tasks, language

Communications & marketing manager: regeneration and housing, Lambeth

As part of our excellent communications team, you will help to deliver a first-class service. Motivated by success, you will use your innovation, flair and expertise to help improve and enhance the reputation of the council among residents, stakeholders and partners. If you have a positive attitude and think you can contribute to our growing success, we are looking to recruit… (*PRWeek*, 3 November 2006: 48)

(Continued)

(Continued)

Stakeholder & communications executives: London Underground

You'll cultivate relationships with key stakeholders, including politicians, watchdog bodies, business organizations and lobby groups. This will involve organizing events, forums and visits, and using them to engage and influence stakeholders. You'll also provide LU representatives with comprehensive briefings, speech notes and presentations. (*PRWeek*, 3 November 2006: 48)

PR managers: Compass Group

Due to the size and scale of the business we now need to hire three PR managers – skilled media specialists who can advise on a number of issues and build long-term relationships with key journalists, maximising media opportunities. These brand new roles are multi-disciplined and span three business sectors: business and industry; sport, leisure and hospitality; health, education, defence and government. The PR manager for each business group will be tasked with the development and implementation of a proactive and creative media relations-led PR programme specifically tailored to its industry sector. (*PRWeek*, 29 October 2006: 36)

Internal communications manager: British Airways

...we want you to design and implement our employee communications and involvement strategy. Working in line with and contributing to the formation of the business plan you'll provide communications support for all internal and face-to-face events and develop a communications plan in close conjunction with our corporate media relations team. With clear and effective communication skills that span a range of formats you'll be skilled in translating complex messages into simple and understandable language ... you'll be an engaging and innovative communicator.... (*PRWeek*, 27 October 2006: 44)

Media liaison executive: Primary and Secondary National Strategies

To continue to positively impact on teaching and learning in schools. ... You will have excellent writing and communication skills ... [to secure] a consistent presence in a range of publications including national and industry press, academic journals and other stakeholder publications and websites. (*PRWeek*, 27 October 2006: 40)

Head of government & external affairs: AstraZeneca

We are one of the world's leading pharmaceutical companies, our business is focused on providing innovative, effective modern medicines that make a real difference in important areas of healthcare. Our success is based on a commitment to discovery, finding new ideas that are inspired by life and which in turn help to inspire the lives of our stakeholders. ... You will be responsible for understanding and anticipating issues and opportunities arising from Government and other policymakers and delivering a business-led public affairs strategy... (*PRWeek*, 27 November 2006: 41)

CRITICAL REFLECTION

Personal development

- What qualities seem important to PR practitioners, and why?
- Do you have or can you develop these qualities?
- How can you write your CV to demonstrate that you have these qualities?

PR definitions

- You may notice that jobs in PR carry widely different titles. Why do you think this is? (One job describes PR as 'Media manager', a term that is also used to describe those who manage media organizations.)
- Notice that PR work is referred to as 'translation'. What skills do you think this sort of work requires and why?
- In some cases job ads emphasize the terms 'strategy' and 'relationship' but the tasks described seem focused on media relations. Why do you think this is?

You can read all sorts of stories and get up to speed with current developments in the PR industry in the UK by reading *PRWeek* or equivalent professional journals and trade magazines. However, you should bear in mind that many of the stories that you read are one-sided accounts from the perspective of the agency or client.

To sum up, contemporary PR is:

- present in all changes – technological, economic, social, political, legal
- issue-driven (reactive and proactive – bringing things on to the public agenda as well as responding to new developments)
- dynamic and flexible
- problem-solving
- involves standing back from immediate problems to view the wider picture and the complexity of organizational relationships and overlapping networks
- integral to complex post-industrial societies and takes place in a wide variety of contexts: politics, science, health, the arts, sport, entertainment, leisure, education, commerce.

Consequently, public relations is varied and responsive in different contexts and can entail:

- interpreting perceptions of the organization
- gathering intelligence from the environment to shed light on issues that might affect publics' motivations

- identifying problems that may emerge from publics
- understanding others' perspectives
- assessing relationships
- establishing contexts for discussion, debate, denial, apologia
- being silent
- resisting lobbying attempts
- reaching agreement/consensus/compromise
- advocacy – promotion
- public service
- rhetoric/persuasion
- diplomacy
- debating issues
- democratic education
- building coherent identity – cohesiveness/consensus
- communication acts

Some of these raise ethical problems. For example, is consensus necessarily a desirable social goal? Do attempts to achieve organizational cohesiveness run the risk of being little more than management propaganda?

There are also other more pragmatic problems. There may simply be limits to the way in which some organizational relationships can be improved. Some writing about public relations is open to the criticism that it is over-idealistic. Some writing about public relations (usually from journalists and media sociologists who focus on the media relations aspect of public relations practice) condemns the practice out of hand as manipulative and anti-democratic. These are all important ideas, but it is only through detailed research of particular cases and historical events, or through philosophical discussion, that we can really be in a position to make judgements. It is also useful to look at the way in which practitioners go about their business.

Public relations: key processes

What processes enable public relations practitioners to get that 'wider picture', to understand relationships and to help organizations and publics change? How can the busy practitioner step back from the hustle and bustle of office life, the writing of promotional literature and the constraints of administering publications schedules and researching the detail required for annual reports?

First of all, what do we mean by 'processes'? In public relations literature these are usually defined as linear steps – a basic checklist. Typically, these are expressed as:

- research
- objectives

- publics
- messages
- strategy and tactics
- evaluation

Note that strategy in this context means the articulation of an overall concept or approach to a campaign, problem or a public prior to the selection of particular communication techniques that will have the potential to *reify* (realize or make real or concrete) the strategy. Shortly, I shall raise some critical questions about the concept of **strategic PR**.

You can find many such lists in public relations texts. What they have in common is their linear structure, their clarity and their rationalism. They are one way of making sense of working life and of imposing structure and order. It is, nevertheless, worth thinking about aspects which are not alluded to in such lists, which are, oddly, all the aspects of relationships with which public relations is supposed to take account. For example: emotions, feelings, relationship states.

Take one example in a popular text which includes a chapter on 'Starting the planning process'. This begins with the headline 'Getting in control' and highlights aspects of planning that benefit the individual practitioner and his or her workload. For example: 'it focuses effort ... it improves effectiveness ... it encourages the long-term view ... it helps demonstrate value for money ... it minimises mishaps ... it reconciles conflicts of interests and priorities ... it facilitates proactivity' (Gregory, 2000: 34–37). However, such points do not tell us whether it helps public relations practitioners achieve their aim in terms of improving organizational relationships. It only looks at public relations from the organization's perspective and not in terms of assessing relationships from a variety of perspectives. Thus it introduces a power relationship between the organization and its publics. In the qualitative paradigm of social science, this process of positioning an audience or a research subject is referred to as **Othering**.

So, while broadly useful, many checklists are somewhat formulaic and can raise lots of questions.

The following list offers a little more detail and explanation but still is linear in structure:

- environmental scanning and research (including issues analysis)
- situation analysis (historical review plus developing scenarios)
- organizational/market strengths, weaknesses, opportunities, threats
- benchmarking against competitor organizations
- combining internal and external intelligence
- identifying key publics, researching, understanding and classifing (1) in relation to organization and current issues and (2) in relationship and emotional terms

- defining and conceptualizing stakeholder/public relationships in relation to ideal
- prioritizing
- aiming and supporting researchable objectives (including those for the state of relationships)
- messages
- technique selection (in the light of budget/time constraints)
- communication
- evaluation, review and re-analysis involving key publics (taking on board positive and negative feedback)

What is the problem with linearity and checklists?

There is a problem for those who seek to position public relations as an occupation that seeks to establish *true dialogue* between an organization and its stakeholders. Because the managerial approaches outlined above necessarily begin with the strategic aims and objectives of the organization, they set a particular agenda for change which does not necessarily involve stakeholders. In other words, although PR is seen as managing relationships, those relationships may not be suitably prioritized. An alternative approach would be to engage stakeholders in the process of defining aims, objectives and desirable outcomes at the outset (Coalter, 2006). This could help prevent ill-defined or ill-informed programmes and public relations could potentially act as a catalyst for organizational development and learning via consultative relationships. The critical point I am making here is that common models of the sort I have outlined do not fit with the normative (idealistic) dialogic models. In other words, there is a discrepancy between some of the idealistic values expressed and the mechanistic methodology. If PR practitioners (and their organizations) are really serious about establishing 'dialogue', then inviting stakeholders to define objectives and outcomes might be a first step. Useful applications of this approach might be made in employee relations and corporate social responsibility programmes. As this book went to press Ströh made some similar points when she claimed, 'Publics...do not want merely to be identified, described, researched and communicated to (as suggested by most models of strategic corporate communication management); instead they want to be part of strategy formulation...' (Ströh, 2007: 210).

There are also some more pragmatic concerns with the linearity of a checklist approach:

- Any elements of processes need to be carried out concurrently, on an ongoing basis, not consecutively.
- They create the illusion of discrete steps and a controlled process which does not reflect reality, thus being of limited assistance to the busy practitioner.

Empirical research into managerial work (see Chapters 8 and 9) showed that scientific and administrative approaches to management did not reflect managerial reality and were therefore of limited assistance to managers. It can be argued that the same limitation may apply to public relations. Step-by-step approaches may provide a simplified guide and are a starting point, but do not help interpretative processes. Ultimately, more is needed than checklists. Understanding and engaging in relationships requires commitment and time. Public opinion and media processes are complex and sometimes contentious. Public relations practitioners need some specialized knowledge and a way of codifying it for those outside the field. Judgements and recommendations made by those in public relations need to be based on a system of knowledge. They need to be capable of some conceptual analysis and to be able to conduct empirical research – if they cannot do so, then they are no more than organizational witch doctors!

Knowledge and theory: research and evaluation

What is meant by **system of knowledge**? The phrase refers to frameworks of linked concepts that form theories that explain the world and help us to understand problems. For public relations, that system is necessarily complex. Public relations practitioners will need to draw on a range of communication and media theories, management and organizational theories. However, to carry out research public relations practitioners need some understanding of systems of knowledge (*epistemology*), and to carry out programmes of corporate social responsibility they need to understand *ethics* and *public policy*, they need a grasp of *philosophy* and *politics*. **Public relations**, as we shall see later, is a *cultural practice* and so it is important to understand the fundamental principles that structure society (*anthropology*). In short, one cannot have too much theoretical knowledge to practise public relations intelligently and effectively! Indeed, there is a very famous quote from the social scientist Kurt Lewin that 'there is nothing as practical as a good theory'.

Effectiveness in public relations, is, however, usually presented as a question of achieving specific relationship and organizational policy objectives. In order to assess effectiveness, public relations practitioners must use a variety of research techniques to establish if their efforts have had any impact (bearing in mind that there will have been other influences affecting the situation and publics – public relations does not happen in laboratory conditions). Designing good social research is therefore a key skill for the competent practitioner and

I would go so far as to argue that this skill (and the underpinning knowledge) alone has the ability to deliver professional status to public relations. Research needs to be understood at the strategic (epistemological and paradigm) level, not purely as a technical skill. It is the deeper knowledge that empowers the practitioner to make intelligent and sophisticated choices. Checklists should be reminders and not reified to the status of a theory.

To sum up, the ability to research and evaluate:

- has the potential to bestow credibility on the occupation and is the route to gaining professional status
- provides some comparability with other management disciplines (though this can be a disadvantage in that these may be overly in favour of quantitative approaches)

In our evidence-based scientific culture that emphasizes rationalism, public relations needs to possess, employ and demonstrate its facility with high-level intellectual knowledge and the ability to apply such concepts to data. In the past, practitioners were criticized for their subjective 'seat of the pants' approach. Aware that the failure to evaluate caused credibility problems, **evaluation** has become and remains something of a 'holy grail' for public relations. Because of this, the Chartered Institute of Public Relations (CIPR) in the UK worked hard to draw up a standardized approach. While this has been a useful intervention, it has weaknesses simply because it *is* standardized and used as a 'bolt on'. Only when practitioners have a good facility to understand and carry out a variety of research can the occupation move forwards to professional status. As English philosopher Francis Bacon said in 1597, 'knowledge is power' (www.quotationspage.com, accessed 23 January 2007).

One important issue that remains a problem in public relations practice is over what it is that is to be evaluated. Many practitioners concentrate on media output but do not try to determine knowledge, attitude, understanding, behavioural change in key publics, relationships or networks. Media evaluation is useful in determining that a campaign has succeeded in bringing an issue to media attention, but should not be seen as evidence that media consumers have actually noticed or been influenced by media content. This often means that their objectives and evaluation do not actually link to each other in the way they should. Box 2.3 analyzes some brief examples reported in *PRWeek*. It should of course be noted that the synoptic accounts presented in *PRWeek* may have edited out important details that were present in original campaign documents. Box 2.4 offers top tips on writing objectives and planning evaluation.

Box 2.3 Comparing objectives with evaluation procedures

1 **London Youth Games Ltd (*PRWeek*, 10 February 2006)**
   Objectives: To increase awareness of competitive sporting opportunities available to young people in London and promote positive images of the city's youth. To help partner organizations such as Sport England to increase participation in sport.
   Measurement and evaluation: Media coverage.
   Results: Participation in games with a breakdown of figures by minority backgrounds and disability. Media coverage.
   Comment: Objectives should specify how much awareness and whose, and define what is meant by 'positive images'. Media coverage should be specifically related to that objective and specific publics. Why was media coverage important? What did readers/target publics make of the coverage? Objectives should specify how much participation. Research and evaluation should attempt to identify whether the event encouraged those who did not normally participate in sport to do so.

2 **Camden Council (*PRWeek*, 30 June 2006)**
   Objectives: To increase voter turnout and voter registration.
   Measurement and evaluation: Coverage was 'balanced'.
   Results: Voter turnout increased. More than 2,500 people canvassed for views on voting.
   Comment: Objectives should be made quantifiable. Specific attitudes and behaviours could be spelt out in detail. Which media and why? What counts as positive and negative coverage could be specified. Did voter registration increase and if so by how much? How did turnout compare to other local elections nationally and historically? What other issues and news coverage might have influenced motivation to vote?

3 **Science Museum events (*PRWeek*, 15 September 2006)**
   Objectives: To position the exhibition as an examination of fame, photography and image management in the Victorian age. To reach out to a new corporate audience from the engineering sector.
   Measurement and evaluation: Exhibition received media coverage in trade titles.
   Results: Energy firm booked exhibition for corporate event.
   Comment: Objectives should specify among whom the exhibition is to be positioned and why. Why is the corporate sector important and what attitudinal/ behavioural change is desired? Who reads the media in which coverage was received and how did this help towards achieving objective?

Box 2.4   Writing objectives and planning evaluation: top tips

- An objective should be specific and researchable.
- Avoid generalities such as 'raise the profile', which are too broad and rather meaningless. Be as specific as possible.
- Spell out what changed knowledge, attitude or behaviour you are seeking, whose, why and by when.
- Make sure you link such desired changes to overall aims and strategic objectives which are likely to do with reputation or market position or particular important relationships.
- Do not assume that media coverage is the be-all and end-all even though media coverage may be a by-product of actions you take.
- Think about who reads the media.
- Remember the media and readers are active, not passive, recipients awaiting organizational communication and instruction.
- Focus on relationships, reputation and public opinion (of which media coverage is a part), which can be examined in terms of quality as well as quantity.
- Make sure that research and evaluation includes research besides media content analysis and that it is precisely targeted at the initial audiences you defined at the outset.
- Consider surveying or interviewing key members or experts about an important issue.
- Above all, link evaluation to your core objectives.

In short, if you set objectives that entail change-making (a relationship, an attitude, a behaviour) the research should evaluate and measure that change element directly. Assessing or counting media coverage on the assumption that this will necessarily directly influence the change item is misguided. Evaluating media explains media, not stakeholders, although media can play an important role in public opinion. Therefore, the evaluation of objectives is likely to require multi-method research to understand media coverage and change processes. Where media coverage is set as an objective, this focus should be justified, and supported by qualitative and quantitative targets.

Public relations: the occupation

Public relations work is relatively unstructured and jobs are often not well defined. This has advantages and disadvantages. For the ambitious there is often the ability to develop their job into the areas of work which interest them – and maybe to achieve promotion along the way. On the other hand, it can be difficult to manage career moves. For example, the term 'Account

Executive' in consultancies can include a very wide variety of tasks and require different levels of experience and seniority in small or large consultancies.

Consultancies have their own specific culture and mystique, often appearing to be 'glamorous gurus' who participate in 'beauty parades' – promotional pitches for business – which can be 'exhausting but exhilarating' (Hinrichsen, 2001: 454).

In reality, the work can be long and hard. Public relations has remained an un-unionized occupation despite the attempts of the National Union of Journalists (NUJ) in the 1970s, which worked on behalf of those journalists who had crossed over into PR. Although the NUJ won a number of cases over pay, by 1967 they had given up the quest for a minimum salary and PR became subject to the vagaries of the market (L'Etang, 2004: 129). This means that the pressures of the business can, and do, lead to excessive hours of work (Box 2.5).

Box 2.5   Working in a public relations consultancy

If public relations is seen as a glamorous field then public relations firms may be viewed as 'Glamour Central'. There can be prestige and excitement, and there is always a fast pace. Some other advantages are ... variety ... big budgets ... the collegial atmosphere can be stimulating and motivating. ... On the flip side, agency life can be rigorous, stressful and demanding. Some of the issues are ... the long hours ... people usually work late in the day and on weekends ... pressure ... the agency environment is like a pressure cooker ... turnover ... could be attributed to resignations over working conditions ... some agencies must let people go if they lose big accounts. (Hinrichsen, 2001: 452–3)

'Strategic' public relations

'Strategic' PR can be seen as a Holy Grail for some PR academics and some PR practitioners. Thus it is worth reflecting on the following questions:

- What is strategic PR?
- Does strategic PR exist?
- Is strategic PR interesting?
- Does strategic PR matter?

Within general PR discourse, strategic PR is assumed to be high-status, important, desirable, intelligent, far-seeing – and it is taken for granted that it is 'a good thing'. Yet strategic public relations can also be read as cunning, clever, self-interested, pompous and powerful. *Strategy* was originally conceived as rationally intended purposeful thought to guide action – and is clearly self-interested (Pettigrew et al., 2002b: 11–12). The field of *strategic management* has traditionally lacked critique or reflexivity, and only a small critical paradigm (composed largely of European scholars) has discussed strategic management as an ideological practice, focused on domination and power (Pettigrew et al., 2002b: 11). In other words, 'strategy' is not neutral, though the term may be used to disguise power and politics in public relations, especially in the fields of *issues management* and *public affairs* (see Chapter 5). Critical independent public relations students and researchers might want to ask themselves and others:

- What sort of strategic management are PR practitioners signing up to?
- What sort of strategic management are PR practitioners actually doing?
- What assumptions underpin strategic public relations (theory and practice)?

Finally, and more provocatively, could we see 'strategic PR' which uses a range of research skills, social psychological and sociological concepts as a form of civilian political warfare or *psyops*?

Psyops

Psyops or *political warfare* is a research-driven effort to persuasive communication that draws upon communications theory and research, media research, analysis and tactics, planning skills, messaging, group dynamics, teamwork and spin, or 'accentuating the positive' (Cooper, 1982: 310–312). Definitions include:

> Psychological operations ... is a communicative act or program, since its purpose is to affect other's perceptions, attitudes, and opinions – and through that effect to influence their behavior. (McLaurin, 1982a: 2)

> [Psyop programmes require] critical information about ... targets (friendly, neutral, hostile) ... [and] must include the following:
>
> 1 The definition of key audiences (both friendly and enemy) within the society.
> 2 The beliefs, attitudes, opinions, and motivations of key audiences as individuals and groups.
> 3 The analysis of current vulnerabilities of specific audiences within the society.
> 4 The determination of message content and the most effective (best) communication channels to reach the target.
> 5 The impact or effect of PSYOP communication. (Katz, 1982: 123)

While psyops is normally defined a part of the military's propaganda effort it is clear that it is methodologically linked to PR. That connection goes some way to explaining critiques of the PR function and its methods. The role of persuasive communication in a society raises questions over its sponsors and its accountability.

Complex societies need to exchange ideas, develop and advocate policies without infringing media freedom and citizen rights of access to information. The occupation of public relations is necessarily ethically challenged because it is situated at centres of power; seeks to influence decision-making; and is unregulated.

Public relations: historical and social role

It is beyond the scope of this chapter to give a respectable account of PR history. Most PR textbooks give a somewhat bowdlerized account of US history plus a few references to Greeks and Romans to suggest that PR has long been connected to the promotion of cultural identity and political debate. The common notion that prevails is that Americans invented public relations and then exported it everywhere else in the world. In the case of the UK, this is patently not true and it is becoming clearer that in many countries forms of public relations were carried out at various stages (Muruli, 2001; Borghetti, 2003; Murphy, 2003; L'Etang, 2004; L'Etang and Muruli, 2004; Toledano, 2005; Puchan, 2006; Al Saqur, 2007; Ismail, 2007). Remembering that public relations arises at points of change and over issues where there is disagreement over policy and practice, we can appreciate that there are many contexts in which formal organizational communication is required. Governments have long appreciated this and have had the resources at their disposal to try to influence key groups of citizens and public opinion more widely. Governmental communication has often been accused on 'being propaganda', and so this chapter explores some of the issues that bear upon a discussion of the relationship between public relations and **propaganda**. This discussion naturally takes us into a discussion of ethics, and from thence to a consideration of the terms professionalism and professionalization.

This section does not explain how to practise public relations, but alerts readers to the importance of the occupation's development, its aspirations for professional status and the challenges its faces for social legitimacy. To some extent it looks at the nature of arguments that have been made against public relations in the past and those that exist right up to the present day. Thus this section opens up debate on public relations' social role through discussion of:

- history
- propaganda
- professionalism and professionalization
- features of the occupation

History and development of public relations

While it is not possible here to review the emergence of public relations on a global basis, it can be noted that:

- academics are still recovering PR history around the world
- understanding different paths of evolution will generate insights into practice and potentially could lead to new concepts, frameworks and theory
- in many countries PR evolved as part of nation-building and national identity processes, sometimes as part of de-colonization or freedom-fighting
- in many countries PR developed as part of political propaganda, sometimes during times of war
- there will in due time be multiple histories (corporate, political, biographical, sectoral, liberal, Marxist, etc.) and interpretations for any one nation or stateless nation
- theoretical frameworks derived from historical evolution in one country cannot be sensibly applied as interpretative models in other cultures
- PR was not invented by Americans and then exported elsewhere
- PR practice is not necessarily morally progressive

Public relations and propaganda

For some (Ewen, 1996; Schlesinger et al., 2001), PR is intrinsically about political control:

> The rise of PR as an occupation began at the turn of the [twentieth] century in the US and slightly later in the UK. Universal suffrage and other democratic reforms were a key factor in increasing the influence that could be exerted by the people on decision-making. In short, PR emerged in response to the democratization that followed increasing social unrest and the rise of organized labour. At the same time, new communications technologies were being developed and it became possible to reach a new mass market. (Schlesinger et al., 2001: 14)

The conceptual relationship between public relations and propaganda is both controversial (particularly for practitioners who fear moral opprobrium) and difficult. First of all, as has been noted by other authors, particularly Fawkes (2006: 267–287), many basic definitions of propaganda could be equally well used to describe public relations. Box 2.6 shows some of the many definitions of propaganda.

Box 2.6   Definitions of propaganda

Propaganda in the broadest sense is the technique of influencing human action by the manipulation of representations. These representations may take spoken, written, pictorial or musical form. (Lasswell, 1934/1995: 13)

Propaganda is ... the deliberate attempt by some individual or group to form, control or alter the attitudes of other groups by the use of instruments of communication, with the

(Continued)

intention that in any given situation the reaction of those so influenced will be that desired by the propagandist. (Qualter, cited in Hazan, 1976: 11)

Propaganda is the preconceived, systematic and centrally co-ordinated process of manipulating symbols, aimed at promoting uniform behaviours of large social groups, a behaviour congruent with the specific interests and ends of the propagandist. (Hazan, 1976: 12)

Propaganda is not neutral, it aims to further the aims of the propagandist. (Wright, 1991: xiii)

For others propaganda is 'brainwashing' – akin to religious conversion, political indoctrination, the changing of delusional beliefs by mentally ill patients. (Watson, 1978: 289)

All modern societies are inundated with propaganda from every quarter. The vast bureaucracies which dominate all institutional arenas generate their own propaganda, for both internal and external consumption. Bureaucracies produce propaganda, among many other reasons, to divert attention from unpalatable hard choices; or to dress up organizational performance when soliciting appropriations or investment; or to mollify employees wary of organizational aims. (Jackall, 1995: 7)

Propaganda is a form of communication that is different from persuasion because it attempts to achieve a response that furthers the desired intent of the propagandist. Persuasion is interactive and attempts to satisfy the needs of both persuader and persuadee. (Jowett and O'Donnell, 1986: 13)

[Old propaganda] was characterized by the attempt of the few to impose a picture of reality on the many. ... [New propaganda] underlined a process of negotiation among many participants ... the audience has always had the power of resistance ... as our media allow us to interact globally with others in a community of interest, we need a new way to think about reality construction. (Edelstein, 1997: xiii)

CRITICAL REFLECTION

Read through the quotes in Box 2.6. Once you have reflected on their meaning and implications, read them again, this time replacing the term 'propaganda' with that of 'public relations'. What is the outcome and implications of this exercise?

The definitions shown in Box 2.6 indicate some overlaps between public relations and propaganda. For some analysts, public relations *is* propaganda. And if that was not enough, the historical evidence in the UK shows that a number of early PR practitioners graduated from careers in wartime propaganda to peacetime PR, thus suggesting shared concepts or *modus operandi* (L'Etang, 2004: 49; 2006b: 149–152).

In addition to historical evidence which shows that regimes and governments and their appointees have used their power to filter and distort information, there are also some intrinsic problems concerned with trying to make public relations activity transparent to members of society. This also raises issues of access to public relations services in the first place, and the relationship between public relations and the media. For some writers, propaganda, as compared to public relations, is a question of whether or not 'the truth' is told and propaganda equated with 'lies'. For others, propaganda is simply persuasion. Reasons why this is a difficult area include the following:

- People tend to come to the debate with fixed ideas about the relationship between public relations and propaganda.
- Definitions are often relativist according to the communication act that is being debated. In other words, one person's PR is another's propaganda depending on what side you take in the debate.
- The hierarchy between the concepts has altered over time partly as a consequence of 'propaganda' becoming a pejorative term or 'devil word'. At various stages 'public relations' has been seen as a propaganda technique and propaganda as a public relations technique. During the inter-war period, and, to some limited extent after the Second World War, British practitioners used the term interchangeably.
- Attempts to define terms are complicated by moral judgements about 'good' and 'bad', 'right' or 'wrong' (L'Etang, 2006a: 23–40).

Table 2.2 Propaganda sponsors, type and media

Sponsors/types of propaganda	Propaganda media
Religious	Books
Regime	Literature
Colonial	Film
Territorial	Poetry
Royal	Articles
Bureaucratic/administrative	Architecture
Political/ideological	Symbols
Terrorist/freedom-fighter	Music
Corporate	Posters
Activists	

CRITICAL REFLECTION

Can you think of an example of what you perceive to be 'propaganda'? What are your reasons for doing so? How are you making the decision? On the basis of apparent motivation? Effects? Accuracy? Manipulation? Your own views of protagonists, sponsors, rhetoric or impact?

Figure 2.7 shows some of the many levels at which propaganda can be analyzed and suggests some key criteria.

Box 2.7   Analytical approaches to defining propaganda

Level of analysis

- State
- Ideology
- Organization
- Individual
- Text

Criteria

- Intent of communicator
- Nature of established relationships (historical review)
- Areas of exploitation/coercion
- Authenticity
- Fairness

CRITICAL REFLECTION

Compare and contrast:

- propaganda and psyops
- pysops and persuasion
- psyops and PR
- persuasion and PR
- propaganda and PR

The connection with propaganda has almost certainly impacted the public rela-tions occupation in its ability to achieve professional status. Public relations is still not 'respectable' and lacks 'social legitimacy'. In this next section, public relations' attempt to achieve professional status is briefly reviewed, along with key definitions of the term 'professional'.

Professionalism and professionalization

As an occupation public relations suffers from a lack of delineation, weak boundaries, and 'encroachment' from other disciplines such as marketing and human resources. It is not unionized so its workers are open to exploitation, and it is barely regulated since most practitioners are not members of professional organizations and there are only legal restrictions (in the UK) in relation to lobbying. However, as Magda Pieczka pointed out:

> When all is said and done, above all else the industry values having the flexibility of a practice unconstrained by statutory regulation. But the price for this freedom is evidently paid in the reputation granted to the public relations industry. (Pieczka, 2006b: 317)

The *public relations of public relations* remains an issue, as Elspeth Tilley reminded readers not so long ago:

> The profession's own reputation remains a major concern with serious implications for practitioners, scholars and therefore also for clients and businesses who use public relations services. Has public relations become a term misunderstood beyond redemption, its use tarnishing not only those who practise it, or study it, but also those that purchase it? (Tilley, 2005: 1)

Tilley argued that media relations specialists should not describe themselves as public relations specialists because it devalued both specialisms. She suggested that: 'We ... need to rename the public relations role in organizations as Transparency, Consistency and Responsiveness Manager ... to reflect and inspire our most important functions' (Tilley, 2005: 1).

On transparency, Julia Jahansoozi commented that:

> Transparency is considered a necessity for PR practitioners interested in opening up decision-making process and ensuring accountability and in pre-empting issues and averting expensive crises. ... If the process is transparent then publics are able to view the interaction and internal behaviour and can decide whether the organization actually does what it claims to be doing. ... Transparency contributes

to the organization's reputation management through numerous benefits ... increased trust, credibility, co-operation ... the transparent organization is one where both internal and external [aspects] are transparent ... the translucent is where either internal or external are transparent and the opaque is where both internal and external are hidden or secret. (Jahansoozi, 2006: 80–81)

CRITICAL REFLECTION

Read the quotes from Pieczka, Tilley and Jahansoozi (above) and consider:

- Is transparency a necessary condition for professional status?
- Is transparency achieveable without regulation and, if so, how?
- Who could monitor transparency?
- What might motivate the drives to (a) transparency and (b) translucency in terms of (a) the PR occupation and (b) organizational work?

DEFINITIONS

Lay terms of 'professional', 'professionalism' tend to imply efficiency, effectiveness and responsibility. However, some sociologists have specialized in analyzing work and professions and this has produced new insights and understandings.

Sociology of professions is a sub-field of sociology along with the sociology of work. These areas give critical understanding and help us to question the role and scope and status and power of occupations in society and in relation to each other. This approach helps us to get behind taken-for-granted norms. 'Professional', as defined by sociologists of the professions, is a conceptually rigorous term and not just 'a jumble of meanings and values, from efficiency to wealth; from prestige through altruism to public service' (O'Sullivan, 1994: 244).

The area *sociology of the professions* seeks to understand institutional structures, such as the Chartered Institute of Public Relations (CIPR), the Public Relations Consultants' Association (PRCA), International Communication Consultancy Organization and the International Public Relations Association (IPRA), and the role they play in relation to the occupation and its societal context (Box 2.8). Sociologists are also interested in social divisions (gender, class and ethnicity) and internal class structures ('management' versus 'technician' is a popular dichotomy in public relations writing). They are also interested in seeing how work affects individuals and groups and their self-identity. Sociologists have pursued a number of lines in defining professional work and professionalization processes. These include functional, descriptive accounts that attempt to define criteria and more critical engagements which explore the way in which some occupations have successfully leveraged higher status, larger salaries, political, economic, legal and social influence.

Box 2.8   Professional bodies in the UK

Chartered Institute of Public Relations (CIPR) (www.ipr.org.uk)
Public Relations Consultants' Association (PRCA) (www.prca.org.uk)
International Public Relations Association (IPRA) (www.ipra.org)
Global Alliance for Public Relations and Communication Management (www.globalpr.org/new)

Key approaches to analyzing professionalism and professionalization

Sociologists have analyzed the professional status of some organizations in order to identify their key characteristics (traits); the common patterns and processes of occupational development that deliver professional status; the experience of those working in such elite occupations; and the way in which professionals and professionalizing occupations acquire and use power, both in relation to related occupations and more broadly in society.

Trait

Early work on professionals (Hughes, 1958; Millerson, 1964; Vollmer and Mills, 1966) tended to assume professions were a benign and stabilizing influence in society – 'a good thing'. Key characteristics of professions were seen as:

- specialized skill and service
- intellectual and practical training
- professional autonomy – independent judgements and notion of what counts as good practice – expertise
- fiduciary relationship with client – trusteeship
- collective responsibility for occupation – ethics
- embargo on some methods
- testing of competence

Process

Other sociologists tried to capture the dynamics of professionalization processes – 'the natural history' – or progression. They saw the key processes as being:

- emergence of sufficient practitioners to form a critical mass
- establishment of training
- founding of professional organizations
- protection by law – status
- adoption of a code of practice or ethics

Ethnographic

Ethnographers are like *social anthropologists* who study the culture (rituals, values, behaviours, social practices, daily life) of an occupation with a view to providing a *rich description*.

Power

The power perspective is critical, drawn originally from Weber and Marx, and takes a less favourable view of professions, which it sees as an elite group in society who have achieved a great deal for themselves and exert considerable power and authority by controlling entry to the occupation and gaining social approval for their work.

Professional project

The 'professional project' approach observes occupations' efforts to translate specialist knowledge and skills into social and economic rewards. This perspective focuses on market control, social closure and elite status.

Systems

Occupations can be seen as a series of related systems. So for public relations, any changes in emphasis or practice in journalism or marketing are likely to be important and vice versa. The growth and formalization of public relations in the UK post-Second World War greatly affected the journalism occupation in terms of working practices and also in terms of status and career progression (PR practitioners were more highly paid than journalists in the 1950s).

A key concept which has emerged from the sociology of professions and which is very important for public relations is that of *jurisdiction*. Jurisdiction is the crucial mechanism for professional status because jurisdiction, and control over tasks that are themselves defined by knowledge systems, permits the erection of boundaries (Pieczka and L'Etang, 2001). This is a big problem for public relations, especially in relation to marketing and particularly social marketing. While the discussion about porous boundaries between public relations and marketing is often presented as an issue of power (financial resources) or historical accident, it is actually about the ability to define a unique knowledge base to public relations.

What role does education play in the
professionalization process?

Education is vital to professionalization because it provides the *cognitive core* and knowledge base which underpins the specialist expertise sold in the market place. Education can build a body of knowledge and improve practice. It also provides credibility, and qualifications may be used for gatekeeping purposes to achieve social closure and limit who can and cannot practice.

At present, the main gift education can offer public relations practice is that of social scientific expertise, especially that which may be applied to the process of evaluation. The ability to evaluate PR work is the academic skill which has the most potential to deliver professional status because:

- it is complex knowledge requiring individual design and judgement on each occasion
- it includes quantitative as well as qualitative elements and so puts public relations on a footing with other organizational managers by enabling them to share a language

Historical models of professionalism and
professionalization applied to PR

Research in Europe in 2004 showed that although PR is seen as a 'professional domain' and a 'specialized management area', it 'lacks an image of professionalism'(van Ruler et al., 2004: 3). So it seems that education has so far made a rather limited impact. Maybe an alternative framework can help to explain this.

Betteke van Ruler, Professor at the University of Amsterdam and 'at the pinnacle' of European scholars (Grunig and Grunig, 2004: xiii), laid out an alternative framework for thinking about professionalism and professionalization (see Box 2.9).

Box 2.9   Van Ruler's framework of professionalism and professionalization

Knowledge model

- Professions are organized experts who apply expert knowledge to particular cases in practice.
- The professional group develops the profession to maturity – experts who implement knowledge.

Status model

- A means to get status and money.
- A professional ideology.
- Apprenticeship culture.
- Emphasis on professional practice.

(Continued)

Competition model

- An exclusive task that meets market needs.
- The client, not the occupational group, defines what is good.
- Competition with other occupational groups (marketing).

Personality model

- The client defines the individual qualities that are needed in a consultant ('they know our business', 'we can work with these people').
- A good professional is someone who coaches his or her client in difficult times ('emotional intelligence', 'charisma', 'creativity').

Source: adapted from van Ruler (2005: 159–173)

CRITICAL REFLECTION

- Which of the above models would you expect PR academics to support and why?
- How do these ideas make you feel about your own educational experiences and career ambitions?

In the UK professional status is still an elusive goal for PR practitioners, since entry to the occupation is not controlled by qualification or membership of a professional body. There is also a confusing plethora of job titles, a lack of general understanding about the practice in society and considerable media criticism (ongoing in the UK since the 1960s) of public relations as persuasive communication.

Thinking critically: public relations in society

Remembering that part of the agenda for this book is to challenge readers to think critically and to ask questions, here are some ideas to consider...

The practice of public relations is a contentious one. Historically, in some cultures, it has had links to propaganda. As a practice it does seem to entail persuasion and it is quite right and proper that such activities are challenged. Because of this it has struggled to defend itself against attacks, especially from journalists, and it is clearly important for students to be clear about the nature of the work they are engaging in and to consider their own moral stance. It may be argued that PR is a social good if it facilitates information-sharing, educates citizens and thus enhances democracy. PR can contribute testing debate to underpin decision-taking. But issues of partiality, connections to power and uneven access to PR services remain a societal as well as a PR issue. Important questions to consider at this stage are:

- Am I comfortable working like a lawyer and working for any client to the best of my professional ability?
- Am I comfortable working for a cause or organization in which I believe and about which I am passionate?
- Am I comfortable working for a very rich or elite organization that has tremendous resources (power/financial) that may have the ability to effect real change?
- Am I comfortable working for a resource-poor group and using my skills to ensure that they are better heard?
- Am I comfortable representing an organization, cause or product which does not align with my personal views?
- Am I content for my opponents or competitors to have access to the same PR services and expertise?

As noted in the first chapter of this book, critical thinking is not necessarily negative, although since it is drawn from critical theory it tends to draw attention to imbalances of power or representation. It is useful for public relations because it alerts us to the fact that some voices may not be heard and some relationships may be disregarded or given insufficient respect. As Paul and Elder (2004) pointed out, independent thought and analysis means sometimes going against traditional organizational practice or confronting organizational mores or values in order to:

- raise questions and problems
- use abstract ideas to interpret information and feed back critical insights
- develop well-reasoned conclusions tested against clear criteria
- think open-mindedly within alternative systems of thought, bearing in mind their assumptions, implications, and practical consequences
- communicate effectively (Paul and Elder, 2004: 1).

Thus, critical thinking is invaluable for public relations practitioners in understanding and resolving public relations problems.

Exercise

Contrast your own views on PR education with those of some American public relations students shown in Box 2.10.

Box 2.10 'I thought it would be more glamorous': US students reflect on PR education

'I don't have the same feelings for it [public relations] now, I thought it would be more glamorous.'

'I thought it would be more fun, just working with people, but I found it to be much more stressful.'

'I thought it was mainly special events and party planning.'

'I don't like it any more. I thought it would be more planning events, taking out clients, and social aspects.'

'I did not realize the journalism aspect in PR. It's not just if you are a good people person, there are big writing responsibilities.'

'I wasn't aware of all the writing involved – I didn't think it would be part of the job.'

'I thought we would learn to do press releases, press packets, media relations, and it turned out to be much more management and research.'

'There's much more responsibility and stress, but there's a wide variety of directions to go in the PR career. It's not just image building.'

'I'm excited it offers more of a challenge, more responsibility, that I can be managing people and making big, important decisions.'

Source: Bowen (2003: 199–214)

CRITICAL REFLECTION

The quotes in Box 2.10 are examples of students who made assumptions about public relations and had their expectations confounded. To what extent do they seem legitimate or surprising?

Box 2.11 displays quotes from senior practitioners about 'the next generation – 29 young PR professionals who have already made a major impression on the industry' (Chandiramani, 2006).

Box 2.11 The next generation

Julia Mitchell, Director, Toast, age 29: '[Her] aim is to "become an ambassador for the industry – lecturing, speaking and writing books"'.

Liz William, Account Manager, Threepipe Communications, age 24: 'belongs to several private members' clubs. "I want to push myself beyond the realm of PR"'.

(Continued)

(Continued)

Kim Blomley, PR Shell Chemicals, age 24: 'Kim's skill in relationship building is far beyond her years'.

Louise Angel, Account Director, Geronimo, age 25: 'embraces any challenge ... even those that stretch beyond her imagination'.

Zaki Cooper, Director of Business of New Europe, age 29: '[His] contacts book is an eclectic mix [and he] lectures to students at Brunel and City universities but also makes use of his PR skills in charity work with the Council of Christians and Jews'.

Tom Cartmale, Head of PR, Oakley, age 27: 'his networking is ... prolific: he attends CIPR and European sponsorship association forums and breakfast meetings'.

Ben Howes, PR Morrisons, age 28: 'diligent with a keen nose for news'.

Katie Jamieson, Account Director, Lewis PR, age 27: 'no-nonsense, down-to-earth results orientated approach...'.

Chris Clarke, Director, Clark Mulder Purdie, age 29: 'He aims to raise the quality of PR in the UK and generate respect for it in the boardroom'.

Source: *PRWeek*, 30 June 2006

CRITICAL REFLECTION

- What themes emerge from the quotations in Box 2.11?
- Do any comments resonate with your own plans and ideas of your future occupation and self-identity?

REVIEW

This chapter has reviewed a range of concepts, frameworks and debates that go some way to explaining the existence and purpose of public relations. Now is the time to return to your response of the questions asked of you at the beginning of the chapter. You might like to consider:

- To what extent have my expectations been met?
- To what extent have my expectations been confounded?
- How do I feel about this occupation?
- Has anything changed about my view of PR as my future career?

In conclusion

This chapter has offered pragmatic definitions and descriptions of PR work, its role and scope. It has offered a further critique of technocratic functionalism and highlighted the limitations of a checklist approach. It has demonstrated potential flaws in PR evaluation practices. Reflecting on the PR occupation itself, the chapter has explained definitions of professionalism and professionalization and related these to the public relations occupation. According to strict sociological criteria, PR is not a profession. The chapter's critical tone is also applied in relation to the rather reverent note sounded by many PR practitioners and academics in relation to 'strategic' PR. Here, readers have been alerted to a range of sources in critical management that have de-bunked idealistic (and ideological) ideas about strategic management. In reviewing some historical trends that have facilitated the evolution and growth of PR, this chapter has not shied away, as some texts do, from the subject of propaganda. Furthermore, it has also introduced the concept of 'psyops' into the public relations context.

RECOMMENDED READING

There are many useful standard texts that provide introductions to PR which would serve well as a complement to the ideas and approach put forward in this chapter. In particular, see Lee Edwards' reviews of PR theories in Tench and Yeomans (2006) and, in the same volume, chapters by Anne Gregory (planning), Rudiger Theilmann and Gyorgy Szondi (research and evaluation) and Johanna Fawkes (propaganda and persuasion). Histories of public relations are available in L'Etang (2004) and in L'Etang and Pieczka (2006), where different cultural historical perspectives are presented by Puchan (Germany), Tilson (Spain), Larsson (Sweden) and L'Etang (UK). A comprehensive review of the literature on professionalism and professionalization can be found in Pieczka and L'Etang (2001) in Heath's *Handbook of Public Relations* (2001). Kevin Moloney's *Rethinking Public Relations* (2nd edition, 2006) focuses in detail on conceptual and applied aspects of propaganda and political communications.

Reputation, Image and Impression Management

BEFORE YOU READ A SINGLE WORD...

- How is reputation formed?
- What do we mean by 'images' and how are they formed?
- How do we impress ourselves upon others?
- What tactics do we use to give a good impression?

Keep these notes and refer to them at the end of the chapter.

Key concepts

Identity	Impression management
Image	Reputation

Introduction

This chapter will give you a good understanding of the terms 'impression management', 'reputation', 'image', and 'identity', and their relevance and application to the world of public relations and its work. It takes a broad approach, linking interpersonal and organizational communication concepts. It includes 'Discipline boxes' on impression management and psychoanalysis which explain the relevance of these sub-disciplines for public relations.

In this chapter a number of important linked concepts will be analyzed and discussed, or 'unpacked' as philosophers say. This means reflecting deeply on the word, its apparent meaning and common useage and trying to distinguish the relationship between linked terms. This is not easy work but it is important in terms of intellectual development, especially in terms of developing the ability to think independently. The relevant skills here are clarity of expression and depth of thought. Clarity can be aided by the use of examples; depth is achieved by explaining what makes something a difficult question (Paul and Elder, 2004: 9). In the next section I shall present and discuss definitions, give examples and suggest ways in which you can relate these ideas to your own experiences and observations.

CHAPTER AIMS

On completion of this chapter you will be able to:

- explain our desire to influence what others think of us
- discuss the relationship between image and identity
- understand the implications of these concepts for individuals in their private and professional lives

Box 3.1   Journal source

Corporate Reputation Review (www.ingentaconnect.com/content/pal/crr)

Reputation

Public relations is often defined as 'reputation management' by practitioners and journalists. For example, PR consultancy Fleishman-Hillard state that they:

> provide reputation management counsel. ... We know that reputation is a corporation's most important asset. Strong and durable reputations are built over time by doing the right thing across the organization and by taking appropriate credit for achievements. (www.fleishman.com/capabilities/practice_groups/rep_management, accessed 25 July 2006)

The Daily Telegraph's business correspondent commented rather more cynically:

> Reputation management is big business in the City, which employs just as many – if not more – spin masters as Westminster. No company, however small, is without a public relations firm. They can earn handsome wages for trying to put the best gloss on industrial accidents, fat cat salaries, or boardroom rows. (Wallop, 2006: 81)

Likewise *Media Guardian* reported, under the headline 'Boom time for PR':

> The public relations industry is experiencing soaring demand as companies wake up to the importance of 'reputation management'. ... Analysts are underscoring a new long-term role for PR firms in managing reputation after some high-profile upsets at big names this summer. Cadbury was hit by a salmonella scare in June, British Airways and airport operator BAA have squabbled over security clampdowns and Thames Water has enraged some customers in its sluggishness to tackle leaks. Danny Rogers, the editor of *PRWeek*, said those press reports had stimulated demand for public relations which was already enjoying the benefits of cyclical upturn. (*Media Guardian*, 14 September, 2006)

Reputation is one of a number of linked concepts which form the basis of public relations work. Dr Eisenegger, from the University of Zurich, argued that the concept of *reputation nurturing* is the central function of public relations:

> The primary function of public relations is the long-term assurance of the survival of the agents involved. This presupposes that these agents can be positioned as positively as possible in their field of action, and also distinguished from any competitors. This is precisely the function performed by reputation: it is the product of the social process that assigns agents their ranking in society. To this extent, PR can at its core be understood as reputation nurturing. (Eisenegger, 2005: 1)

The emergence of corporate reputation as a concept and practice signifies the complex structures, instant communication and symbolic sophistication of contemporary developed worlds. Those specializing in corporate reputation aim to help organizational insiders and outsiders make sense of organizational behaviour and media interpretations and to answer the questions:

- What is this organization all about?
- Why does it do what it does?
- Why has it done what it's done?

Reputation is popularly defined in dictionaries as what is generally believed about a person or organization. It is worth noting here, however, that general beliefs may be influenced by public expression of opinions which implies information-sharing and networks of communication, such as rumour or the 'grapevine' – the popular metaphor to explain the intertwined connections of social organizational discourse. As Surma explained:

> An organization's reputation depends on what others think about it (the term reputation comes from the Latin *reputare* – to think over). More importantly, for an organization to be defined by its reputation is for it to be defined according to an individual or group's judgement of its trustworthiness and its integrity – that is, according to its judged capacity to act ethically and responsibly in all its interactions and practices. (Surma, 2006a: 1)

In other words, reputation is formed outside the organization on the basis of subjective impressions.

According to key reputation theorists Charles Fombrun and Cees van Riel (2003: 225–230 *passim*), several different approaches have been taken to analyzing reputation: economic (related to leveraging reputation to inspire investor confidence); strategic (the unique aspects of the organization and its mission); marketing (reputation as both brand and *stereotype*); organizational culture (links between reputation and the cultural life and practices of the organization); accounting (reputation as an indicator of social legitimacy). Public relations is often subsumed under 'marketing' in many literature reviews of the field. Fombrun and others have focused on key facets of reputation, such as financial performance, product/service quality and social responsibility. However, such approaches fail to take account of 'stakeholders' active roles in enabling an organization to be defined as reputable or disreputable' (Surma, 2006a: 2).

The concept of reputation

Professor Bromley, a psychologist, alerts us to some important features of reputation, pointing out that reputation:

- is distinct from personality
- is a valued resource (a good reputation creates happiness and security; a bad reputation causes guilt and anxiety)
- can be manipulated
- is worthless if not authentic and based on truth
- is partially a caricature since it centres on distinguishable features and selectively emphasizes good and bad points thus using the process of stereotyping (Bromley, 1993: 1–18, *passim*).

According to Bromley, personal reputation is seen as belonging to that person while the notion of public image emphasizes the distinction between a person and the images that others hold of them – hence the importance of *social networks* in the formation of reputations. Thus reputations are partially derived from social discussions in which individuals exchange views about the images they hold of third parties. Even so, one must bear in mind that they will only express the views they feel are publicly acceptable so dominant views emerge and shape reputation. Gossip and rumour play an important role (DiFonzo and Bordia, 2000; Kimmel, 2004).

Reputations are derived from an individual's or organization's actions and words (and the relationship between these), and the relationships and experiences that others have of that individual or organization. They are also derived from stories, histories and dramas, mediatized versions of these and public appearances. In other words, reputation is in a constant dynamic process of evolution, subject to review and re-evaluation. Personal reputation is something that individuals have some control over, but corporate reputation is a collective responsibility and the consequence of multiple individual and collective interpretations of public images (mediated information). In other words, we may make judgements about a company's reputation without having had any direct experience ourselves of that organization.

We should be cautious, however, about how we evaluate reputational claims, for, as Bromley (1993: 1) pointed out: 'One must not confuse ... what is in fact generally said or believed with ... what people think is generally said or believed. People can be mistaken in their appreciation of group opinion.' This points to the importance of formal research by public relations practitioners to establish a sound understanding. It also suggests that reliance on focus groups could be misleading and that a mixed-method approach combining qualitative individual and group interviews plus quantitative research will produce the best understanding of public opinion.

While reputation may be seen as some sort of generalized 'public opinion', it is also the case that there may be varying or several reputations of an individual or an organization. For example, an organization may have a reputation with a funding body or government for being worthy and reliable, and yet be regarded with cynicism and dislike by its own employees. Likewise, employees may be seen as keen, ambitious and promising management material by their employers but resented by organizational peers for toadying behaviour and for stealing ideas, and distrusted in a friendship group for the way in which they treat the opposite sex.

Trust

Trust, reliability, sincerity and authenticity all contribute to a good reputation. Trustworthiness is essential for communicators and failure to demonstrate the quality convincingly has threatened the reputation of public relations practitioners, particularly those who specialize in media relations and crisis management. In such situations, media's trust of PR sources is appropriately low, given the inevitable self-interest of organizational representatives. While media effects cannot be assumed, it is reasonable to surmise some linkage between media trust (or distrust) and public trust. Professor Dr Gunther Bentele argued that: 'Public relations, journalism and the media act as trust mediators' in the process of public trust formation (Bentele, 2005).

German literature since the 1950s has linked 'trust' with 'transparency' (Szyska, 2005), an approach consonant with the relational approach in public relations first developed by Ferguson (1984). 'Transparency' means that we can 'see through' processes, decisions and communications so that there is no opaqueness or obscurity – no organizational veil or fig leaf. As noted by Jahansoozi:

> Transparency is very important for organization–public relationships and can be viewed as a relational condition or variable that is a pre-requisite for other relational elements such as trust and commitment. It provides the atmospheric conditions that allow trust, accountability, cooperation, collaboration, and commitment to flourish. ... Because of the link between transparency, trust and accountability, there is naturally a strong interest in it as a notion for instantly restoring confidence [at a time of crisis] to the organization–public relationship. (Jahansoozi, 2006: 80, 82)

Reputation is dependent on trust and transparency and the interplay between the concepts of identity and images. These terms are confusingly presented in a variety of literatures because authors define them differently or even use the terms interchangeably, as though they referred to the same concept. Likewise, the term 'image' is sometimes used interchangeably with 'reputation'. How are students of public relations supposed to make sense of this multiplicity of definitions? The most important step is to understand that authors from different backgrounds employ terminology variably and that when speaking or writing about reputation, image or identity one should specify how one is using the terms to facilitate a shared understanding. My task here is to make clear distinctions between key concepts.

Identity

According to Woodward (1997), **identity** is the consequence of processes of comparison and differentiation both at personal and organizational levels. Identities arise from economic and political conditions, are apparent in local and virtual communities and may be biologically determined or socially constructed (Woodward, 1997: 1). Identification processes align with national, ethnic and religious affinities and loyalties. There is an interplay between the social and political conditions which frame our individual choices and subsequent lifestyles; our introspections; and our lived reality. Identity implies authenticity and 'gives us an idea of who we are and of how we relate to others and to the world in which we live' (Woodward, 1997: 1).

Exercise: Personal identity – who am I?

- What makes you, you – and why?
- Who are you?
- What has influenced your identity in the past?
- What recent and current influences affect and have affected your identity?
- How do we communicate our identity to others?

In contemporary developed societies individuals can choose to construct their own identity partly through symbolic brand choice that aligns them with values of organizations (in a secular world) (du Gay, 2000). Corporate branding helps stakeholders/consumers to simplify choice and provide reassurance through emotional, functional even spiritual consistency. Cultural studies theorists suggest that: 'Consumers are constituted as autonomous, self-regulating and self-actualising individual actors seeking ... to optimise the worth of their existence to themselves by assembling a lifestyle or lifestyles, through personalised acts of choice in the marketplace' (du Gay, 2000: 69).

Organizational identity

Exercise

Choose an organization of which you have experience (your college or university or where you work) and think about the following questions:

- Who or what is your organization?
- What makes it recognizable and distinct – and why?
- Does your organization have a 'personality'? If so, what is it?
- How does the organization communicate its identity to others?
- How does your experience of the organization compare to its publicity and formal presentations of itself?

For some authors (Meech, 1996: 65–81; 2006: 392–393), there is a case to be made for distinguishing corporate identity from corporate personality. Cornelissen makes a distinction between organizational identity and corporate identity, contrasting the existence of the organization with its representations:

> The spectrum of identity involves at one end deep-seated questions concerning what the organization is and what it stands for, often referred to as the organization's identity or organizational identity. At the other end, identity involves the act of expressing an image of the organization to stakeholders through all communications campaigns, employee behaviour and products and services. The management of all such communications and expressions towards stakeholders is conceptually referred to as corporate identity ... [which] can be defined as the picture of the organization as presented to various audiences. (Cornelissen, 2004: 69)

Organizational identities develop through their histories, cultures, people, political affiliations, formal and informal positioning in relation to other organizations. For this reason it is useful to see organizational identity as something that is open to negotiation and co-creation among a number of actors.

It is important to distinguish between the identity that is a consequence of organizational policy, experiences and 'managed identity'. Managerial efforts to direct and control identity may be referred to as 'corporate branding', 'corporate culture' or 'corporate identity', depending on the extent to which marketing, design or public relations specialities, ideas and discourse dominate.

Internal regulation of identity is controlled by *top management* of an organization and so the concept of 'corporate identity' has come to imply an aspect of the organization which can be manipulated or indeed purchased from specialized consultants as a complement to, and part of, *corporate culture*. The symbolic aspects of this – visual, aural and environmental identities – are more readily altered than the human behavioural and relational aspects fundamental to organizational life.

Organizational identity can be understood as the 'essence' of the organization, comprising the multiple aspects and core components which make it distinctively recognizable. It is also part of the *lived experience* of those who work in the organization and therefore a feature of *organizational culture* (which focuses on behaviours, rituals and practices – explored in detail in Chapter 9). Nevertheless, at the same time that there exist core elements, there is opportunity for change – new market opportunities, organizational mergers and other developments. Moingeon and Soenen (2002: 17) usefully distinguished five types of identity:

- The **professed identity** – what a group or organization professes about itself to define collective identity.
- The **projected identity** – the way the professed identity is communicated via different media (including, but not limited to, mass media).
- The **experience identity** – 'the lived experience' referred to above and the beliefs members hold about the organization's character.
- The **manifested identity** – the core historical aspects referred to above as the 'essence'.
- The **attributed identity** – attributes ascribed to the organization by the organization's audiences and stakeholders.

Interpretations of the organizational identity, both internal and external, may be varied and multiple – which makes this a good moment to consider the concept of 'image'.

Image

The serious study of images requires an interdisciplinary approach since the topic has been tackled by philosophers, artists, literary figures, scientists, critical theorists and cultural studies experts. Since the 1960s the interest in images has often arisen from debate about whether contemporary developed societies are in fact *image cultures* (Manghani et al., 2006). Image as a concept is employed in religious and philosophical tracts, archaeology, iconography and art history, linguistics and semiotics, phenomenology, poetry, psychoanalysis, cinema and ideology (Manghani et al., 2006). These fascinating and complex debates are sadly outside the scope of this volume, but awareness of these connections is important for PR students, researchers and practitioners.

The term **image** is derived from *imitari* meaning imitation or reproduction (Bromley, 1993). The PR role may be defined as the projection or organizational reproductions. In other words, PR communicates organizational 'essence'. One difficulty with this view is that PR practitioners and senior management are part of the scene they are trying to project and their view may be consequently limited. The term 'projection' also connotes a filmic quality suggestive of creativity and some artistic licence. The first president of the Institute of Public Relations in the UK and a prominent British practitioner of the 1920s and 1930s, Stephen Tallents, was closely associated with the British documentary film movement and author of *The Projection of England,* which formed the blueprint of The British Council, the organization responsible for cultural diplomacy (L'Etang, 2004: 36–38). Projections, however, are consumed and interpreted by many individuals who construct various 'images' in their heads of the organization. Images and experiences and 'readings' of media come together in the construction of organizational reputation (see Figure 3.1).

It is useful to reflect at this point on the ideas of Walter Lippman, US political philosopher (1889–1974). Lippman commented extensively on public opinion, media and public relations, and developed the concept of stereotypes, a term to describe the 'pictures in our heads' as distinct from 'the truth' or 'reality'. For Lippman, the process of forming stereotypes was a way of making sense of what we observed, of piecing together and relating new information to old. This process is also described by psychologists in discussions of perceptual processes, the way in which we made perceptual representations and how we are able to distinguish what it is that we observe. Experience and learning help us to interpret new information and objects. One of the early

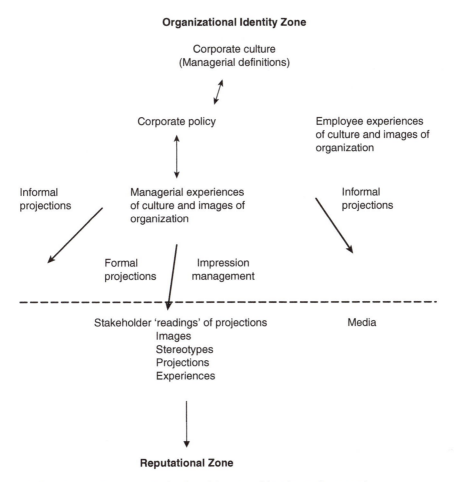

Figure 3.1 Concept map: organizational images, identity and reputation

psychologists, William James, famously described the baby's world as 'one giant, blooming, buzzing confusion' (Lippman, 1991: 81), something that we can appreciate as adults when we travel and experience cultures whose languages we do not speak or, indeed, if we are short sighted. In order to speed up the process of interpretation we rely on cues and short-cuts, as Lippman argued:

> For the most part we do not first see, and then define, we define first and then see. In the great blooming, buzzing confusion of the outer world we pick out what our culture has already defined for us, and we tend to perceive that which we have picked out in the form stereotyped for us by our culture. (Lippman, 1991: 81)

From this quote you can see why contemporary useage of the term 'stereotypes' emphasizes its value-laden and simplistic aspects. To sum up, stereotyping processes are the consequence of interplay between individual perception, the environment and cultural constructs and values. Although we can apply these ideas widely in human communication and discussions of culture, they are also invaluable in considering organizational communication. As Curtis (1991) explained:

> Social reality ... is not just out there to be understood. It has to be constructed from the social context in which we live. The role of the observer is always selective and usually creative. We all have an image of the world we have built. (Curtis, 1991: xxvi)

Stereotypes are therefore part of culture and are effective devices because they simplify life. But Lippman's analysis shows exactly how deeply they may be embedded in our daily lives:

> The system of stereotypes may be the core ... an ordered, more or less consistent picture of the world, to which our habits, our tastes, our capacities, our comforts and our hopes have adjusted themselves. They may not be a complete picture of the world, but they are a picture of a possible world to which we are adapted ... we feel at home there. We fit in. We are members. We know our way around ... we do not readily admit that there is any distinction between our universe and the universe. ... A pattern of stereotypes is not neutral ... not just a short cut. It is all these things and something more ... it is the projection upon the world of our own sense of our own value, our own position and our own rights. The stereotypes are, therefore, highly charged with the feelings that are attached to them. (Lippman, 1991: 95–96)

CRITICAL REFLECTION

- Thinking about the concept of stereotypes, what does this suggest about the values attached to the notion of consensus, both culturally and in the public relations discipline?
- Is the term 'political correctness' an attempt to counteract stereotypes or a stereotype itself?
- Does public relations influence or use stereotypes? What are the implications of these ideas about PR's role in society?

The discussion above should make clear how difficult it is to know what we are referring to when we talk about organizational identity or images. Yet it falls to public relations to 'work the hyphens', to understand stakeholder perceptions and images of organizational identity and actions and to discuss these with top management who will have their own cluster of perceptions, experiences and images. Managers frustrated at a perceived gap between their own perceptions of organizational reality and those outside the organization may harshly follow the dictum of advertiser Bernstein who wrote:

> Image is a reality. ... It is the result of our actions. If the image is false and our performance is good, it's our fault for being bad communicators. If the image is true and reflects our bad performance, it's our fault for being bad managers. Unless we know our image we can neither communicate nor manage. (Bernstein, 1984: preface)

This instructive quote has had some impact in PR business and in marketing and is sometimes heard in common parlance as 'image is reality'. One of the well-known British PR consultants whose career started in the late 1940s, Tim Traverse-Healy, argued: 'Perceptions are facts ... if a perception is right, one has the task of maintaining it. If a perception is wrong, then the communication task is to make sure that it is changed' (lecture, 1994).

Pieczka's ethnographic research into practitioners' conceptual frames showed that while they distinguished differently and variously between facts and perceptions and between perceptions and reality, perceptions were seen as entities that could be manipulated by PR experts thus 'creating the space for occupational existence in the world of action' (Pieczka, 2006a: 292). In other words, the ability to conceptualize, explain, discuss, apply and operationalize these terms defined an area of work that could be claimed as within public relations expertise.

In summary, here are some important points to note from Bernstein:

- Image is *a* reality, not reality itself, even though receivers see the images they construct as reality.
- There will always be multiple images, not just one.
- There is a distinction to be made between the image that the managers would like others to have and the images that are constructed.
- Images contribute to the development of an overall judgement about an organization's reputation. (Bernstein, 1984)

These summary points imply the importance for ongoing research in order to understand changing identities and their construction processes. A *co-orientation* approach, drawn from *mass communications* is useful here, because it shows the importance of researching internal and external stakeholder knowledge and beliefs about the knowledge and beliefs of other parties in relation to themselves. As Duherich and Carter pointed out:

> How insiders think outsiders see the organization may not be identical to how outsiders actually see the organization ... when organizational members believe that critical outsider stakeholders see the organization in a negative, identity-inconsistent way, they are motivated to attend the negative cues by engaging in *reputation repair* ... [but] the external image may not be an accurate portrayal as to how outsiders see the

organization ... some organizations seem almost paranoid, blowing negative reputation cues out of proportion, others seem to be oblivious to the negative feedback that
they receive. (Duherich and Carter, 2000: 103, emphasis added)

Critical perspectives on reputation management

Questions have been raised about PR's claims to be responsible for 'reputation
management'. An empirical study of Fortune 500 companies in 2001 raised some
serious questions about reputation management as a concept that can be managed
and measured (Hatton et al., 2001). The researchers pointed out that reputation
was affected by elements outside the control of communicators (financial performance, quality of employees, products, organizational ethics) and that corporate
communications as a function was disintegrating rather than integrating.
Consequently, they suggested that it was dangerous politically to claim control
over and responsibility for reputation. Their further challenge to assumptions in
the field was to point out that 'reputation' is a more diffuse concept and:

> Far more relevant to people who have no direct ties to the organization, whereas
> relationships are far more relevant to people who are direct stakeholders of the
> organization. A reputation is generally something an organization has with
> strangers, but a relationship is generally something an organization has with its
> friends and associates. Brands represent the middle ground between relationship
> and reputation. (Hatton et al., 2001: 247–261)

Campbell, Herman and Noble (2006) suggested that increased use of the term
might be to gain status, avoid negative connotations of the term 'PR' and thus
be part of the public relations of public relations. They also argued that reputation was partly created by publics and was thus not controllable: 'Viewing "reputation" as both independent of the organization, yet within its control, is a
difficult balancing act, but one that public relations is trying to achieve'
(Campbell et al., 2006: 193).

CRITICAL REFLECTION

Hatton et al. raised the following fundamental questions for reflection and discussion:

- How important are celebrity CEOs to organizational reputation?
- Should public relations abandon relationships as its central tenet in favour of reputation
  when marketing, and other fields focus on relationships?
- Is reputation management the most appropriate guiding philosophy for public relations?

Concepts in practice

Pieczka's ethnographically inspired work produced a partial map of public relations expertise and the relationships between key concepts, public relations tools and their effects (Pieczka, 2006a: 291–292). Her model is depicted in Figure 3.2 and shows the organizational core being projected to stakeholders, who form their own images and judgements which come together as reputation. Her empirical research showed how PR practitioners linked symbolic concepts with business measurement, for example:

- reputation – share value: 'the management of reputation improves share value'
- identity – financial performance: 'a strong sense of corporate identity is as important as slavish adherence to business financial results'
- culture – competitiveness: 'nurturing corporate culture is useless unless the culture is aligned with a company's approach to competitiveness'
- corporate – brand: 'there is almost a straight line relationship between product recommendations and excellence of corporate image' (Pieczka, 2006a: 291).

The threat of damaged reputation requires organizations to engage with concepts of *apologia* and *reputation repair* – to restore the face of the organization by presenting a convincing account of organizational actions that persuade and legitimate. Apology means that injury must be acknowledged and responsibility accepted even though legal implications may limit this. More commonly, organizations acknowledge human tragedy fulsomely, and express intention to investigate the causes and prevent reoccurrence. Organizational apologia are rhetorical performances aimed at redeeming and legitimating the organization (Hearit, 2001: 502). As such, they may entail some less than savoury impression management tactics, such as denial or claims of unintended accident, shifting blame or scape-goating, reminding audience of past good actions, making claims or promising that it will not happen again and discrediting those who blame the organization (Giacalone and Rosenfeld, 1989, 1991; Rosenfeld et al., 1995; Hearit, 2001: *passim;* Rosenfeld et al., 2002). For example: 'Wal-Mart CEO H. Lee Scott Jr apologised for the company's problems by citing a management failure for not telling its story better' (Burson-Marstellar (Hearit, 2001: 502) promotional document, 2006, *The Road to Reputation Recovery*).

Exercise

You might like to consider:

- Who creates reputation?
- How do you control reputation?
- How can trust be established?

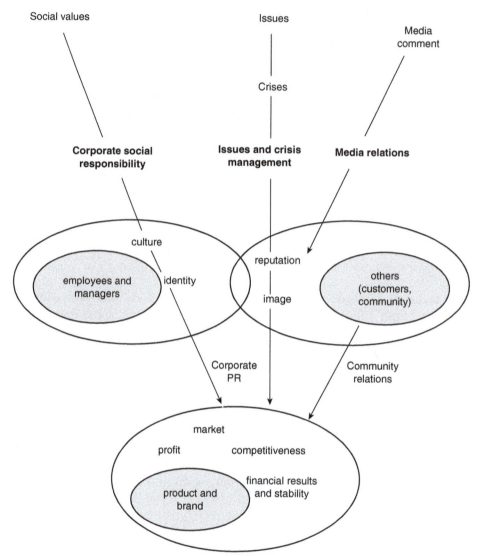

Figure 3.2 Public relations brings together the symbolic and the material
Source: Pieczka (2006a: 291)

Impression management

The field of **impression management** is of fundamental importance to PR and reputation management. It is an area which has always had a strong 'pop' side to it, illustrated by Dale Carnegie's book *How To Win Friends and Influence People*, first published in 1936. The main focus of Carnegie's book was on how to ingratiate yourself with work colleagues at all levels. Mark MacCormack, founder of International Management Group (IMG), the international sports agency, was author of *What They Don't Teach You at Harvard Business School* (first published in 1984). In a chapter entitled 'Creating impressions' he wrote:

> It is an artful form of manipulation. One of life's big frustrations is that people don't do what you want them to do. But if you can control their impressions of you, you can make them want to do what you want them to do. (MacCormack, 1984: 37)

MacCormack's advice included:

> Dressing as though you mean business ... confounding expectations [such as delivering ahead of time] ... mean what you say ... being yourself ... emotion management ... making a notable gesture ... let people off the hook ... drive a soft bargain ... flatter legitimately ... make friends and mentors ... be discreet ... do something for the kids [of client and customer]. (MacCormack, 1984: 37–60 *passim*)

CRITICAL REFLECTION

- What do you think about MacCormack's advice?

Concepts underpinning impression management

Impression management is about the devices that we use and the symbols we choose to create a particular persona with a view to influencing perceptions or images of ourselves and behaviours towards us. In this sense, impression management is the individual version of corporate visual identity programmes. Impression management is based upon the following beliefs:

- You never get a second chance to make a first impression.
- Decisions about you are made within the first few seconds of meeting.
- It is possible to manipulate certain variables to affect the impression others have of you.
- We do this anyway, so we might as well reflect about identities, personalities and how we project ourselves (Giacalone and Rosenfeld, 1989, 1991; Giacolone, Riordan and Rosenfeld, 1995, 2001).

Key elements that can be subjected to impression management are:

- physical appearance
- behaviour

- verbal communication
- non-verbal communication

There is room for manipulating our physical selves. A consideration of common techniques suggests that such practices are gendered with greater pressures on women to conform to a type or 'the look'. It should be acknowledged, however, that male anorexia and steroid abuse are increasing – as are products for male skincare and make up. Height can be added by wearing high heels, hair can be dyed and cut or permed, contact lenses or surgery can replace glasses or change eye colour, weight can be lost (and slimness is positively associated with a whole range of other successful attributes), muscle can be acquired through hard work or steroids, fake tan can be applied, teeth whitened and straightened, Botox injected and, ultimately surgery can 'lift' faces, plump lips, straighten noses and enhance or reduce breasts. Voices can be altered, manner of speaking and use of language can be manipulated, accents can be lost and found, physical gestures, cultural and gender-specific roles can be learned. Make-up and clothing are easiest of all. Thus impression management comprises individual strategies and tactics that can be seen as the negotiation of social identity. Our expectations for our self-presentation have changed as we commodify ourselves.

Visual identity management: clothing and impression management

Choice of clothing is the easiest way in which to create an impression, hence the ubiquitous classic dark suit and brands. Black is often selected for its slimming properties and has become a real uniform. Ambitious new entrants to many occupations are advised to 'dress for the grade above', although many organizations deliberately break their own conventions with 'dress-down Friday' or 'jeans day' to facilitate more informal relations. Organizational dress is an important feature of organizational and corporate culture (these terms are explained fully in Chapter 9).

Key elements of impression management practice

Successful impression management requires a confident belief in oneself to integrate physical appearance, self-presentation, beliefs and appropriate social networks. Therefore, impression management goes beyond mere physical appearance to require certain props or 'front', such as the right clothing, appropriate interests and outside activities, and membership of clubs. There are key moments when impression management skills are tested to the full, for example in interviews, important meetings with senior colleagues, and at times of organizational political uncertainty.

Key skills for impression management include:

- Ingratiation – flattering, agreements (public and private), voluntary favours.
- Self-promotion – publicizing personal connections, demonstrating market value by obtaining extra qualifications and being open to head-hunters.
- Distancing oneself from negative events.
- Finding senior patrons. (Giacalone and Rosenfeld, 1991).

Key impression management moments in public relations include:

- Job interviews
- Pitches
- Client handling
- Negotiation
- Networking
- Role-play
- Fitting in to organizational culture

Examples of impression management include:

- Tidying your room before a friend visits.
- Agreeing that you like some music to which you are actually rather indifferent.
- Keeping a clear desk and filing loose papers out of sight.
- 'Official' friendliness and 'customer care' type interpersonal relations.
- Exaggerated body language to indicate listening or sympathy ('I hear what you say').

Those influenced by impression management ideas argue that: 'The public presentation of self is always a staged activity in which the human actor presents a 'front' or 'face' to others while keeping a significant portion of the self in reserve' (Rojek, 2001: 11).

Academics from the impression management field argue that we use these tactics anyway so we might as well hone these techniques to improve our own organizational chances and to spot their use against us!! Indeed, even a simple act may in fact be staged and much more complex than appears, as R.D. Laing pointed out:

> It is not so easy for one person to give another a cup of tea. If a lady gives me a cup of tea, she might be showing off her tea pot or her tea-set; she might be trying to put me in a good mood in order to get something out of me; she may be trying to get me to like her; she may be wanting me as an ally for her own purposes against others ... the action could be a mechanical one in which there is no recognition of *me* in it. A cup of tea could be handed to *me* without *me* being *given* a cup of tea. (Laing, 1974: 106)

Laing's research drew upon interactional processes, especially *dyadic* (between two people) communication from a *psychoanalytic* perspective. It was based on listening

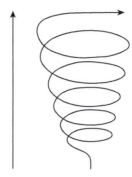

Figure 3.3 Dance's spiral of communication, a helical model showing the dynamic nature of the communication process

Source: Dance (1967: cited in McQuail and Windahl, 1981: 16)

to insights from patients and led to the development of a notation to illustrate the fact that our relationships are built on our imagined interpretations (Laing used the term 'phantasy') of that person, the existing relationship, their behaviour and what we believe it connotes about their imaginings and perceptions of ourselves. The complexity and challenges of communication, even at an interpersonal level, have been tackled from various perspectives. For example, the communications scholar, Dance (1967, cited in McQuail and Windahl, 1981), devised a simple but effective diagram to illustrate how communication events are the consequence of previous history. His simple spiral (see Figure 3.3) suggests dynamism and developmental aspects of relationships shaped through communication and relationship histories. This is similar to the approach taken by management theorist Mary Parker Follett in the early twentieth century (described in Chapter 8).

Discipline box: Psychoanalysis, psychology and PR

Psychoanalysis emerged from Freudian psychology and other psychologists, such as Jung, Adler and Klein, developed their own approaches and terminology. For example, Jungian analysts refer to themselves as **analytic psychologists** (Rycroft, 1972: 130) whereas psychoanalysis encourages free association and the interpretation of feelings towards the psychoanalyst whereas 'Psychotherapy' refers to any therapy involving reflexive discussion with an empathetic counsellor. (Rycroft, 1972: 130–131). Psychological therapies include cognitive behavioural therapy (CBT), which is used in the treatment of depression and also addiction (and therefore useful to those who wish to alter habits such as smoking).

(Continued)

The most commonly quoted link between psychoanalysis and PR is the career of US publicist Edward Bernays, a nephew of Sigmund Freud. However, while Bernays claimed to use Freud's ideas in practice, it should be remembered that this was only at a superficial level similar to contemporary marketers' concept of psychographics. Bernays studied agriculture at college so his interest in psychology and psychoanalysis was necessarily that of a lay person. A reading of his work shows that his ideas about symbolism and human motivations were not based on methodical (scientific) analysis and research or therapy. Bernays should be remembered for his considerable efforts to get Freud's work published in the USA – and for his use of the Freud name to legitimize his work (often retrospectively) as part of his own individual impression management strategies and publicity tactics (Tye, 1998).

Personal image consultancy

Our promotional culture has triggered an industry which advises individuals on their impression management skills for the workplace. This may be as limited as assessing physical shape, colouring and skin tones to advise on appropriate styles and colours of dress, or it may involve more in the way of personal coaching to help individuals develop confidence, emotional intelligence and networking skills. These techniques have entered popular culture through various popular media make-over programmes. In the UK a good example would be Trinny Woodall and Susannah Constantine's BBC1 series and associated books (Woodall and Constantine, 2003).

Box 3.2   Useful source

The Federation of Image Consultants (TFIC) (www.tfic.org.uk) –
This professional body in the UK was set up in 1988 and has its own qualifications.

*New developments in education and training:
personality PR*

In 2005, the University of Klagenfurt in Austria launched a part-time further education course for communicators on 'Personal communication management', which incorporates personality marketing and branding strategies for senior managers and communicators (www.pcm-lehrgang.at). This is aimed at helping them to 'personalize' their organizations, to present a 'human face' and to maintain personal credibility.

Exercise

Read the quote below and discuss the extent to which you agree with the author's views on female dress in public relations:

> I get impatient with young professionals in my company who ask for career advice and then spend thirty minutes planning who is going to bake the cake, provide the streamers and bring paper plates for the next birthday celebration. There are many ways to be human in business and to celebrate a colleague's birthday at lunch. Women say that they want role models. Well, they do not see executive men or women directing birthday parties at the office. And then these women whine they are not viewed as professionals. ... A woman at our last IABC [International Association for Business Communicators] meeting in Atlanta complained that her President did not seem to have confidence in her. I stood there and looked at her multi-coloured dress, lace hose, cute little earrings shaped like cats and green eye shadow and wondered how on earth she even got employed by the conservative corporation she is with. I have an idea she was hired for a public relations speciality, with little thought given to how she was going to influence top management. If she does not have enough sense and reasoning to project a serious image, why should top management have confidence in her? (Stewart, 1988)

Discipline box: Impression management

The academic origins of the field of impression management lay in the work of Erving Goffman, a sociologist. In 1959, he wrote a book called *The Presentation of Self in Everyday Life*, which was partly based on his PhD entitled 'Communication conduct in an island community', a study of Shetland crofters. Goffman's argument was that people make calculated decisions about their behaviour in order to create or maintain a particular impression so that they fit in with group norms or to distinguish the individual in a particular way. Even though Goffman's work showed that impression management was a natural part of the normal routines of behaviour, it took a long time for this to be

(Continued)

accepted. In the 1960s impression management was seen as something artificial that interfered with 'real' and 'authentic' relationships. In the 1970s it was acknowledged as a form of behaviour but seen as invariably negative and as deceptive and manipulative. In the 1980s organizational theorists explored impression management in organizational politics.

Impression management draws on sociology and social psychology to determine motives behind social behaviours that could influence other's impressions. Applied impression management is a relatively new academic area that aims to (a) make people more effective for organizational success and (b) help people recognize strategies that are being used against them. The field is presented as being necessary to organizational survival, not as Machiavellian. Impression management can be a useful tool for managers to help employers create strategies for success by creating and visualizing success, thus creating self-fulfilling prophecies. Managers who make subordinates feel that a lot is expected of them will raise subordinate's expectations of themselves and in this way impression management can be a tool for shaping performance expectations.

Source: Giacalone and Rosenfeld (1989)

Impression management therefore:

- enlightens understanding of pitch processes and consultancies
- enhances our understanding of human interactions in organizational as well as social contexts
- highlights the challenges for public relations of performing impression management on behalf of an organization to protect its reputation

Exercise

- How do PR practitioners present themselves to students? (You might like to think about visiting speakers you have seen, their dress, their mode of address to you, their language style, degrees of formality, openness, flexibility.)
- How are individual PR practitioners presented in public relations and business professional magazines?
- In the UK, PR practitioners since the 1950s have bemoaned bad press and a lack of social status for the occupation, arguing that there is a need for the 'public relations of public relations'. Why do you think this is? What could be done about it? Could you devise a credible campaign to improve the reputation of the industry?

REVIEW

Think back to the questions at the beginning of this chapter and consider:

- What images do you think are constructed of you?
- What impression management strategies do you employ when preparing for (a) a presentation, (b) an interview, (c) a night out?
- What do you think you are known for, and why?
- What would you like to be known for and why? What strategies could you use to achieve that goal?
- Is the field of impression management, and the strategies that emanate from it, manipulation or self-promotion?

In conclusion

This chapter has shown how concepts of identity, image, reputation and impression management are applied to individuals (including PR practitioners) and organizations. To some degree it hints at the existence of promotional culture to be discussed more fully in Chapter 10.

RECOMMENDED READING

Useful collections that include practitioner perspectives on reputation are available in Balmer and Greyser (2003) and Schultz, Hatch and Larson (2000). Published as this book was going to press was van Riel and Fombrun (2007), which combines conceptual discussion with many case studies from the authors' consultancy. Jahansoozi (2006) gives an excellent review of the literature relating to the concept of *transparency*. Kimmel (2004) is fascinating and very readable. An invaluable source book is the reader *Images* by Manghani, Piper and Simons (2006), which includes historical, philosophical, aesthetic, semiotic, psychoanalytic, cultural and visual contributions. The final section presents a manifesto for image studies. Impression management is still a small specialist field within management and psychology, and the most recently available text from some of the most prolific authors, Rosenfeld, Giacalone and Riordan (1995) explores psychological, organizational and communication approaches to impression management; ways of building and protecting reputation; and the influence of impression management on human resource management and organizational life. If you want good advice on how to apply impression management strategies in your own job searches and organizations, then Huczynski's *Influencing within Organizations* (2004) is useful.

Risk, Issues and Ethics

BEFORE YOU READ A SINGLE WORD...

- What is 'risk' and how do we evaluate something as 'risky' (a) as an individual and (b) as a member of an organization?
- What risks might organizations take and why?
- How can an organization be 'good'?
- Should organizations be punished for bad behaviour and, if so, how and why?

Key concepts

Business ethics	Issues
Corporate governance	Issues management (IM)
Corporate punishment	Metaphor
Corporate social responsibility	Outputs
Criminal liability	Others/othered
Disciplinary society	Public affairs
Equilibrium	Risk assessment
Feedback	Risk management
Homeostasis	Systems theory
Inputs	

Introduction

This chapter explores a range of interlinked issues that are central to public relations work in reputation management. It is argued that PR practitioners need to collaborate with risk managers, ethicists and organizational strategists in order to understand areas where future issues may develop that impact on reputation. Also considered are voluntary philanthropic or charitable activities an organization may engage in, sometimes with the avowed intention of enhancing reputation. The moral issues that this approach raises are also subjected to critical review. This chapter combines both *functional applied* concerns and *critical ethical* questions. It is intended to help you to question ideas in public relations textbooks, to ask hard questions in practice and to develop anticipatory skills.

The chapter begins by explaining a popular framework (systems) that provides the rationale for the functions of public affairs, issues management and corporate social responsibility. This facilitates a deeper understanding of (a) public relations analysis and (b) the dominant paradigm within the public relations academic discipline. It provides the rationale for public affairs, issues management and corporate social responsibility, which are the focus for discussion in this chapter and the next.

The use of systems analysis and environmental scanning helps managers to notice and track emergent issues and benefit their organizations by early response. Unmanaged issues may become crises, which necessarily involve many more uncontrollable elements. Intervening in crises may solve problems, resolve relationships and allow the organization to shape debate so that their view is understood. Issues are debated in organizational and public space (the public sphere) and policies are subjected to review. Issues management cuts across a variety of literatures, including business ethics, project management, public relations, public affairs, risk communication, management, and marketing management.

CHAPTER AIMS

On completion of this chapter you will be able to:

- explain the origins and function of issues management and link it to the conceptual framework of systems theory
- define 'risk' in relation to ethics and reputation nurturing
- explain the moral dilemmas which underlie corporate social responsibility, organizational misdemeanours and concepts of punishment

(Continued)

- define the role and scope of corporate social responsibility, community involvement and cause-related marketing
- understand the relevance of moral theory and that moral concepts underpin legal systems

Systems theory

Systems theory is a *metaphor* that can be applied to many contexts. A metaphor is a creative language device that transfers meaning from one context to another to generate new insights, either by helping us to see something in an entirely different light or by 'making strange' something we habitually take for granted (Grant and Oswick, 1996). In Chapter 9, metaphor is applied to organizational culture and management.

The systems metaphor sees the world as living, interacting organisms. It is an holistic approach which can be seen to provide an understanding of any set of relationships or domains. For example, an ecosystem is a pond: single-celled organisms, algae, plants, water beetles – all responding to inputs such as temperature and light and to each other. Systems theory emerged in academic thinking in the late 1960s and early 1970s and came from a number of different subject areas such as physics, information theory, biology, communications and media studies (Pieczka, 1996b, 2006c). Systems theory was taken up by public relations theorists in the early 1980s and became linked to the American 'Excellence' project, in which US researchers sought to explore PR communication effectiveness in the USA (Pieczka, 1996b, 2006c). Therefore, the systems framework was used to understand the functional benefits of PR (Grunig and Hunt, 1984: 8–11). This way of thinking still dominates many of the books and articles you will read. Here, a brief summary of key terms is presented, together with a short outline of the pros and cons of the systems approach based an organizational theorist Goreth Morgan's interpretation (Morgan, 2006: 38–45).

Systems theory suggests that while systems have their own distinct boundaries, they also relate and interact with their environment and other systems. The relationships and interdependence between multiple systems and subsystems creates an holistic web of connections. As systems grow and develop they become more complex and differentiated, requiring alterations in structure and function. New specialized parts also adjust, leading to further alternations and refinements. Therefore, the organization is always in a state of flux in terms of its internal structures and functions and requires formal efforts to ensure social and internal integration to hold the whole thing together. This is where the public relations function and system comes into play in order to facilitate internal communications and a shared culture (identity).

The organization takes material goods, energy and information – *inputs* – from the environment and translates them into goods or services or expertise – *outputs*. Successful organizations, it is argued, are relatively 'in balance' with their environments and manage that balance through *feedback*, making adjustments when necessary. This is done through information systems and market intelligence processes. An organization, which does not respond to external circumstances will *atrophy* and fail.

Imbalances may lead to discontent and difficult issues arising on the public agenda that could threaten the organization's reputation. Therefore organizations seek to maintain a balanced state of **equilibrium** with their environments using **intelligence gathering**, **environmental scanning** and other feedback techniques.

Each of the key organizational environments (political, economic, socio-cultural, technological, legal) is a system which has its own arrangements, subsystems and ways of relating between other environments. Each environment thus has relatively porous boundaries across which information and issues and publics flow.

Figure 4.1 depicts an organization and its external systems to illustrate the overlaps between different aspects of the external environment within which issues arise, which **media** (specialist and news) and **stakeholders** and **publics** (who may become media sources) debate. Bear in mind that this model is a static snapshot whereas in reality environments are fluid, responding to world events on a daily basis.

We could also think of the organization as a spider in its web as shown in Figure 4.2. Parts of the web represent socio-cultural, political, technological, economic and legal environments, which are all interconnected. At times the spider is closer or more concerned with certain environments in response to activity in those environments (the flies). The spider's web metaphor emphasizes network capacity between environments and the need to respond to change.

The systems approach to analyzing organization has a number of key benefits:

- It broadens our perspective.
- The organization of a system makes it more than the sum of its parts (captures the synergy of processes and relationships).
- The relationships between parts influences the shape and attributes of the system, thus implying a key role for interactive communication and language.
- It emphasizes order and stability in a chaotic and changing environment.
- It provides a clear rationale for issues management and public affairs work.

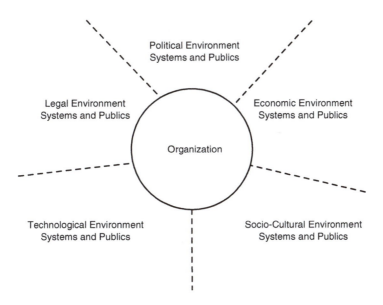

Boundaries between domains are porous, for example political decisions and policy affect all other environments; the economic context and technological opportunities affect the socio-cultural envioronment.

Figure 4.1   Organization in its environment

From a public relations perspective, systems are useful because of their emphasis on relationships, interaction and communications. The notion of feedback is of particular interest to public relations because it is likely to be most engaged in the problems of relationship management. Of particular concern to public relations theorists is the desirability of practitioners maintaining relatively open rather than relatively closed systems. An organization which is open and receptive to its external environment, and changes within it, is more likely to be able to respond and adapt to changing circumstances than one that does not. Thus, according to most PR interpretations of systems theory, public relations as a function is concerned to maintain relationships (*homeostasis*) to support the system.

Negative aspects of systems theory as used in public relations theory:

- It underplays the ability of the organization to take action and express *agency*.
- It underplays the importance of power and elites.
- It is a totalizing theory in the sense that everything is connected to everything else (because everything is a system or subsystem of something) (Morgan, 2006: 39).

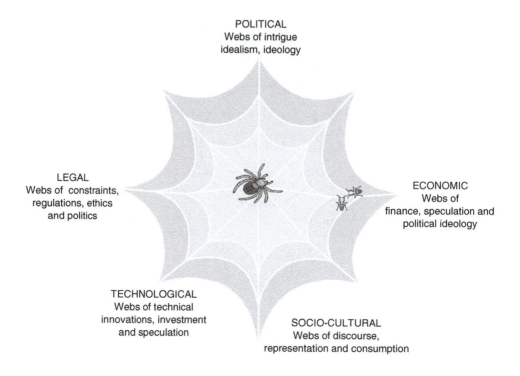

The economic sphere and networks require attention.

Figure 4.2   Spider's web of organizational environments

CRITICAL REFLECTION

In what specific ways might a systems approach impede PR practice?

Challenges to systems theory

Systems theory emerged in the 1950s but was challenged in the late 1970s by organizational theorists who moved on from asking questions about organizational control and order to questions of power and the nature of organizational reality. Organizations came to be seen not as static, but as cultural and political processes involving rhetoric and ideology (Pieczka, 1996b: 132).

Systems theorists from biology (such as Varena, Maturana, Uribe) later developed the concept of *autopoesis*, which presented an entirely different view of the system (Pieczka, 1996b, 2006c). Autopoetic systems are driven by the need to survive: 'but survival is understood as the maintenance of self-identity ... environment exists for the system only as a projection of its self-identity – or, to simplify, it is constructed by the system' (Pieczka, 2006c: 339).

As Pieczka pointed out, the living system was seen as a network of interactions, but social scientist Niklas Luhmann proposed the revolutionary interpretation which suggested that organizations needed to maintain autonomy and closure, rather than openness, to survive. This is a radically different version of systems and has implications for the PR role. Systems came to be seen as self-referential and self-producing. It is the PR practitioners that produce 'images of reality as expressions or descriptions of ... [their] own organization' (Pieczka, 2006c: 340).

CRITICAL REFLECTION

- What are the implications for PR theory and practice of the alternative view of systems?

Organizational environments are host to stakeholders, publics, media and issues, and it is to the latter that I now turn.

What is an issue?

An **issue** can be defined as a topic of debate, a trend or a recurring theme that moves from the private sphere into the *public sphere* and on to the media agenda. (The concept of public sphere is discussed in Chapter 5.)

The developmental aspect of an issue means that in the early phases it is open to negotiation with regard to its definition and significance. Issues are represented in the literature as having life-cycles: potential, emergent, current, crisis, resolution, declining, dormant. Here is a list of issues that have moved on and off the agenda over the past 20 years or so in the UK:

- food and product safety
- child obesity
- gun crime
- corporate governance
- ethics in politics
- smoking in public places
- extended hours for sale of alcohol
- music piracy

- terrorism – security
- world hunger and poverty
- globalization and anti-globalization
- global warming

Once issues have been on the agenda for a while they are often presented by the media according to a set frame. This is because the media classifies events into types for simplicity so that a repeated event becomes 'another one of those' packaged in a similar way.

Exercise

Look through three newspapers (same day) and discuss their handling of current issues.

- What are the most important issues of the day?
- If you were Public Relations Officer (PRO) for any of the organizations relevant to the key issues you have found in the newspapers you have reviewed, what would be your major concerns?

'Issues' became constructed in managerial *discourse* as areas of policy or public debate or concern (often with a legal, political or economic focus) that are relevant to the organization. The connection between the issue, media coverage and public debate could thrust the organization into the public eye. This was well captured in the 'kite' communication model devised by McLeod and Chaffee (cited in McQuail and Windahl, 1981: 23), shown in Figure 4.3.

The 'kite' model developed from the *co-orientation tradition* in *mass communications* (see Discipline box below). This drew on values of balance, congruence and supportive information and emphasized inclusive interactive communication (McQuail and Windahl, 1981: 23). The model was subsequently adopted by the systems paradigm within public relations to emphasize the importance of researching both organizational and stakeholders' opinions about an issue and the extent of agreement as well as the accuracy with which both parties understand the other's views (both of the issue and of their own views) (Broom and Dozier, 1990: 83).

The connection between issue, media coverage and public debate can thrust an organization into the public eye. Questions may be asked about the organization's stance on tough issues such as ethics, recycling, or age discrimination. Rather than waiting until the organization was put in the spotlight, management strategists suggested that it was more helpful for organizations to try to anticipate trends and debates, and to consider issues in relation to organizational function. This required a process of anticipation, preparation and

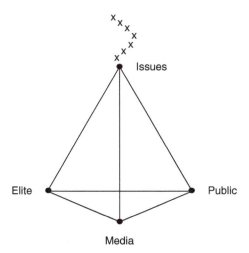

The 'kite' model shows relations (relationships, attitudes, perceptions, channels of communications) between elites, media, publics and issues.

Figure 4.3 The 'kite' communication model
Source: McQuail and Windahl (1981: 23)

planning that could ultimately protect the organization's reputation. Two organizational specialisms have developed to anticipate and prepare for contingencies: **issues management** and **risk management**. Both of these functions require a communications focus even if they are not carried out by communications specialists.

Discipline box: Mass communications and communications science

Public relations has borrowed extensively from mass communications theories and methods. Mass communications emerged in the 1940s when academics began to apply technological terminology (much drawn from telephony) to communications in order to clarify and explain processes (McQuail and Windahl, 1981). Language included terms such as 'feedback' and 'signal', and processes were partly explained through graphics or 'models'. One of the main benefits of the models for

(Continued)

(Continued)

researchers was that they facilitated quantitative research. Mass communications' level of analysis is the society, hence the interest in media (McQuail, 2000). Public relations connects with this via the notion of institutional communication that engages with media and public debate. Later mass communications adopted qualitative approaches to research socially constructed meanings. Public relations research still privileges quantitative research, although alternative approaches are emerging (this is discussed further in Chapter 12).

Issues management

The concept and definition of issues management is normally attributed to the work of US public relations consultant W. Howard Chase in 1977 (Holcombe, in Harris and Fleisher, 2005: 41–42). For some authors such as Harris (2005: 98), issues management (IM) is defined very much as part of **public affairs** and operates primarily in the governmental political domain. Issues management is intertwined with public affairs and *lobbying* and connects PR to public policy: 'The ultimate aims of issues management is to shape and respond to public policy for the benefit of the organization' (Harris, 2005: 98). Harris usefully identified key questions for practitioners which are displayed in Box 4.1.

Box 4.1 Key questions facing practitioners in relation to an emerging issue

1 Will the issue/s affect the bottom line?
2 What is the probability and time scale of this issue impacting on us?
3 Can corporate action change the outcome?
4 In the light of this analysis are our present corporate policies and practices correct?
5 Do we have the resources and the will to do something on this at present?
6 What will be the cost to influence this?
7 What are the financial or policy benefits to us of doing this?
8 What can we learn from this for the benefit of our organization?
9 How can we evaluate the effectiveness of our actions?
10 What can we learn from this situation to ensure future competitiveness?

Source: Harris (2005: 101)

Issues management implies a strategic role for public relations that can highlight communication challenges and reputational threats and help the organization to think through in advance its stance and policy in relation to emerging and future agendas. This necessarily involves researching external opinions, internal *communication audits* (see Chapter 9), scenario planning, risk assessment and crisis planning. Specifically, PR specialists can take the initiative to engage with stakeholders, emerging publics and policy-makers, which is the point at which issues management merges with public affairs (discussed in Chapter 5).

Risk assessment and the communications function

Defining risk

In this section I have followed closely the analysis of Tulloch and Lupton (2003: 2), who point out that 'risk' is a slippery term which may be used simply to mean 'danger' or it may be seen as a social construction or cultural convention about appropriate behaviour.

Risk assessment may be presented as being about statistical calculation, but risks are not reducible in this way because emotion, cultural context, mediatization and power all play a role (Boyne, 2003). Some risks are taken by those in power on behalf of others (nuclear power or weapons). Therefore, risks may indeed be real dangers that might happen, but they are also perceptions manufactured partly through our own sense-making and judgements. Our perceptions may be influenced by key sources (from social contacts or media) (Adam et al., 2000: 2). Thus there is a risk 'out there' but there is also what we all make of it individually and collectively in the various communites of which we are members; and thence how we position it socio-culturally in relation to our everyday lives, in our conversations, attitudes and behaviours (Adam et al., 2000: 2). Risks and risk debates make productive copy for journalists because they offer storylines such as: doom and gloom scenarios; threats to innocent parties; villains to blame; contradictory explanations; human interest; political intrigue.

'The risk society'

The term 'the risk society' was famously coined by the German sociologist Ulrich Beck as part of the title of a book in 1992 (Beck, 1992). Beck argued that specific risks are produced alongside benefits as a consequence of industrialization, modernization and globalization (Tulloch and Lupton, 2003: *passim*). Risks were portrayed as unwelcome 'side effects' (to use the economic and philosophical term). Beck argued that in a risk society, risks are seen as the consequence of human action (rather than fate or God) and that the scale of modern risks makes them incalculable. As Beck suggested there is considerable public debate about risks, their extent and their impact, and he pointed out that these discussions have heightened and continue to sensitize us at an individual level to dangers that can threaten us (Tulloch and Lupton, 2003: 3). However, Beck's ideas were not totally pessimistic because he thought that heightened awareness or increased perceptions of risk could be potentially productive in opening up areas for debate in society and thus encouraging democratic discussion (Tulloch and Lupton, 2003: 5).

Professionalization of risk knowledges: management, assessment and communications

The pervasion of risk awareness has had effects on various occupations and stimulated the growth of others. Risk awareness has projected scientists and health workers into the public arena, positioning them as 'media experts' and 'professionals'. Some occupations therefore benefit from the risk society in terms of their own status. For public relations, risk is a two-edged sword, since its practitioners may be seen as apologists for inexcusable dangers or accidents, rather than responsible communicators explaining levels of risk and degrees of danger. This has led to a particularly negative interpretation of public relations work in sociological literature. For example, Beck refers to 'big corporations' use of media to structure knowledge (power and research) and disseminate it', even though he acknowledged that 'there are counter usages (by special interest and advocacy groups)' (cited in Tulloch and Lupton, 2003: 5). In common with others, Beck pinned a lot of hope in the institutions of media and law to redress the balance, and anticipated that they would provide arguments that could be taken up by citizens who would be empowered to co-create meaning in the public sphere (Tulloch and Lupton, 2003: 5).

The creation of risk experts might actually disempower lay people, who are often presented with conflicting knowledge claims from different experts – something which can only add to anxieties. Risk assessment and management processes have developed into a new occupation, industrial phenomenon and part of the organizational and social economy.

Risk assessment requires extensive social and organizational practices of *surveillance* and *self-discipline*, activities which Michel Foucault explored in his analysis of society, as the political target of governments concerned to ensure orderliness and the reduction of risk (Rabinow, 1984). To illustrate the rational efficiency of surveillance that could be conducted and justified on utilitarian grounds, Foucault pointed to the utilitarian philosopher Jeremy Bentham's *panopitcon* – a large courtyard within which is situated a tower from which inmates in the courtyard cells can be observed. Since inmates could not see the guardian in the tower, they must always behave as though the guardian were present, thus serving as their own guardian (Rabinow, 1984: 19).

CRITICAL REFLECTION

You might want to ponder the role of public relations in relation to these concepts - is public relations part of surveillance processes organizationally or societally?

Risk assessment is now formally part of management discourse and there are qualifications in risk provided (in the UK) by the Institute of Risk Management (IRM) (http://www.theirm.org/thediploma/Dldiploma.html).

In the UK, the Institute of Chartered Accountants in England and Wales (ICAEW) published the Turnbull Report, which was issued to the private sector and contained guidance on what disclosures needed to be made about corporate governance and internal control, thus implying the requirement for risk management (www.icaew.co.uk, accessed 12 January 2007). Risk in this context is understood as an issue which has the potential for negative impact on an organization's mission. Notions of risk may come from compliance and legal issues (health and safety, discrimination). A risk manager in a higher education institution explained:

> The greatest general risk to a university is loss of reputation – damage to this can make it hard to recruit staff and students, to win research and other funding, to grow and develop. ... But reputational risks don't emerge out of a vacuum – if we fail to live up to our legal, ethical and general good practice standards, we risk not only the financial fallout, but also the loss of reputation, which is a lot harder to recover from. ... We do have to say, what if? What could happen if something goes wrong here? How can we prevent it? How can we minimise the impact? By doing this we can often ... identify opportunities to improve what we currently do. To use an HR example, if we were hit by a flu pandemic and 25–30 per cent of our staff weren't in work, what absolutely has to be done? Payroll. We can put back some training issues, and reschedule meetings and other activities, but people need to be paid and on time. ... I'm closely involved with crisis management: what are the risks? How likely are they to materialise and what will the impact be? What do we need to do and who is going to be responsible for it? I'll also do a fair amount of information gathering and communicate back to a crisis management group. ... [In terms of] employee communications and the media, I'll often work directly with the PR department to come up with a form of words and decide the best means and media for communicating this, though responsibility for communication is always with PR. (Interview, 5 July 2006)

CRITICAL REFLECTION

- What do you think of the relationship between the risk manager and PR as described above?
- What are the implications for PR of the professionalization of risk management?

In the organizational context it is important for public relations practitioners to understand and relate their own function to risk processes, as I shall now discuss.

PR perspectives: risk, issues, crisis and social responsibility

If one accepts Beck's view that risk is the result of industrialization, globalization and late capitalism, then it is clear that responsibility (blame) for such side-effects may be attributed to modern organizations. This provides a clear link to theories of **corporate social responsibility**, which suggest that part of the motivation for embarking on such programmes is to redress the balance of any potential negative effects and to pay some sort of social debt or meet a *social contract*. These ideas have not had much airing in public relations literature, which tends to emphasize the interests of the organization and the responsibility of practitioners to protect organizational reputation. Public relations literature suggests that PR practitioners should build up some 'goodwill wealth' and accrue this against the day when there is a crisis. It is argued that in the event of a crisis, the accumulated goodwill will effectively inoculate the organization against potential anger and protest of publics.

In risk management literature, risk is often defined as the threat or possibility that an action or event will adversely or beneficially affect an organization's ability to achieve its objectives. Likewise, crisis is 'seen as a very unusual situation that may threaten an organization's business, reputation, image, and relationships, or ... harm its publics ... threats are regarded as external threats from the market or the surrounding environment' (Falkheimer and Heide, 2006: 3).

Risk management takes strategic issues analysis to consider organizational risk and response, for example, to national security threats, energy crises or flu pandemics. Risk management has also developed from the bottom-up as an extension of health and safety at work initiatives which relate to legal requirements. In the UK, breaches of health and safety can incur *criminal liability* – 'an offence against the state' (Duncan et al., 2006: 3). Civil action, in contrast, involves negligence and/or breach of legislation. In a globalized workplace this type of risk management is complex, encompassing emergency procedures, insurance provisions, safety of equipment, violence and specific workplace problems such as manual handling, hazardous substances, stress, noise, vibration, machinery and vehicles. Other risk areas include insurance, legal and contract, competition and information systems. **Corporate governance** codes were designed to rebuild public and investor trust following a number of scandals in the 1980s (*McKinsey Quarterly*, 18 April 2004). These issues, which impact directly upon reputation are therefore of central importance to the PR function.

Box 4.2   Useful sources

Corporate Governance: an International Journal (www.blackwellpublishing.com)
Corporate Governance (www.emeralinsight.com)

A major difficulty in dealing with the terminology of *issue*, *crisis* and *risk* is that such concepts are subject to individual interpretation, peer pressures (and these are very present in organizations, especially when reinforced by lines of authority and power to emphasize team-building) and cultural context. Despite globalization we live in an inequitable world and what may be deemed as risky in one culture may not be seen as such elsewhere. As Smith commented:

> The term 'crisis' is often used to describe events and situations that are difficult to deal with, but not necessarily potentially damaging or destructive. There is also considerable overlap, at least in common useage, between the related terms of 'disaster', 'business continuity' and, to an extent, 'risk'. There has been discussion within the literature around new ways of conceptualising the relationship between 'risk' and 'crisis' management ... in practice the distinction often made ... was that risk management was seen to have a focus in the identification of potential problems, whereas crisis management was concerned with the management of the crisis event itself. ... Crises can be constructed within a spatial setting ... display emergent properties and are represented as complex non-linear events that generate problems for those who are responsible for attempting to manage them. (Smith, 2006: 1)

Issues, risk and crisis management have global dimensions and: 'the nature of emerging threats is of central importance to PR practitioners' because 'risk and crisis communication are the core of public relations theory and practice' (Falkheimer and Heide, 2006: 15). The link between risk, crisis, reputation repair and corporate social responsibility is recognized as a linear connection by Burson-Marstellar:

> A reputation that took a lifetime to create can be destroyed in seconds ... a mishandled response, inappropriate act ... poorly timed reorganization. ... However, the well-managed and reputation-conscious company need not remain defenceless when faced with a damaged reputation. ... Restoring a company's reputation is a monumental – but not impossible – task ... the most effective strategy is an apology from the CEO ... the second most recommended approach to reputation recovery is commitment to being a better corporate citizen. Corporate responsibility was once a marginal issue but it has ascended into the mainstream. (Burson-Martstellar 2006) *The Road to Recovery*. Corporate promotional document)

Therefore, the issues management function of PR needs to liaise closely with organizational risk management processes. Pontential risks need to be incorporated into issues and crisis management planning and, likewise, PR's issues management and media scanning may produce new topics that could be potentially risky for the organization and its reputation.

Issues management defined as 'anti-activism': a critical perspective

Early issue management literature included something of a corporate bias. Opponents were positioned as organizational threats and *othered* as 'activists' with the implication that they were illegitimate. In this way, we can see that the dominant paradigm in public relations is firmly rooted in the concerns of US capitalism. Anti-activist discourse is apparent in the following typical quote:

> A new era of social and consumer activism has emerged. Special interest groups and activist organizations use technology to put their causes on the pubic agenda. They force the hand of corporations and pressure government to react. Business must respond to these challenges and take an active role in setting the public agenda. ... Activists are successful in getting access to policymakers, are popular among consumers and understand how to get media attention. (Daugherty, 2001: 396)

Activists appear to be constructed as problematic in public relations. They are *the other*, the implied organizational opponents, and the term that defines them encapsulates that process. Professor Larissa Grunig described an activist group as: 'a group of two or more individuals who organize in order to influence another public or publics through action. ... Its members are committed and organized ... to reach their goals which could be political, economic or social' (cited in Smith and Ferguson, 2001: 504). Similarly, Professor James Grunig argued that:

> Critical scholars seem to ignore the countervailing power that publics have when they organize into activist groups and use tactics such as media advocacy ... litigation, legislation, and regulation to accomplish their goals. Indeed, many public relations practitioners believe their organizations have lost control to activist groups. (Grunig, 2001: 18)

Demetrious (2006) argued that the term 'public relations' is a loaded term and 'has specific connotations for activists as a self-serving capitalist activity deeply rooted in exploitative corporate history and tradition', and that consequently activist literature does not engage in public communications 'nor public relations literature deal adequately with activism' (Demetrious, 2006: 107).

Exercise

- How many 'activists' has your university invited as visiting speakers to your course?
- What is the difference between 'a public' and 'an activist group'? (Give examples)
- Is there a difference in societal legitimacy between organizations that produce goods and services and those whose mission is to try to change beliefs? (If so, what and why?)

Issues management as 'futurology': the role of scenario planning

'Futurism' and 'crystal ball gazing' generate options that make scenario-planning possible and it is in this role that issues management is primarily serving the crisis planning and management functions. The danger here is that the focus of the role is altered, thus risking the possibility that the management of ongoing issues and the development of useable policy is compromised.

Some have seen issues management simply as preliminary research prior to developing a communications campaign, but such instrumentalism may inhibit an ongoing process that feeds into corporate strategy in general. Restricting IM research to a campaign focus alters the function and loses the benefit of broad environmental level scanning and intelligence.

One of the identified benefits of IM has been its role in helping organizations develop corporate social responsibility (CSR) programmes by identifying emergent key social issues before they move on to the media agenda in a major way and adapt policies accordingly. Such strategic opportunistic responses may be advantageous although there is also a danger that CSR policy becomes incoherent and overly reactive. As will shortly be argued, organizations need to explore and define their moral principles internally first and use these as the basis for external activities.

Sources for futurologists include think tanks, conference key notes and specialist magazines such as *Blue Skies* in the UK, the by-line of which is 'Debating the policies of our future'. (www.epolitix.com/EN/Publications/Blue + Skies + Monitor)

Issues management as 'surveillance': a critical perspective

Issues management recommends 'environmental scanning' and employs the military term 'intelligence gathering' – which could equally well be described as 'surveillance'. What are the implications of this language and the activity? I would suggest that this practice, and its accompanying discourses, contribute to what social theorist Michel Foucault termed the **disciplinary society**.

One might also want to note that surveillance tactics may entail collaboration with other businesses, industry bodies and governmental organizations which have shared interests. Such partnerships reinforce institutional legitimacy in surveillance practices and have hegemonic potential. In a globalized world, such practice has implications for international society and communications. Indeed, the growth of the public relations occupation itself can be seen as an institution (professionalization) that contributes to surveillance culture.

Box 4.3   The disciplinary society

Michel Foucault saw the growth of discipline in specialized institutions (prisons) or in organizations concerned with human and social functionality (schools, hospitals) or state apparatuses to ensure discipline reigned over society (police, law) as a precondition of capitalism (Rabinow, 1984:). The consequence of technological and statistical capabilities makes it possible for 'the power of the state to produce an increasingly totalising web of control' and to define ever more clearly definitions of 'normality' (Rabinow, 1984: 22). Foucault argues:

> The judges of normality are present everywhere. We are in the society of the teacher-judge, the doctor-judge, the educator-judge, the 'social-worker'-judge ... the network with its systems of insertion, distribution, surveillance, observation, has been the greatest support, in modern society, of the normalising power. (Foucault, 1979: 304)

CRITICAL REFLECTION

- Are PR practioners 'judges of normality'?
- What might be the implications of this for the PR role in society?

PR as spying, subterfuge and sabotage: a critical perspective

Professor David Miller, media sociologist and PR critic, has commented on the surveillance activities of PR in relation to activists and the overlap between corporate spies, intelligence agencies and think tanks. He has suggested that:

The internet can be used in a variety of different ways and prophets said that it was about democratization of civil society and the impossibility of our rulers exerting control. … I'm sceptical of the approach that technology determines political outcomes. … It can be used in other ways by corporation and governments for spying, subversion, monitoring and surveillance. (Interview, 6 October, 2006)

CRITICAL REFLECTION

- In what contexts might organizations 'spy' and on whom?
- How might public relations be implicated in this role?

BEFORE YOU READ A SINGLE WORD OF THE NEXT SECTION...

- What is your view of the obligations, if any, of profit-making organizations to (a) local, (b) national and (c) international society, and why?
- Should profit-making companies that pay large taxes contribute extra funds to society, and if so, why?
- What benefits might profit-making companies gain from gift-giving?

Business ethics

The field of business ethics gained momentum in the 1960s and 1970s when there was much criticism of corporations. The social role of business and its responsibilities to society beyond economic contribution and taxes spawned a host of issues to which companies were forced to respond. *The Journal of Business Ethics* was set up in 1980 and numerous textbooks and conferences (academic and practitioner) followed.

Business ethics is the study of moral issues in organizational life. Initially it started as an investigation of the role of corporations in society and then widened into the public rather than the private sector. Early work focused on fundamental principles of justice and fairness and the role of private enterprise. It thus engaged with debates about the ethics of capitalism and socialism, and the role that corporations could play in distributive justice and creating benefits for society. Issues of philanthropy followed on from this and in a famous article by free-market economist Milton Friedman, 'The social responsibility of business is to increase its profits', published in *The New York Times Magazine* in

1970, considerable focus was given to the practices of corporate philanthropy (which I'll come on to later) (L'Etang, 1996b). Big questions were therefore asked as to whether business should act in its own self-interest and those of its shareholders or in the interests of the larger society.

Business ethics is thus the broad field within which corporate social responsibility sits. It is both internally and externally focused. Externally, it includes issues relating to consumers, product safety, communication ethics (ethics of advertising and PR), the environment, product safety, pollution, liability, regulation, multinational business and issues of globalization. Internally, it focuses on issues such as discrimination, the quality of working life, employee relations, HR practices, employee rights, employee privacy, governance and structure (power and accountability).

Why is business ethics relevant to public relations?

Ethics are the foundations for values and ideals and therefore form an important part of organizational culture. Ethics are a part of organizational identity and of course a vital part of the organization's reputational stance. But it's a tough area because the organization has to live up to publicly stated ideals. These are usually found in Codes of Ethics or Codes of Practice (L'Etang, 1992).

Since ethics and moral issues touch on all aspects of human life, it is unsurprising that business ethics, or an understanding of its importance in terms of reputation, makes it a crucial area for public relations. 'Issues' are often 'moral issues' and are very likely to be couched in such terms by journalists.

Corporate social responsibility has been on the business agenda for the last 30 years. Its antecedents in the UK were the Quakers and other social reformers, who recast the business role and social expectations of business by establishing practices that were designed to improve the communities within which they were situated during industrialization (L'Etang, 2006: 407–408). The history is important because too many business and PR practitioners and authors claim that it is a new issue or practice (L'Etang, 1996b, 2006d). CSR and PR have become closer, however, as I have remarked elsewhere:

> The concept of corporate responsibility has become ever more closely associated with public relations as the function has extended its strategic scope. The emergence of issues management in America in the 1970s coincided with that of corporate responsibility. Issues management is linked to corporate social responsibility at a strategic level because it is seen as the way in which companies can predict emerging issues, often of a social nature, to which they can respond either through issues advocacy advertising, public relations campaigns or through programmes of corporate social responsibility. The danger is that corporations can develop an incoherent, reactive approach to their social responsibility programmes, responding to external issues or trends rather than defining their moral responsibilities in a rational manner (L'Etang, 1996b: 85–86)

A key consideration for PR is whether CSR programmes are embarked upon as a moral duty or purely for their organizational advantage or whether they also seek to make positive changes to disadvantaged lives. The evaluation processes engaged in may reveal underlying motivation: programmes evaluated purely in terms of media coverage and organizational reputation indicate strong self-interest. Evaluation that engages CSR beneficiaries in programme development and evaluation is clearly rather different in terms of moral orientation.

CSR philosophies: free market or social contract?

Free market view

This approach was famously articulated by economist Milton Friedman, who argued that business was being socially responsible in its profit-making, wealth-creation role. For Friedman, business was intrinsically ethical because it promoted free enterprise (Friedman, 1970). On this account, government regulation of companies should be limited. Friedman opposed CSR because it turned companies into unaccountable (unelected) instruments of public policy. CSR was only be acceptable to Friedman if it was motivated entirely out of self-interest and justified on those grounds (Friedman, 1970).

Contractarian account

This approach attempts to balance conflicting rights and duties of citizens and business. Contract theory has been debated in business ethics literature but the concept of contract theory in relation to CSR is not straightforward. A business–society contract is not the same as a government–society contract because citizens do not vote for business leaders. Yet one can imagine an implicit contract that becomes established as convention if CSR is shown to be of intrinsic benefit to society. This follows the notion of contract envisaged by Scottish philosopher David Hume (Hume, 1980: 498). This interpretation of contract implies that it is a technique to achieve and formalize a particular type of relationship. Indeed:

> The practice of corporate social responsibility is potentially a way of redressing the balance and redistributing benefits and burdens in society on the grounds that business benefits from publicly funded infrastructures and considerable economic, social and political power and that this accumulation of power should lead to increased responsibility. (L'Etang, 1996b: 89, 2006d: 413)

Anthony Giddens, academic architect of New Labour's Third Way, articulated CSR principles as:

Fair commercial competition, monitoring corporations; incentives for corporations to act ethically; ecological safeguards placed on corporations; protection of civil society and freedom of expression; employee share ownership; and unions' protection of workers from corporate excesses ... the more aggressive forms of shareholder capitalism and thus corporate excess risk destroying the social fabric and the civil frameworks that underpin capitalism. (cited in Mackey, 2006: 4)

Cause-related marketing (CRM) is the term used to describe programmes such as Tesco's 'computers for schools', whereby the more a product or service is sold, the more money goes to charity. Other terms used, such as *community involvement (CI)* or *corporate community relations (CCR)*, are self-evident.

CRITICAL REFLECTION

- Should companies be required to redistribute further profit beyond the taxes they pay?
- How should benefits and burdens be distributed in society and why?
- Why might it be important instrumentally (functionally) for companies to organize CSR on a long-term basis?
- What issues face PR practitioners in relation to CSR programmes?

The uses of moral theory

Moral theory helps us ask questions in an informed and logical way. Here are some important questions that could be usefully directed at those running CSR, CRM, CI or CCR programmes to help them make good choices:

- How does this CSR activity relate to previous practice and existing relationships?
- Why is this CSR activity proposed? What is the motivation?
- Who is going to benefit from CSR, in what way, by when and how will we know?
- How is CSR to be evaluated?
- Should CCR (corporate community relations) be used for competitive advantage?
- Is CSR about 'being good, looking good or doing good'? (L'Etang, 1989)

Discipline box: Philosophy – ethics and morality

Philosophy asks basic questions about what we can know, how we know it and what it means to know something (epistemology) and analyzes knowledge, politics, beauty (aesthetics), knowledge structures and arguments (logic), the mind and morals (or ethics) (Lacey, 1976: 176–177). Philosophy analyzes concepts and methods such as

(Continued)

those of science or social science (epistemology underpinning research methodology). In theory, there could be a 'philosophy of public relations', although very few people have tried to think about PR in this way. Two academics who have taken on this challenge have been Arthur Sullivan (Sullivan, 1965: 240–249) and Professor Latissa Grunig (L. Grunig, 1992: 65–92). Ethics and morals are exchangeable terms to describe how people ought to behave. Systems of ethics define good and bad, right and wrong behaviour but arrive at these definitions somewhat differently. Key frameworks in Western philosophy include:

- utilitarianism – obliges us to maximize happiness
- deontology – emphasizes duty and obligations that we owe

  The ethics of public relations is usually discussed in relation to:

- professional codes of conduct
- propaganda, where propaganda is defined as lying as opposed to truth-telling
- 'spin-doctoring', where such practice is seen as manipulation
- corporate social responsibility
- business ethics, regarding organizational culture

The interest in contentious issues that arise from ethical considerations has led to the development of a number of specialist applied fields such as medical ethics and business ethics (within which debates about corporate social responsibility and public relations are properly located).

Box 4.3   Examples of corporate social responsibility

GlaxoSmithKline community investment activities in 2005 were valued at £380 million. GSK responded to various natural disasters, including the Asian Tsunami and the New Orleans floods (*Human Being*, GSK Annual Review, 2005).

W.K. Kellogg Foundation undertakes the following investment activities:

- It funds women with seedcorn money in rural South Africa to start and sustain. small businesses.
- It supports native artists to market their work as a cultural and development tool for self-determination and poverty reduction.
- It revives schools in the Bolivian Andes (W.M. Kellogg Foundation, 2005).

Citigroup Asia Pacific committed more than US$20 million to support over 140 community programmes in Asia Pacific, prioritizing microfinance and the reduction of poverty; financial education/literacy; educating the younger generation; disaster response; sustainable development in China and Indonesia; and volunteering (Citigroup, 2005).

(Continued)

(Continued)

Chelsea Football Club was the first major football club to commit to a CSR programme in January 2007 (Rogers, 2007: 19).

Human rights: companies can seek guidance from the UN's Draft Norms of Responsibilities of Transnational Corporations and Other Business Enterprises with Regard to Human Rights (www.umn.edu/humanrts/links/businessresponsibility-comm-2002html) (Amnesty International, 2003).

Working in CSR: practitioner perspectives

Those whose careers take them into CSR tend to become very passionate and committed to their work. They are evangelists for their specialism who see the human as well as the organizational benefits of such work. Box 4.4 presents key quotes from an interview with an expert CSR specialist:

Box 4.4 Working in CSR

I got involved because my job is head of corporate affairs. ... I could help the company communicate with its stakeholders and community relations was one of the things that was an important part of that. ... There are two really valuable things for companies about CSR work. One is that all employees are members of communities and customers are members of communities, and the second is that staff actually want to do things and they want the company to be involved in their local communities. They feel good, they want to do things and they also like to do things together as teams as well because organizations are social as well as work – that's a very big driver for our community relations strategy.

There's a community expectation that corporates will act in their total capacity as a responsible organization but that in addition to being a good employer and having good work practices and behaving ethically ... the company will have a community strategy and give back to the community...

It is a question of where we could add value and answering the question: what should the world's largest financial company be doing in these communities and we felt that one was to provide disadvantaged groups the opportunity to get access to financial services and the second was providing financial education, helping people understand money better, especially people who didn't have access to a lot of money, or making customers more aware and responsible. ... We are an advocate for financial education...

Evaluation – the hardest part is to measure impact but we fund impact studies because we recognize it's important to demonstrate proof of the value of the effort. Financial education is difficult [to evaluate] because you can't measure the long-term

(Continued)

impact of education through a single programme, but we will put a quiz at the end to see if they learnt anything...

The Micro-entrepreneur of the Year Award would bring tears to your eyes, they are so incredibly inspiring. These women (some men but in microfinance more borrowers are women than men) – you see them getting out of poverty, having small businesses that hire people so they become managers, sending their kids to school and their kids getting an education. One of the most critical things for women's empowerment is financial security ... organizations have a power to influence and this is the way to get the voice of the poor into the public sphere. (Interview, senior practitioner, September 2006)

CRITICAL REFLECTION: CSR AND THE COMMUNICATIONS INDUSTRY

Wayne Drew, CEO of the International Visual Communications Association, was reported in *PRWeek* as raising critical issues for the PR industry:

Globally, communicators could be accused of pollution at a devastating level – a pollution that consists of ignoring or trivialising important issues, or promoting mediocrity and unsustainable values... (Cowlett, 2006c: 22)

• How could the PR industry address this criticism?

CRITICAL REFLECTION: CSR AND CORPORATE UNACCOUNTABILITY

Professor David Miller, media sociologist and critic of PR since the 1990s, has commented:

There are progressive elements in the business classes and there are people inside corporations who want to do the right thing ... and there are people in business corporations who genuinely believe they can make corporations more ethical and if they give something back to the community that will change what the corporation is like. ... So I think there is a struggle inside the corporation [and] an element of dispute ... some of the CSR people come across as dangerous radicals to some ... of the accountants and the straight executives. ... The key problem for me is that [CSR] is about replacing functions that should be exercised by democratically elected governments ... it's stopping the possibility of the democratic regulation of corporations ... it's a means to pursue corporate strategy... (Interview, 6 October, 2006)

Curiously, the point about unaccountability was also made by the radical right wing free market economist Milton Friedman (L'Etang, 1996b: 87; 2006e: 412).

- Is CSR about being good, looking good or doing good (L'Etang, 1988)?
- How can companies best use their resources?
- How should CSR be evaluated and why?

Corporate punishment?

The other aspect of corporate social responsibility relates to the liability of organizations in the case of accidents. Key considerations here are:

- Who is to blame?
- How are blame and punishment handled and why?
- How are communications and apologia handled?
- How are accidents and subsequent fall-out handled in the organization? What, if any, change follows?

A major problem is whether those at the scene of the accident are to be held responsible or whether managers are responsible for safety/risk processes and therefore it is they who should be accountable (L'Etang, 1996b, 2006d). In legal philosophy, this tension is expressed as the dichotomy between the 'hands' and the 'brain' of the organization.

Exercise

- Should senior managers or those who were directly involved in an organizational accident be held accountable and punished? Give reasons for your answers.
- How can organizations be punished since they are not people? What sort of punishment might be appropriate and why?
- Thinking back to Foucault's insights on the disciplinary society, should the state or management regulate organizational action, and if so, why?
- How might PR be included or implicated in blaming processes, and why?
- If PR is part of the management team, should it accept partial responsibility for corporate accidents? If so, how should PR be punished and why?

REVIEW

Reflecting more deeply upon this chapter's contents and the questions asked of you at the beginning, you may now like to consider the following:

- What moral obligations prevail upon the practice of PR and why?
- How may a PR practitioner assess and manage organizational risk?
- When might relationships become intrinsically risky, and what can PR do about it?
- What ought a PR practitioner to do if an organization has been negligent or has failed to meet public (as opposed to legal) demand?
- What is the role of internal PR (employee communications) of an organization (a) threatened by risk, (b) accused of malpractice, (c) involved in an accident that has resulted in injury or death?

In conclusion

This chapter has reviewed some key concepts and raised critical questions about their assumptions and implications. In particular it has linked the study of public relations to challenging questions about moral values, social organization and control, which suggests connections between PR practice and power.

RECOMMENDED READING

The most comprehensive critique of systems theory and its associated links to the 'Excellence project' can be found in Pieczka (1996b) and (2006c). These are best read alongside Professor Grunig's response to criticisms (2001). The *Handbook of Public Affairs* (Harris and Fleisher, 2005) brings together a range of academics from public affairs, marketing and politics, together with public affairs practitioners to provide a valuable collection of insightful contributions. Students will notice, however, that contributors and editors see 'public affairs' as quite distinct from PR. On the subject of organizational and managerial ethics, Maclagen (1998) provides useful insights, including discussions of corporate social responsibility. Parsons (2004) provides an introductory and commonsensical account of PR ethics, which raises important issues, although it lacks theoretical treatment. For this, turn to Somerville (whose PhD was in philosophy) (2001), or indeed my own work (L'Etang, 1989, 1992, 1994, 1996b, 2006e).

Public Affairs and the Public Sphere

5

BEFORE YOU READ A SINGLE WORD...

- What is 'public opinion', and how can we find out what it is?
- How can ordinary people make their views known in the public arena?
- Why does public relations need to understand public opinion?

Key concepts

Interest group	Public affairs
Lobbying	Public opinion
Political communication	Public sphere
Political marketing	Stakeholder
Private sphere	Think tank
Public	

Introduction

This chapter begins by highlighting important environmental features that influence public affairs and political communication. It starts with a descriptive review of some fundamental terms used in public relations discourse, drawing out implications for practice. It then proceeds to sketch out major conceptual issues which provide the backdrop for public affairs and political communication in the context of democracy by providing an account of the public sphere. The review positions public affairs and political communication within political and sociological theory, and links it to concepts of 'spin' and propaganda. Following a critical and theoretically driven account, a more functional approach is taken to describe public affairs work, linking theoretical literature with practice.

CHAPTER AIMS

On completion of this chapter you will be able to:

- define and explain key terms and their application of these terms to PR practice
- describe the fields of public affairs and political communication and their practices
- critically review and discuss the impact that public relations has on democracy and the public sphere

Box 5.1   Key factors that frame public affairs and political communication

- political philosophies, values and ideologies that have shaped historical developments and underpin political arrangements
- political architecture and relationships between state, royalty, religion, subjects/citizens and the media
- legal framework
- transparency of state and corporate organizations
- historical and current international relationships and diplomacy
- political economy and trade relationships
- cultural/ethnic composition and relationships
- globalization.

Source: adapted from Harris (2005: 23)

Terminology of the field

Many of the key terms discussed in this chapter share the root term **public**, a sociological term which means a group of people who identify a common issue and organize themselves to articulate concerns through campaigning or lobbying. **Public opinion** may be used either to refer to an understanding of the common, outwardly expressed consensus or to a statistically researched numeric account of outwardly expressed views of a representative sample of the population. The **public sphere** is a concept used to refer to the domain in which issues are debated, in contrast to the *private sphere*, which is personal, domestic space. The public sphere includes work, formal institutional communications, public relations work, media, politics, and policy formation and implementation. Those active in the public sphere may be deemed *public individuals*. Each of us has a public face and a private face (though this separation can be threatened in the case of celebrities), but public individuals are those who lead institutions or causes that shape policy. Since policy dictates the immediate legal, economic, socio-cultural environment, its development and process is the area of prime concern for all organizations. These processes (political, legal, administrative and communicative) and the interplay and debate between concerned actors defines the field of *public affairs* in common parlance. Public affairs is also a public relations 'strategic' specialism that makes sense of environmental change especially in relation to *public policy,* which it may attempt to influence through **lobbying**. Publics may be defined as active or passive or as activist groups, and are distinguished by some authors from **stakeholders**, who are seen as those who have a legitimate stake (investment, relationship) in the organization. *Political communication* is a catch-all phrase used variously to refer to party-political communication, lobbying and public affairs, whereas **political marketing** refers explicitly to the application of marketing theory and techniques, including *political advertising, market research* and *public opinion polling* using *quantitative* (numerical, statistical) and *qualitative* (focus group) techniques. *Political public relations* is a less commonly used term because some political work in public relations is subsumed under the term 'public affairs', which in any case overlaps with issues management and lobbying. Some public affairs practitioners see themselves as an outcrop of the legal profession or as political affairs specialists who have received their grounding as political researchers or assistants to politicians. Political public relations may now be a less common term because of the popularity in common discourse of the pejorative phrase 'spin-doctor' – a term which suggests a skilled wordsmith or expert in rhetorical persuasion, but which also perhaps connotes webs of deceit and hidden influence as well as media manipulation.

Public opinion

Public opinion is a challenging topic that has intrigued and fascinated generations of thinkers. The origin of the concept is credited to Rousseau in 1750. However: 'generations of philosophers, jurists, historians, political theorists and journalism scholars have torn their hair out in the attempt to provide a clear definition of public opinion' (Noelle-Neumann, 1993: 58). To summarize crudely the outcome of much philosophical debate, the concept can be subdivided into two main interpretations:

- public opinion as the *general* will or overall *consensus*
- *a majoritarian* definition – it is the majority opinion that matters and that should count.

The concept of public opinion is used rhetorically by politicians and journalists, although they do not always make clear which definition they are using.

The first definition above derives from Rousseau and captures the sense of *climate* rather perfectly (discussed in the context of organizations in Chapter 9). The concept of the general will raises some interesting questions about how consensus develops, who influences it and whether minority views can be articulated or get an equal hearing. Noelle-Neumann's research argued that 'the climate of opinion depends on who talks and who keeps quiet' and she suggested that peer pressure created a snowballing effect that deters from alternative views being expressed, certainly in relation to the expression of voter intention (Noelle-Neumann, 1933). Noelle-Neumann also proposed that the cumulative effect of peer pressure could result in a spiral of silence, whereby minority views were increasingly suppressed. This phenomenon has some similarities with processes of groupthink – a term used by theorist Irving Janis in relation to the quality of decisions made by small groups of policy-makers. Research into groupthink by social psychologists has shown that it has application to political, corporate and other spheres (Janis, 1972; Janis and Mann, 1977). These ideas are returned to in Chapter 9 in which the politics of organizational life is given some consideration. Political organizations, too, have their own internal politics and ideological debates as well as public policies.

Because the general will is difficult to pin down, the majoritarian definition is useful in our scientific culture and is also the concept which underpins opinion polling.

Why does public opinion matter?

The fundamental democratic value requires that policy is supported by public opinion. Taking account of public opinion minimizes the possibility of dictatorship. However, all politicians attempt to 'manage' public opinion to drive through their policies efficiently. Efforts at politically inspired persuasion are inevitably open to charges of propaganda. The media have a crucial role in representing non-official views but are themselves part of an institutional elite. Alienation from political processes is a worrying sign for democratic health, hence the concerns about low voter rates in recent local and national elections in the UK.

Public opinion matters to public relations practitioners whether or not they work in the political sphere. It is dynamic, fluid and a *shape-shifter* – which is why public relations is always focused on change. Public opinion intersects interpersonal and mass communication and is relevant to processes of reputation formation. All organizations need to take account of the current climate and to participate in open debate. PR practitioners in their intelligence-gathering and environmental-scanning roles need to perceive trends and developments whether they are political, commercial or social. Public opinion polls, think tanks, newspaper leaders, current affairs programmes, conferences, media coverage and scientific research are all sources of information.

Here are some alternative definitions of public opinion:

- the majority opinion aggregated from individual citizens
- the qualitative climate of opinion
- the opinion of elites
- the opinion of the media
- the consequence of media opinion (which assumes media consumers are passive recipients incapable of exercising their own independent judgement)
- a meaningless fiction (see discussion in section below on public opinion research)

Exercise

- Listen to any news programme and note the use of the term 'public opinion' by different contributors. How do they use the term?
- How and when have you encountered 'public opinion' in your daily life?

Public opinion intelligence potentially forms a key part of public relations jurisdiction and requires the ability to commission research such as surveys, and to understand statistics.

Exercise

- What political action have you been involved with and why?
- What are your reasons for voting or abstaining?
- How could you engage further with public affairs?

Use your answers to the questions above to reflect upon your views about the democratic process and your own responsibilities as a citizen. Then consider how you could engage differently in public affairs (through political action or volunteering for a charity) in a way that could help provide you with valuable experience when applying for public relations jobs. Improving facilities locally for the elderly might not seem very glamorous but you will learn a lot about local politics and media.

Public relations and public opinion: a critical perspective

Lana Rakow, one of the first to use critical theory to analyze public relations, put forward the following arguments to understand the complex relationship between public relations and public opinion:

> Advertising and marketing textbooks assert that a business or industry only succeeds by the approval of the buying public. Public relations textbooks state that public opinion is the *raison d'être* for the existence of public relations ... authors see no contradiction between ... [the] view of public opinion as powerful and their accompanying statements that the goal of public relations is to manage it ... If individuals, can, must and should be persuaded, where does the power actually lie? In the individuals? Or in the hands of those who do the persuading? Rather than locating public opinion as the *source* of power, it is more accurate to locate public opinion as a *site* of power ... In sum, the marketplace metaphor provides a justification for the competition of organizations for public opinion under the guise that the public, not organizations themselves, is a powerful actor in, and arbiter of, public affairs. Along with this justifcation is a belief that all groups and organizations are free and equally able to compete for resources and favour in the marketplace, which is a belief in pluralism (Rakow, 1989: 173–174).

Critical exercise

- Review the indices of a range of introductory public relations text books to see what they have to say about the public sphere and the role of public relations - what does this tell you about the state of the field?

The role of public relations in identity construction of collectivities and in facilitating influence in the public sphere raises a number of critical questions regarding equity and influence.

Lana Rakow argued that the public should be able not only to reflect upon and discuss issues but to 'exert decision-making authority' and collective action (Rakow, 1989: 178). She argued that, 'To divide individuals into publics, markets, clients or audiences is to maintain the flow of communication from the institution *to* people, preserving the institution's position of authority over them and preventing collective discussion or decision-making among these groups' (Rakow, 1989: 178).

Instead she suggested centring the public to direct the actions of organizations which would be objects of the public's will, thus truly becoming 'an active public' (Rakow, 1989: 178). Rakow was very clear to distinguish her definition of an active public engaged in dialogue from the version proselytized by the dominant paradigm in PR:

This is not the same as calling for a reciprocity of interaction between institutions and individuals or publics, however, as implied by James E. Grunig and Todd Hunt's (1984) two-way symmetric model of public relations and Ron Pearson's (1988) ethic of dialogue in public relations. It is one step to say that, contrary to the amount of power typically exercised by institutions, individuals or publics should have equal power in an interaction with an institution. It is quite another to suggest, as is being suggested here, that institutions should not have a right to as much power as people, that is, that institutions have no right of dialogue, but that people do *with other people*. Only when institutions are sublimated to the publics, can we entertain the possibility of authentic discussion, the necessary basis for genuine democracy. (Rakow, 1989: 181)

Public relations and public opinion: the need for research

A great deal of research has been conducted into public opinion in relation to voters, elections, polling, policy-making, democratic processes, non-democratic contexts (collective opinion in authoritarian, totalitarian and tribal contexts), technological change, and the mass media. A remarkable study was conducted by Susan Herbst, in which she interviewed political actors (journalists, activists and legislators) about public opinion and found that they tended to reject 'the voice of the people' as 'uninformed and nebulous, relying instead on interest groups and the media for representations of public opinion' (Herbst, 1998). An important question that has yet to be answered is: how do public relations practitioners understand, employ and operationalize the term 'public opinion'?

Public opinion research

Public relations practitioners are urged to set *measurable* objectives and to conduct quantitative research (and quantitative research still dominates the public relations academic discipline). Yet some serious questions have been raised about public opinion research. For example, media sociologist Pierre Bourdieu, in a famous article provocatively entitled 'Public opinion does not exist', challenged the value of the majoritarian approach to public opinion when he wrote:

> Every opinion poll supposes that everyone can have an opinion ... it is taken for granted that all opinions have the same value ... the simple fact of asking everyone the same question implies the hypothesis that there is consensus about the problems, that is, agreement about which questions are worth asking. (Bourdieu, 1973)

In other words, questionnaires set an agenda and put a value on the majority. There are some key questions that public relations practitioners need to bear in mind and try to ascertain when planning public opinion and other quantitative research as Price (1992: 68) pointed out:

- Where does opinion come from? What or who has influenced the individual?
- What alternative choices have framed or constrained the response? Whose agenda?
- How close is the public response to privately held views?
- How stable are these views?
- Is one person's 'very strongly' the same as the next person's?
- Is the response rational or emotional?
- What is the relationship between opinions and actions/behaviours?
- How important is this issue to the individual? (Price, 1992)

Publics

The term **public** has been around since the turn of the twentieth century and developed out of research into public opinion. As Price points out (1992: 24–29), the term can be contrasted with:

- **crowd** – a group who share simultaneous experiences in an anonymous setting where emotions can spread quickly. So the crowd could turn into a mob (e.g. support for a band or a football match).
- **mass** – a shared but individual experience such as watching television (this might be particularly of interest if what is viewed is a major media event such as early footage of 9/11, the Asian tsunami, *Big Brother*, or *X Factor* finals).
- **mob** – a riot or violent uprising, implying hysteria and hypnotism relevant to studies of riots or mass panics (e.g. celebrations and riots following Pinochet's death in Chile).
- **public** – 'A group of people confronted by an issue, divided in their ideas about it and who consequently engage in discussion to resolve the issue. A group who face a similar problem, recognize it exists and organize to do something about it' (Blumer, 1948, cited in Price, 1992: 24–29) (e.g. local action group in Stirling, Scotland, protesting about the proposed erection of giant pylons).

The concept of publics in public relations has become theoretically and ethically problematic. As Leitch and Neilson point out:

> ...the organization may attempt to create publics that have no existence outside of public relations discourse. ... Members might have experienced no sense of shared identity or solidarity prior to becoming the object of public relations attention. ... Publics appear to come into existence only when an organization identifies them as publics. ... Publics ... appear not to be actively involved in the ongoing construction of their own identities, strategies or goals ... [this] can make practitioners blind to the presence of important publics. (Leitch and Neilson, 2001: 136)

In other words, public relations practice *others* and *objectifies* publics who become *subjects*. This matters because it affects the balance (and potentially the quality) of the relationship between the organization and its stakeholders/ publics. (This is also a problem in quantitative research, such as public opinion polling, in which the agenda for discussion is laid out clearly by the researcher). In such contexts it is challenging for public relations not to be implicitly bound up in power structures.

Public relations perspectives on 'public'
and 'stakeholder'

There are many usages of the term 'public' in public relations practice and public relations writing. Why is this? Because the concept which 'public' and other terms attempt to describe are *multi-discursive*, value-laden and sometimes controversial. Usage may depend on what the author or speaker wishes to convey about organizational relationships. According to the PR author, Kim Harrison:

> The term 'stakeholder' originated in the physical act of miners staking a claim: in the past, miners marked each boundary of their territory by hammering a stake into the ground. The term is now commonly used to describe individuals and organizations who have a stake in the corporation. They have something at risk and therefore something to gain or lose as a result of corporate activity. (Harrison, 2003: 499)

Steve Mackey who teaches PR at Deakin University, Australia has argued against the over-use of the term 'Stakeholder'.

> A ... pervasive pathology of stakeholder theory is the way users frequently co-opt journalists as stakeholders. 'The media' are often listed as stakeholders both in business management literature and in public relations literature. ... This co-option is anathema to the principles of democratic civil society. ... People in the public relations sphere are ... well aware of the concept of information subsidy ... underfunded and corporately owned journalism organizations apparently rely more and more on pre-produced material from public relations sources. ... If journalists have a pre-existing investment or reciprocal connection of some sort – a stake in the organization they are scrutinizing – then credibility is lost. If some pre-existing special relationship is not what casting journalists as stakeholders means, then why use the term? (Mackey, 2006: 10)

He suggests that when the term is applied to groups such as 'voluntary groups, protest groups, trade unions' they become effectively incorporated into relationships with the state and business organizations and 'beholden to the rest of society' instead of retaining independence in civil society (Mackey, 2006: 5). This argument is consonant with that of Leitch and Neilson (2001), quoted earlier, which showed how powerful organizations construct publics.

Box 5.2 Summary

- The sociological term '**public**' describes a group that gets together in response to an issue that affects them, yet public relations practitioners and academics use the term to describe large groups which share similarities (shareholders, employees) but who may never have had any direct contact with each other, as Leitch and Neilson (2001) point out. To get around this problem, PR Professor James Grunig developed sub-categories of active, passive and latent public in situational theory, which drew on Blumer (1948) and Dewey (1927) (Pieczka, 1996a: 59–60, 2006d: 427).
- Some use the term 'public' only for 'active publics', whereas others use the terms 'publics' or 'audiences' (some may use these terms interchangeably).
- Some use the term 'activist' to stand for the original meaning of the term 'public' (i.e. a group that faces an issue and organizes).
- An alternative term to 'activist' is the issue-based concept of **interest group** and sometimes these are combined as issue-based activism.
- Some use the term **stakeholder** for all those who have an interest in, or relationship to, an organization and use the term 'public' in its original sense (i.e. a group that faces an issue and organizes).
- Some define the media as a public, which is not technically correct except, perhaps, in instances of a media-instigated campaign (disclosure of information), in which case the media could be seen as an 'activist public'.
- Some argue that the media is not a 'public' because it is a channel for reaching publics/stakeholders.
- Some public relations theory does not seem to engage with the sense of identity that groups may have of themselves, rather than those imposed on them by practitioners.
- The term 'general public' is not generally used in public relations because it is thought to be too broad to be meaningful. This may partly be the influence of marketing which segments large populations using demographics and psychographics.

What these different views tend to show is that concepts of public and public opinion are *constructed* from various subject positions based on specific sets of assumptions about values and relationships that are open to interrogation.

CRITICAL REFLECTION

- What do you think is implied about an organization's relationships if the terms 'public', 'activist', 'stakeholder' and 'audience' are used?
- Can the media be accurately defined as (a) a channel, (b) an audience, (c) a stakeholder, and (d) a public? What issues might arise from such definitions?

- Is the term 'general public' another term for 'public opinion'?
- Is the term 'public opinion' another term for 'media coverage'?
- Review the indices of a range of introductory public relations textbooks to see what they have to say about the public sphere and the role of public relations. What does this tell you about the state of the field?

CRITICAL REFLECTION

- Are all stakeholder groups of equal importance?
- On what basis could one distinguish them and why?

Well-known business ethics writer Norman Bowie argued that organizational obligations to different stakeholders need constant monitoring and reassessment. In what might seem a radical step, he suggested:

The interests of employees often take priority over the interests of other stakeholders. ... I reject the view that treats all stakeholder interests as equal in all cases ... the primary purpose of business is to provide meaningful work for employees and that if managers focus on this goal, business will produce quality goods and services for consumers and profits as beneficial by-products. (Bowie, 1990: 8)

CRITICAL REFLECTION

- How should public relations practitioners assign priorities to stakeholders and on what basis?
- How might PR practitioners convince top management to reconsider their own prioritization of stakeholders?

Management specialists picked up on the importance of the stakeholder concept and soon it was being proselytized in business schools as a route to business excellence and corporate advantage. For example, Rosabeth Kanter, the well-known management expert, argued: 'corporations that will succeed and flourish in the times ahead will be those that work in partnership with all their stakeholders to continue to create new value' (cited in Solomon, 1994: 278).

In 1995, an international group of scholars embarked on a large research project, *Redefining the Corporation*, the goal of which was to: 'develop a broad conception of the corporation as a vehicle for advancing the interests, and responding to the concerns of multiple and diverse "stakeholders" defined as persons or groups that stand to benefit from, or be harmed by, corporate activity' (Clarkson Centre for Business Ethics, 1999: v). The project developed 'stakeholder principles' to define the scope of 'stakeholder management', which emphasized the role that stakeholders should play in decision-making and the importance of open communication and co-operation. Corporations should minimize harms and distribute benefits and burdens fairly among stakeholders as well as: 'acknowledge likely tensions between their own role as corporate stakeholders and their legal and moral responsibilities for other stakeholders and should address such conflicts through open communication, appropriate reporting and incentive systems and, where necessary, third party review' (Clarkson Centre for Business Ethics, 1999: 4).

The Clarkson principles offered a contrast to the overtly managerial ones which recommend stakeholder analysis purely in terms of their strategic value to the organization. Such approaches are exemplified by Harrison (2003: 506) and the strategic business and management scholars, Johnson and Scholes (2002: 208—215), whose work is often cited in core public relations texts. They suggest mapping stakeholders against organizational aims and current issues in terms of their ability to influence and affect developments. Stakeholders can be mapped in terms of their access to media, policy-makers, their influence and likely motivations and subsequently assessed in terms of their power.

The public sphere

Public opinion research is largely associated with discussions about political and democratic arrangements that deal with questions of how citizens or subjects can articulate their views and where. For Jürgen Habermas, the notion of the **public sphere** was of a space where private opinions could be transformed into a more general public opinion in relation to democratic procedures and state policy development and decisions – 'the sphere of private people come together as a public' (Habermas, 1989: 27). Habermas criticized the role of public relations in this process, arguing that:

> Public relations invades the process of 'public opinion' by systematically creating news events or exploiting events that attract attention. ... PR bestows upon its object the authority of an object of public interest about which – this is the illusion to be created – the public of critically reflecting private people freely forms its opinion. 'Engineering of consent' is the central task. (Habermas, 1989: 193–194)

Habermas suggested that PR has the ability to set the agenda and thus intervene and disrupt the bottom-up flow from citizens to those in power. Other media sociologists picked up on these critiques and argued variously that PR was the tool of capitalism; that PR interfered with public communication between government and governed; that corporate resources could buy influence; and that the media can be manipulated by public relations practitioners (Garnham, 1986: 41). Some have suggested that this is achieved through PR's provision of easily usable packaged information that meets media needs in terms of format and news value – *information subsidies* (Gandy, 1992). However, it is important to look beyond a propaganda-model interpretation of the public sphere in which political and corporate institutions that can afford PR services are able to dominate news agendas so that media businesses become 'the gate through which privileged private interests invade the public sphere' (Habermas, 1989: 185). The consequence of extensive commodification and varied entertainment media outlets has led to the evolution of *promotional culture* (Wernick, 1991), in which a major socio-cultural shift has occurred in terms of audience awareness and cynicism of media performances.

To sum up, the public sphere is where issues are debated and policy made, and '[t]he range of effective voices in the public sphere is an outcome of battles over information management in society' (Schlesinger, 1992: 296). In other words, whose views are heard, how views are articulated and, implicitly, by the *structuring absence* of those whose views are not given an airing. *Censorship* is one dimension of this. The concept of the public sphere foregrounds communication and media industries, their interrelationships with each other and both political institutions and capital. *Source-media relations* and the ability of the source to define issues and information in a way that shapes media content (the process of *primary definition*) takes a critical perspective on public relations work. As Leitch and Neilson argued: 'Public relations is about the many ways in which different types of publics interact with different types of organizations, and vice versa on a strategic terrain of competing discourses and unequal access to power and resources' (Leitch and Neilson, 2001: 134).

Leitch and Neilson suggested that the organization's frames of reference and *primary definition* of issues and publics inevitably weights debate in favour of the organization's position. Other public relations theorists take a more optimistic approach, seeing public relations in tandem with new technology as the solution to the problem of unequal access. For example, one of the most established scholars in the field, Professor Ray Hiebert, who has edited *Public Relations Review* for many years, wrote:

> Civil society, or democracy, requires a level playing field in the public sphere, meaning that competing interests must have more or less equal access to the marketplace. But media concentration and corporate globalization have tilted the playing field. We know now that mass media, because of economics as well as politics, are no longer likely to provide equal access, if they ever were. The only possible solution is public relations, not in terms of spin or propaganda but in terms of developing real public relationships in the public sphere. ... The new technologies could be an innovation in public communication that could revitalize civil society, as earlier innovations have done. (Hiebert, 2005: 3–4)

This seems to suggest that PR can contribute positively to a dynamic public sphere constituted by publics keen to be recognized as legitimate and significant, yet 'Publics are not bounded entities but rather are involved in continuous processes of construction and reconstruction, of negotiation and contestation' (Meyer and Moss, 2006: 12).

Public affairs

'Public affairs' has been subject to variable definition and some evolution. Public affairs deals with the public policy implications of issues management and lobbying may be the tactical consequence of public affairs analysis. Thus public affairs is usually portrayed as higher status strategic work, mixing with the 'movers and groovers' in the arena of public policy and government. Public affairs often operates in the areas of reputation, responsibility, governance, ethics and regulation.

Public affairs is becoming recognized as a specialism distinct from public relations and experts are beginning to debate issues such as education and qualifications for public affairs consultants. The discipline of public affairs took a major step forward with the publication of a seminal text *The Handbook of Public Affairs* (Harris and Fleisher, 2005), on which I have leant heavily in this chapter. In this volume a host of research-driven contributions lay out the field relating to the history and development of the practice in various nations, the management of the practice, measurement and evaluation, and theory-building.

The impact of globalization in particular has impacted this specialism for, according to Lord Tom McNally (formally public affairs expert at consultancies Hill & Knowlton, Shandwick, Weber Shandwick):

> We live in a world of instant 24/7 communication which makes the capacity to absorb, analyze, and advise on developing events a key asset for public affairs practitioners. So too is an understanding of political decision making at local, regional, national and international level. The power and reach of regulators and their capacity to adopt best practice from each other, the pace and direction of international trade agreements, the likely impact of new technologies, the opening up of new markets, all need a public affairs understanding and input. So too does the work of non-governmental organizations and pressure groups. (McNally, 2005: xxvi–xxvii)

Nevertheless, although broad societal issues are highlighted as important, recent research and thinking in public affairs have focused on the political environment as being the source of power which most influences key aspects, and which affects business. So business–government relations and public affairs have become inextricably linked with political lobbying. Public affairs has sometimes been used as a title to obscure the fact that the real job is political lobbying.

The origins of the term 'public affairs' have political and diplomatic connotations. The term was used by the Americans in the Second World War to describe posts which 'disseminated essential information and [built] up a programme of cultural and educational exchange between the US and the country to which he has been assigned' (Robbins, 1958: 228). Public affairs work in this context included research and evaluation and 'the more exact established techniques of measurement known to experts in the field of mass media and communications' (Robbins, 1958: 229).

Lobbying has always been a high-level occupation since originally it was the responsibility of the CEO or Chairperson. British public relations practitioners started to get involved in political lobbying in the 1920s, and by the 1950s and 1960s were being criticized for that role. Pieczka's empirical research (2006b: 320) identified the 'circuit of power' between media, PR and politics (see Figure 5.1) and noted that there remains an asymmetrical flow in employment patterns from journalism to public relations in the UK.

> If movements between journalism and public relations ... remain ... based on media expertise, jobs in public relations and politics were swapped on the basis of expertise in policy making and political campaigning ... a number of jobs seem to draw on the same expertise: politicians ... PR consultants, described either as lobbyists or public affairs specialists; PR specialists working for the government (permanent civil servants); special advisers; researchers working for MPs or for political parties and PR practitioners, usually described with labels using the term 'communications', at political parties, trade unions, or other organizations. In comparison with

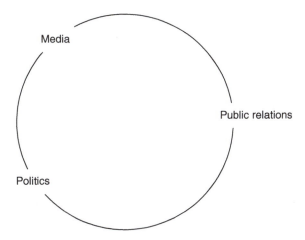

Figure 5.1 'The circuit of power': media, PR and politics
Source: Pieczka (2006b: 320)

media relations and journalism, there is less of a sense of one route in the world of careers in politics and PR. It is possible to build up the required expertise in any one of these jobs and exploit it in almost any other. (Pieczka, 2006b: 323)

The revolving doors syndrome noted by Pieczka highlights the existence of an elite group who work in the same domain, know each other and socialize with each other, if only at formal events such as UK party political conferences where: 'Organized business and "not for profit" interests use the opportunity to gain discreet and relatively easy access to decision-makers to informally talk through the issues that impact on them...' (Harris, 2005: 93–95).

Box 5.3 Working in the political arena: professional insight

Gaining access to PR jobs in the political domain is also network-dependent. Voluntary work for political parties, local constituencies or government, local councillors or politicians is probably a necessary investment unless you already have

(Continued)

(Continued)

connections. In small countries such as Scotland or the Scandinavian countries, overlap between public and private spheres may occur readily through personal contacts. Talent-spotting may happen in this field so careers can change quickly, as illustrated by this professional insight:

I was always involved in politics, a member of a political party at 15, then, when I went to uni I was involved in student politics and ended up as President of the union and also on the executive of the National Union of Students. I always knew that if Scotland got its own Parliament I'd want to be involved...

I took the civil service exams to join the Government Communications Service which I passed and then went to work for the Enterprise Minister. There were three or four of us working very closely in the Private Office and with the Special Advisers. So you go to meetings with those who are actually developing policy and you give advice about how it would actually play out publicly, how the press would view it. On the other side, you are giving advice directly to the Minister about the news of the day and how to deliver the policy, what sort of event should be hosted, what sort of people should be invited, audience-building and the whole communications mix, web strategy, marketing element as well as press and media. It was unbelievably long hours ... often two or three o'clock in the morning...

Then I was asked to go and work with the First Minister. He has an official spokesperson who does on-the-record meetings with the political lobby twice a day and then he has a press team who does all his day-to-day stuff, long-term planning of events, that kind of thing. The First Minister waits till policies are ready from the other teams and then gets it ready, finishes it off and gets it launched. You feel as though you've got a real input into the political process...

Number 10 invite papers each year and on the basis of what I wrote I got invited to work there for a while. It was at the time running up to G8, which was interesting for me because I'd been involved in Scotland with the preparations for the First Minister. The other current issue was the tail end of the bid for London's Olympics. There was the successful Olympics announcement, which was absolutely brilliant, and then the converse the following day with the July 7th bombs. There were two of us in the office because everyone was in Gleneagles for G8. I've never known anything like it and it was horrible because you kept being updated with information and you were very aware of the body count mounting and you were sitting there thinking 'where does this stop?' The media didn't know so they were speculating and our biggest job was to get information and get it out to the public and stop erroneous information getting out like *Sky News*, who claimed [erroneously] that troops were running through Covent Garden. (Interview, August 2006)

Lobbying

Lobbying aims to influence the decisions of government either by approaching local, national or international politicians or administrators. In the UK, theoretically, anyone can lobby, but in practice it is carried out by interested organizations or organized interests. Devolution to the Scottish Parliament and the Welsh Assembly has reshaped public affairs and opened up 'new spaces ... for lobbyists to interact with politicians and officials' (Schlesinger et al., 2001: 255). While lobbying is accepted as a legitimate practice in Western-style democracies, it raises problems of access for individuals and *resource-poor* groups. Lobbying may be seen as underhand and devious rather than as an important part of the political process (i.e. various parties expressing their opinion to the drafters of legislation). Since this text is designed for public relations students around the globe, it is not really appropriate to go into the technical detail of how to lobby in specific national contexts, so this chapter simply indicates the necessary questions and knowledge base that a lobbyist might need.

Lobbyists need to know governmental processes, both administrative and political, constitutional history, forms and structures of states, participation in international organizations, media, election processes, and timing. Lobbyists need to understand how the political system works and the role played by politicians and civil servants. In the UK, it is possible for public affairs and lobbying specialists to take advantage of ignorant clients and charge for knowledge that is freely available, or impress them with social meetings with politicians that are meaningless in terms of influencing legislation. Scepticism has also been expressed as to whether changes achieved are that earth-shattering.

Box 5.4   Lobbying

Lobbygate

Lobbyist Kevin Reid worked for PR firm Beattie Media. During a sales pitch to someone he believed to be a potential US client (but was actually an undercover journalist exploring connections between the lobbying industry in Scotland and the new Parliament), Reid said 'I know the Secretary of State very well because he's my father' (Schlesinger et al., 2001: 226). The incident immediately became a huge news story, partly because sleaze scandals had become such a feature of British politics. There was a major public debate on lobbying, during which lobbyists were castigated as: 'Fixers, go-betweens and influence peddlers ... parasites who inject the body politic ... scavengers of the corridors of power ... pimps who seek to prostitute politics' (Schlesinger et al., 2001: 233).

(Continued)

(Continued)

This criticism was simply a contemporary example of media criticism of PR in politics that dates back to the 1960s when, for example, Harold Wilson (then MP, later Prime Minister) remarked: 'It is an extremely degrading profession ... rather squalid'; and Malcolm Muggeridge commented: 'PR persuasion is ... hidden behind a camouflage of objectivity and hospitality ... wrapped in slices of smoked salmon, aromatic with cigar smoke' (cited in L'Etang, 2004: 148–149).

Herbal remedies

Following changes in EU legislation, the UK Medicines Control Agency began to develop policy to tighten control of traditional herbal medicines and to change the definition and licensing of some products, which would require stricter control of packaging, labelling and promotional literature. The existing legislation had required that remedies should only be made from active herbal ingredients and should not include vitamins, minerals or animal derivatives; they were not to be branded and were to make no medicinal claims. The largest UK supplier of herbal medicines, Bioforce, consequently engaged in a lobbying campaign to explain to legislators the implications of new legislation for some products and to renegotiate the time scale of the legistation.

Sources: Medicines and Healthcare products Regulatory Agency (www.mhra.gov.uk); The Nature Doctor (www.AVogel.co.uk); Bioforce (www.bioforce.co.uk); interviews with Bioforce, March 2005

Box 5.5   Trade associations for lobbyists

Association for Professional Political Consultants (AAPC) (www.appc.org.uk)
Association for Scottish Public Affairs (ASPA) (www.aspa-uk.org)

CRITICAL QUESTIONS

- Does lobbying benefit citizens or those in power?
- What might be attractive about work in the political domain?
- Are you interested or disinterested in this line of work and why?

Political communication

Political communication is carried out by political parties in and out of power both internally and externally. It encompasses media relations, personal public relations (image and impression management for higher-level politicians), speech writing and political marketing (segmentation, demographics, market research). Media relations is sometimes confusingly referred to as *media management,* thus implying the nefarious spin-doctor or even connoting the magical work of the witch doctor, whereas in fact media management is a distinct sub-discipline of media sociology and management which aims to teach students how to manage media institutions (TV stations, video companies, etc.). Political public relations cuts across all these activities and intersects with public affairs work on behalf of political parties. It entails campaign planning, public opinion research, speech writing, political messaging, issues management, gatekeeping and media relations.

In the UK, some form of public relations work is carried out on behalf of government by the Government Information Service, which is supposed to be non-party political. Political parties have their own machinery for public relations, which may be carried out by communications specialists and the ubiquitous research assistants. As media sociologist Jeremy Tunstall remarked: 'All political systems include public relations. It is a peculiarity of the British systems of political public relations that the mechanisms which generate publicity are often remarkably secretive' (Tunstall, 1983: 6).

Discomfort over persuasive communication in a political and ideological context is linked to fears of propaganda and inappropriate controls of information. For some, political communication can never be more than ideological propaganda. For example, the organizations CorporateWatch (www.corporatewatch.org.uk) and SpinWatch aspire to identify practice which benefits the powerful.

Exercise

In your local community try to find out, through local newspapers, the local library, and local government websites how key local decisions are taken. Good examples to research include planning permissions, transport, health and sports facilities.

- How is it possible for local communities to express their view about such decisions?
- Are there local community councils? How do they work? How easy are they to access?
- Who has the power?
- How are views represented in the local media?

Think tanks

In the UK, no discussion of public affairs and political communication would be complete without some reference to **think tanks**. These are comprised of the politically motivated but theoretically driven, who develop policy options and challenging ideas for debate. They are an unaccountable and discrete influence. Little is known of the PR activities of think tanks, their communication strategies and the way in which they facilitate informal or social environments in which lobbyists engage with political elites. Examples include:

- The Adam Smith Institute
- The Bow Group
- The Centre for Policy Studies
- Chatham House
- Aims of Industry
- Commonwealth Policy Studies Institute
- Civitas
- Demos
- The Fabian Society
- The Foreign Policy Centre

- Globalization Institute
- The Institute for Public Policy Research
- Localis
- New Economics Foundation
- New Policy Institute
- New Politics Network
- Open Europe
- Reform
- Royal United Services Institute for Defence Studies (http://politics.guardian.co.uk/thinktanks/ accessed November 2006)

According to Magor (December 2006: 1–2), The think-tank scene has matured in the UK over the last decade and there are now many different types of think tank organizations serving diverse niches ... Think tanks commonly assert and overplay their impact on policy yet few have measurable performance indicators to determine this ... the role of some think tank organizations is more akin to that of management consultants.

CRITICAL REFLECTION

- Are think tanks a form of public relations organization? If so, what?

Discipline box: Politics

Politics developed from philosophy (political philosophy) and deals with questions about power, authority, political organizations, political rights and nature of the state (Lacey, 1976: 181). Politics explores the relationships among state, citizens, religion and, to some extent, the media. Political science studies historical and contemporary institutions while political economy focuses on the control of economic power (Lacey, 1976: 181–182).

In conclusion

This chapter has outlined the key frameworks of the public sphere, the space which is targeted by many public relations practitioners on behalf of their organizations and clients. Questions have been raised as to:

- the implications for democratic practice of that space being taken up by sponsored political communication
- the legitimacy of paid lobbyists
- the emergence of 'spin-doctors' in political life
- the role, transparency and influence of think tanks

REVIEW

Taking into account the questions at the beginning of this chapter and considering the variety of concepts and theories, reflect upon your own individual role as a citizen. You might like to return to issues of identity raised in Chapter 3 and think about how these impact on your approach to citizenship and politics. You might also wish to consider the extent to which the public sphere is dominated by questions of power; issues of distribution of goods; rights and responsibilities; consumer choice; public policy.

- to what extent can individuals make an impact on debates concerning social justice?
- does public relations engage in the structuring of socio-political arrangements, and, if so, how?

RECOMMENDED READING

The most useful contemporary source on public affairs is the major international collection of essays edited by Phil Harris and Craig Fleisher (2005). Antony Davis (2004) also provides a helpful, practical and clear descriptive account. Magda Pieczka's work on public opinion (Pieczka, 1996a, 2006d) is a concise and useful account of the concept in a public relations context. Vincent Price (1992) gives an excellent summary of public opinion theory. Aeron Davis is a media sociologist whose *Public Relations Democracy* is an outstanding book for UK-based students, as it is based on careful and extensive empirical research and cases exploring financial, corporate and trade union PR. It provides a clear link between PR and media studies, and focuses on the growth of the occupation from the 1980s to the present day. Davis explores PR's influence on news production, in particular analyzing which organizations benefit most from PR assistance and which groups are included or excluded from public discourse. Kevin Moloney is a public relations theorist whose *Rethinking Public Relations* (2006) explores public relations as 'weak propaganda' and a 'Niagara of spin' aimed at manipulation or persuasion and a threat to democratic ideals. Moloney's book, which has a wealth of sources and detail, is written as a challenge to dominant idealistic and normative work in public relations.

Media Perspectives: Critique, Effects and Evaluation

BEFORE YOU READ A SINGLE WORD...

- What impact does PR have on the media?
- Watch TV news, listen to the radio and look through a newspaper or two and see if you can identify PR sources for stories.
- Can you identify any stories which have not had any PR input?
- Can PR's impact be evaluated through media coverage? If so, how, and what exactly does media coverage tell us?

Key concepts

Agenda setting	Media sociology
Content analysis	Media studies
Dominant paradigm	Mega-events
Gatekeeping	Primary definition
Journalism studies	Propaganda
Media evaluation	Secondary definition
Media events	Source-media relations
Media framing	

Introduction

This chapter takes a media studies approach in relation to public relations. It begins by defining media studies, media sociology and journalism studies in relation to each other, and key terminology. It is suggested that media studies and sociology of the media offer useful lines of enquiry that could broaden the field of public relations. The chapter reviews the main approaches to understanding media and proceeds to summarize key models of media processes before turning to the question of media effects. There is a brief comment in relation to public relations' engagement with media theories and media evaluation. There are a short summaries of the media environment, the status and ideals of journalists, and journalism and media studies. A sampler of quotes about PR that appear is some current journalism texts is presented – be prepared to be shocked!

To sum up, this chapter addresses the following main themes: media environment and processes; media values and journalism culture and ideology; public relations' relationship with the media; and issues surrounding media evaluation, which have a bearing on public relations practitioners' aspirations to professional status.

CHAPTER AIMS

On completion of this chapter you will be able to:

- understand and engage with the perspectives of media studies, media sociology and journalism, and describe their relevance to public relations practitioners and academics
- understand and describe media processes and concepts
- describe media evaluation procedures, analyze media content and critique public relations approaches to media content analysis

A cautionary word for public relations students: taking the media for granted

In my experience as teacher and external examiner, public relations students are very inclined to assume mass media interest and, indeed, coverage. There may be talk of 'placing stories' suggestive of a somewhat propagandistic relationship with the media. There is often, too, an overdependence on media within PR strategies and campaigns and a lack of imagination in relation to other media, or to networking and interpersonal communication. But fundamentally, the major flaw seems to arise from a lack of understanding of the media environment, its pressures and its autonomy. Sometimes there is a sense that a PR student's close identification with even a hypothetical client or cause may be so great that it becomes hard to believe that a journalist might not be interested! Enthusiasm and evangelism for a cause should not prevail over a rational understanding of news values and the needs of journalists. Sometimes there is danger, especially for the rookie PR trainee, that because someone senior in the (assumed Very Important) organization asked you to get coverage, the media are obliged to do so. Such assumptions may be accidentally communicated, verbally or non-verbally, and are like a red rag to the media bull! This chapter is therefore designed to help you see the world through the eyes of journalists, journalism students, and critical media theorists.

A cautionary word for public relations practitioners: assuming the media is the ultimate audience

In my experience as assessor of public relations cases presented for prizes awarded by professional bodies, it seems that many practitioners are really only interested in one client – the media – and one outcome – coverage. Whether that coverage actually means anything to anyone, is read or interpreted by anyone significant is neither here nor there. That upsets most public relations academics. It seems to show that too many practitioners are only concerned with publicity and not with reputation, communication, relationship-building or behavioural change. In any case, in some contexts mass media has been shown not to be particularly helpful, for example in health campaigns where multiple interventions of various types (interpersonal, community level) have been shown to be more effective. A further criticism of practice relates to the lack of formal (meaningful) research done into the evaluation of media content. It is difficult to resist the conclusion that sometimes rather meaningless information is sold to clients. With increased media literacy, such practices are not going to improve PR's reputation.

Some practitioners regard the media as a technical medium for the transmission of messages to audiences and not as a public in their own right. The latter view is predicated on the notion that media are passive receivers and transmitters. While it is the case that unproblematic, appropriately presented material that fits into *news values* (an *information subsidy* (Gandy, 1982)) may be used verbatim in some contexts, the media need to be understood as active, interpretative and critical agents who operate in a complex web of economic, political, social and technical relationships.

In the next couple of pages I shall explain some terminology and describe some key concepts as well as something of the broad fields of media and journalism studies. In this review I have largely followed the work of Curran (2000), McQuail (2004) Downing et al. (2004), and Curran and Gurevitch (2005), which are all excellent sources for deeper study. In particular, I have lent heavily on the chapter co-authored by the Goldsmiths Media Group, entitled 'Media organizations in society: central issues', which both sets the context and lays out the crucial societal and critical challenges facing the media as well as providing a review of the field and key developments (Curran, 2000).

Media studies, media sociology and journalism studies: the research agenda and critical perspectives

Media studies began with research to explore the effects of media on society and was conducted within the field of mass communication. The presuppositions of this research led to the emergence of a **dominant paradigm** in the field that saw the media as a powerful stimulus that could lead to predictable responses (McQuail, 2004: 2). Consequently, as McQuail points out, the study of mass communications was of interest not only to academics but also to politicians and policy-makers. Indeed the ability of mass communications to influence public opinion was of interest to those in power prior to the establishment of media studies. In the UK, the British Documentary Film Movement in the 1930s and 1940s highlighted the virtue of film as the medium that could educate the populace regarding its rights and responsibilities and the Scottish leader of the British Documentary Film movement, John Grierson, wrote and lectured extensively on the role of public relations and propaganda in democratic society (L'Etang, 2004: 32–35). The research agenda in mass communications has included: the impact of media technology on societies; media effects and audience reception; media texts read in the context of other cultural forms; the cultural role of the media; the public sphere, media ownership, political communication and propaganda; media representation, media as a business, and feminism (Curran, 2000: 1–54).

Media studies has developed into a very broad field which overlaps with cultural studies, sociology, political science and public relations. According to Curran, *mediacentric* research has focused on media ownership and control (the political economy), regulation and public policy, media production and audience production of meaning, internal processes in media organizations (organizational sociology) and the media occupations (recruitment, career paths, education and professionalism, gender) (Curran, 2000: 9–16). *Sociocentric* research has drawn on cultural studies to explore the media as a cultural product and a space for contest, both in terms of access (public sphere) but for the collective fantasies of audiences or an arena for the expression of multiple identities (Curran, 2000: 9–16). *Cultural industries* approaches have looked at the way in which the production of culture has been industrialized by exploring how media industries innovate, maximize paying audiences and make profits (Curran, 2000: 19–65). *News values* is a functional term for news priorities and what counts as news. Elite groups have a natural advantage since their importance makes them newsworthy. Finally, of great importance to public relations is the research focused on sources and access to media, which has largely suggested that sources with political or corporate power, wealth or cultural capital are automatically sought out by journalists for their views, thus structuring the public sphere through **primary definition**. As Curran pointed out:

> All these studies have explored the development of elite sources and their increased interest in managing, and their ability to manage the media. All have also identified the rapidly expanding group of cultural intermediaries – professionals whose job it is to promote elite source organizations and improve communications with the media. This group, which includes pollsters, marketing experts, agents and public-relations practitioners, has drawn increasing attention from academic disciplines and the general media. (Curran, 2000: 29)

Later research suggested that things were not so straightforward and that actually there is a more complex picture, in which resource-poor groups can challenge dominant accounts. Thus primary definition may be open to redefinition by competing or oppositional groups known as secondary definers. The revisionist account implied that media access was the consequence of competitive jockeying between credibility-dependent competing sources.

Media sociology developed out of sociology and political science and focused on power in terms of the way in which the media relates to and represents power via its coverage of political, economic and social issues (Downing et al., 2004: 5). The structuring role of the media and its presumed effects have been a major focus, as is media consumption (Downing et al, 2004: 2). Media sociologists are generally highly critical of public relations and have been so since the 1960s when Stuart Hall (cultural studies) and Jeremy Tunstall (media sociology) produced critiques (L'Etang, 2004: 8, 127). Latterly, criticism has tended to focus on public relations' impact on the public sphere. Few, if any, media sociologists integrate literature or concepts from PR theory into their accounts.

Journalism studies, as an academic area, focuses on the specifics of journalism practice (whereas media studies has the broader remit to cover all media). For example, the academic journals *Journalism Studies*, *British Journalism Review* and *Journalism Studies Review* have published articles from academics and practitioners on topics such as: source protection, secrecy, whistleblowers, freedom of information, journalism education, professionalism and professionalization (utilizing sociology of professions as a framework), objectivity, neutrality, agenda setting, alternative media, blogging, peace journalism, and propaganda versus professionalism in wartime. Aspiring journalists can take degrees in the subject at a number of universities worldwide.

Media studies, media sociology and journalism studies: implications for public relations – future lines of enquiry

What can be learnt from a review of media disciplines? One can observe that public relations research has engaged with some common themes. Specifically, these are PR as an occupation (education, professionalism, gender), as an organizational role, and, to some degree, on PR values and PR's role in society in terms of impact on practitioners, clients, media and society. However the intentions behind much of the PR research seem to be to bolster the status of the occupation; equivalent media research has been from a critical perspective. There is less on PR ownership (though see Miller and Dinan, 2000) or the *organizational sociology of public relations* (the internal processes of PR organizations). The way in which PR and communications companies create services and make profits could enlighten understanding further about the practice and its values in relation to expertise and standards. *Public relations regulation* has been touched on in the context of debates over professionalism and licensing, but the implications of an essentially unregulated market are worthy of exploration, as is the relationship between PR and sources of political and economic power (see Miller and Dinan, 2001; Schlesinger and Miller, 2001). *Public relations effects research* tends to be focused on variables determined by a paying client and media evaluation, rather than in terms of societal impact and side-effects. Relationships between PR and media could be further enlightened in the context of authority and power relations, freedom of information and privacy.

Exercise

Identify other aspects of public relations work and the life of PR practitioners that could complement the media studies research agenda.

Understanding media processes

In this section I have briefly summarized material from core media studies sources. **Source–media relations** is probably one of the most interesting areas for public relations students, even if it is the area which has stimulated media sociologists' greatest criticisms of PR practice and has led some to conflate the term with **propaganda**. It aims to identify those who are able to influence the media and those who are not. Inevitably, sources provide slanted information. Media sociology research has tended to show that the more powerful the source, the more influential it is in terms of shaping media interpretation and content. However, being a reliable newsworthy source brings a great deal of credibility and enhances PR success. Public relations practitioners who do not know which journalist to approach, who write badly, indulge in puffery or who try to sell stories that are not stories, destroy both their personal professional integrity and that of their organization.

According to McQuail and Windahl (1981), the earliest research in this area emerged from **source–reporter relations** (Geiber and Johnson, 1961, in McQuail and Windahl, 1981: 97–99). **Gatekeeping** (White, 1950, in McQuail and Windahl, 1981: 100–101; Schoemaker, 1990; Schlesinger, 1992) studies explored the processes of news selection employing the concepts of *channels* and *information subsidies* (information made easy to use by journalists). Gatekeeping studies have examined the flow of specific news items and the processes by which some are selected (the gates are opened) or filtered out (gates remain closed). Stories need to meet key criteria for selection. Some have argued that the filtering processes, which take place in media institutions that are dependent on profit motives, advertising and information subsidies, lead to conformity and ultimately to a **propaganda model** of societal communication (Herman and Chomsky, 1988). In other words, there are inbuilt biases and distortions in news selections and coverage that are partially dependent on power structures.

News values have been the focus of much research to ascertain core features such as immediacy, scale and impact, unexpectedness, predictability, human interest, which, when taken in various combinations, can be developed into an interesting storyline (Galtung and Ruge, 1965, in McQuail and Windahl, 1981: 106–108). **Media framing** describes the way in which media text is written to help the reader orientate his-herself to the topic (McQuail, 2000: 343). The contextualization of factual data may improve communication and audience understanding but it raises issues of media bias and stereotyping. **Media impact/effects** is a controversial area which explores direct and indirect, intended and unintended impacts on individual and collective opinions and/or behaviour; the public agenda and social change. The influence of effects is apparent in many studies exploring the impact of TV violence. In the UK, the Office of Communications (Ofcom), the independent regulator and competition authority, banned the advertising of junk food in March 2006 (www.ofcom.org.uk, accessed 24 January 2007).

Others suggest that active viewers and readers use media for their own private and personal agendas and interpretations (uses and gratifications) or that those issues that are given more media attention will become more familiar and be perceived as more important (McCoombs and Shaw, 1972, in McQuail and

Windahl, 1981), and that the importance of the media is in **agenda setting**. This is relevant to the formation of private and subsequently public opinion about what constitutes the important issues of the day. The media can also be seen as having a socialization or cultural change role on society through the personal influence of active opinion leaders who take up issues (**two-step flow**; see Katz and Lazarfeld, 1955, in McQuail and Windahl, 1981) or as a consequence of multiple interactions between and within institutions and the media (*negotiated effects*). Also important to public relations is research associated with **media events**, although this has not received much attention in public relations literature. Media events (some of these are predictable **mega-events** such as the Olympics) are a natural partner to crisis and risk communication and to events management. Crises heighten society's needs for information and the media performs the vital link in reporting, framing and sense-making.

CRITICAL REFLECTION

- How do PR practitioners determine gatekeepers and get them to open the gates in (a) media relations and (b) organizations?
- In what ways do PR practitioners attempt to set the agenda?
- How can PR practitioners apply the concept of media framing?
- To what extent does PR practice assume media effects?

The revisionist approaches to media effects had implications for those working in media and related industries. As McQuail pointed out:

> The new sobriety of assessment was slow to modify opinion outside the social scientific community. It was particularly hard to accept for those who made a living from advertising and propaganda and for those in the media who valued the myth of their great potency. (McQuail, 2000: 419)

The public relations industry still promotes the idea of powerful media and of media analysis as the primary tool for its assessment. It seems that media content is used simplistically, often treating media content as 'exposure' and thus assuming direct influence (magic bullet) and effects. **Content analysis** is also a term referred to and used by public relations researchers (sometimes rather sloppily), which is why it is an important technique to understand, along with its strengths and limitations. PR practice also uses the media as a two-step flow (remember that in Chapter 5 I observed that some PR practitioners identify media as a public) and PR influence on the media is seen as a way to shape the political agenda and influence policy-makers (agenda setting). For some practitioners, media content is the same thing as public opinion. Finally, PR campaigns are sometimes focused on short-term woolly aims such as 'raising the profile', 'raising awareness', which seemed to translate as 'media coverage'.

Media evaluation and content analysis

Media evaluation and the research method most associated with it – content analysis – analyzes what is reported and what is not, and how what is reported is portrayed. It is largely based on effects assumptions. As an approach it raises questions about the assumptions of researchers and what is meant by 'neutral' and 'objective'.

Media content analysis uses quantitative method that seeks to count the way that certain items are presented in media to show patterns of treatment in a 'statistical summary of a much larger media reality' (McQuail, 2000: 327). Content analysis research was widely popularized in the UK by critical media researchers, especially the contributions of the *Glasgow Media Group* (GMG) which was a thorn in the flesh of political institutions in the UK in the 1970s and 1980s by showing apparent media bias in the treatment of a range of issues, including trade unions, conflict in Northern Ireland, peace demonstrations during the Cold War, mental illness, health and food scares, children and violence, the developing world. Their work, in books such as *Bad News, More Bad News, Media and Mental Distress, Getting the Message: News, Truth and Power* and *Bad News from Israel*, challenged and continues to challenge stereotypes and misrepresentation. The output of this group of scholars unpicks strategies of accommodation and compliance to argue that media bias exists and privileges some groups above others. While all of the GMG *oeuvre* is important reading for public relations students, *The Circuit of Mass Communication* (Miller et al., 1998) is particularly interesting as it explores the promotional strategies of interest groups and debates the interaction between PR, media coverage and audience response.

Of course, we also have to ask questions of critical researchers, especially those who appear to claim a moral high ground:

- Are they disinterested, scientific, objective observers?
- Are they disseminating knowledge/power?
- What is the role of 'media dons' in society?
- Are academics' agendas always made explicit?

Content analysis: definition, criteria and standards

Content analysis can be used to analyze newspapers, magazines, broadcast media and websites. Content analysis is a way of sorting media content into categories or units according to clearly defined criteria. Content analysis then counts categories to find patterns or the relationship between categories statistically. Content analysis is useful in providing quantitative evidence of dominant interpretations of topics.

Content analysis is apparently objective and quantitative, based on common definitions that can be applied by a number of trained 'coders' who sort materials according to agreed criteria (key concepts defined at the outset of the study). However, it must be borne in mind that choosing criteria at the outset of the study is inevitably a subjective process. Thus content analysis includes an element of qualitatively arrived at definitions of concepts to be measured. Concepts are turned into measurable variables in the process of **operationalization**, for which Riffe et al. provide the following useful example:

> A student's maturity and self-discipline (both abstract concepts) may be measured or operationally defined in terms of the number of classes missed and assignments not completed. Both can be objectively measured and reproduced by another observer. (Riffe et al., 1998: 20)

In content analysis there is no room for coders to make subjective assessments, individual interpretation or 'reading into' content. This means that the results could, if need be, be replicated.

Measurement might be focused on words, phrases, themes, editorials, front pages, pictures, and graphics (Riffe et al., 1998: 24). Numeric values are applied to identify examples, specify location, totals and represent differences (Riffe et al., 1998). A content analysis will assign *values* to a linked hierarchical system of *units* (Riffe et al., 1998). Values should accord with a majority view of what would count as 'negative', for example. Rules to assign values are laid out in a *coding manual*. The consistency and agreement of coders as to the application of the coding manual is what gives the study its *reliability*. The *coding manual* explains how *variables* are to be measured and recorded on the *coding sheet*.

Quantification has the advantage of being able to reduce data to statistics and to assess how representative findings are from a particular sample. Content analyses may be short- or long-term and may compare interpretations across different media.

Content analysis is useful in showing patterns or relationships but it cannot explain causes, reasons or effects. This is why content analysis is best complemented by other research techniques, which might explain background political or commercial issues or the way in which stakeholders or target audiences understand or interpret media coverage. As it is beyond the scope of this book to explain content analysis procedures in detail, here are a few handy questions you should always ask (colleagues or clients) about a content analysis to be sure that it is based on sound scientific principles:

- What research questions were asked and why?
- What was the sample size and how was it justified?
- How were 'positive' and 'negative' defined?
- Where is the coding manual?
- How many coders were used and how were they trained and monitored?
- How was subjectivity minimized?
- What other research was carried out and how does it contextualize the content analysis?

Box 6.1   Content analysis in practice: World Association for Christian Communication (WACC)

WACC is an international ecumenical organization established by communicators whose aim is to prioritize Christian values in the world's communication. Its mission statement is:

> WACC promotes communication for social change. It believes that communication is a basic human right that defines people's common humanity, strengthens cultures, enables participation, creates community and challenges tyranny and oppression. WACC's key concerns are media diversity, equal and affordable access to communication and knowledge, media and gender justice, and the relationship between communication and power. It tackles these through advocacy, education, training, and the creation and sharing of knowledge. (www.wacc.org.uk)

Based in 120 countries worldwide, WACC 'offers professional guidance on communication policies, interprets developments in global communications' and, as part of its brief in 2006, carried out a three-week global media monitoring programme to explore gender issues in relation to the question 'Who makes the news?'. This follows a number of studies beginning in the 1980s, which have reported how much harder it is for women to make the news than men (Bertrand and Hughes, 2002: 182) based on content analysis of international news media carried out by teams of academic researchers in participating countries.

Source: www.wacc.org.uk

Content analysis in public relations

In public relations, the types of question that content analysis might be used to answer could include:

- When, where and why did this issue move on to the media agenda?
- Has promotional material been used by the media and if so in what way, how often and in what qauntity?
- How has the issue been presented and how has it been linked to the organization?

To sum up, content analysis is a rigorous scientific quantitative method that should not be confused with qualitative analyses of content, such as critical analysis, discourse analysis, rhetorical analysis, narrative analysis, structuralist or semiotic analysis, interpretative analysis, all of which have their own methodological procedures.

Box 6.2   Media evaluation companies and public relations

The Association for Measurement and Evaluation of Communication (AMEC) was formed from a number of other organizations in 1996. AMEC had 21 corporate members in January 2007 and provides a variety of services including their own training courses, awards and guidance on evaluation and the briefing and recruitment of evaluation specialists. (www.amecorg.com/amec)

The media environment: working lives, professionalization and occupational culture

Media organizations operate in a highly pressurized and competitive environment. While some media organizations have a public service remit others are more business-focused. The media have formal and informal influence and top journalists inhabit the same shared social political-cultural-economic space as their prey. Technological change constantly impacts media practice.

While newspaper readership has been shrinking in the UK for the last 60 years, newspapers have responded by trying to develop broader appeal, partly through a shift towards 'lifestyle' supplements and coverage. The magazine market is also highly competitive and new titles are only given a few months to prove themselves to readers and advertisers – all media products effectively produce audiences and markets, which can be sold. These are promoted through glossy media packs which articulate the 'demographic' or a caricatured version of the typical reader in marketing-speak.

In the UK news environment the 'national' press is highly concentrated in terms of both location (London) and ownership and, compared to other countries, 'the number of newspapers and their national territorial reach is exceptional' (Schlesinger, 2006: 300). Despite the growth of freesheets, paid-for newspapers are still read by 35 million people (60–70 per cent of the public) (Schlesinger, 2006: 300).

As in the case of public relations, journalists' claim to professional status can be questioned since many who write in the media are not in fact journalists in the traditional sense. In the UK, there has been loosening control of training and professionalization. For example, the National Council for the Training of

Journalists (NCTJ), founded in 1951, had a stranglehold on basic training for years, keeping the subject out of universities until 1993, when Cardiff University took it on board. That was five years after public relations was being taught in universities in the UK. The NCTJ very much focused on basic skills, such as shorthand and a thorough knowledge of the law (legal constraints such as slander, libel and invasion of privacy), and on local and central government. Such training focused on *craft skills*. The NCTJ has been selling courses since 1994 and thus attempts to control its own market and maintain barriers (http://www.nctj.com/index-2.html, accessed 5 October 2005).

The Broadcast Journalism Training Centre (BJTC) accredits various degrees for this specialism (http://www.bjtc.org.uk/, accessed 5 October 2005). It was set up in 1979 when there was a considerable expansion in broadcast journalism and there were concerns about 'where the next generations of broadcast journalists were coming from and how good their training was' (private e-mail correspondence with Jim Latham, BJTC Secretary, 8 October 2005).

Media values and journalism culture

Journalism has its own traditions of occupational ideals, which are important for its social legitimacy and part of its own occupational mythology. These ideals focus on truth, social reporting and democratic education. Journalists are supposed to be independent and objective, reporting facts that enable the democratic process to take place. Journalists should also be critical, and socially responsible, drawing attention to issues that have implications for humanity thus acting as potential catalysts for social change and improvement. They should protect sources to enable revelatory information to emerge and expose wrong-doing, especially in the corridors of power.

Given these ideals, it is possible to see why journalists find it hard to acknowledge their dependence on public relations. Journalists and public relations practitioners are in competition to define news. Though they share many of the same ideals (truth, public service, contribution to the free flow of information in a democracy), the competitive nature of their relationship and the struggle for power (over interpretation) that results leads to a continual tension, which may be uncomfortable, but possibly important for democracy. A further relevant point relates to the relative fortunes of the two occupations. In the context of shrinking newspaper readerships and audiences, and falling advertising, there is intense competition, which means that journalists have less job security and there is a casualization of labour, with increasing numbers of freelances trying to do more work in less time (which is partly what leads to increased dependence on publicity material). The rise of the public relations source and the expansion of the media relations role in society cuts across core occupational values in journalism:

Journalism professionalism is closely tied up with the handling of sources: indeed, for practitioners one major aspect of being a good professional lies in making sound judgements between competing claims and in judging what are credible points of view. Professionalism functions as an all-purpose defence against outside attack. (Schlesinger, 1992: 294)

On this account the journalist should have many of the skills of a good historian, balancing a variety of sources and accounts and taking into consideration the voices that may not be easily heard, for reasons of singularity, unpopularity or obscurity.

What are media studies, media sociology and journalism students taught about public relations?

In Box 6.3, a selection of quotes are presented from a range of texts for students studying journalism. These are intended to give you a good insight into the way in which journalism students are taught to think about public relations. It is worth noting that Stuart Allan's book, *News Culture*, which I've cited, did not even reference 'PR' or 'public relations', only 'spin doctor'!

Box 6.3   What media students are taught about public relations

All government departments, local councils, and moderately sized companies these days have press officers. There is now sufficient media about to make it a full-time job explaining the council's or government's policy and presenting it in a positive light. Councils and the government have long since seen the need to employ people whose particular skill is to present their employer well to the media. This is a mixed blessing to the journalist. It is certainly useful ... but it can be annoying that a part of their job can be to try *not* to tell you things, or worse still, disguise them as something else. At the end of the day, they are just people with a bit of news savvy, intent on presenting information about their employer in a good light – exactly the same as anyone else, but better at it and therefore more of a match for the journalist. Journalists can and should use press officers to their advantage, however. A good PR knows who to speak to in the [organization] ... how to get the information you need quickly and accurately. Don't be afraid to use them in this research role. They can often do a lot of the basic legwork for you. It is important to remember that the press officer will always follow the employer's policy line and so you will also need to build links elsewhere in the organization. The press officer is useful for finding out basic facts and figures, but you may need to talk to someone else to find out

(Continued)

(Continued)

what those facts and figures mean, how they may have been twisted or misrepresented ... never believe anything you are told until you've either verified it or worked out the person's motive for telling you. (Frost, 2002: 26)

The work of the PR industry is visible every day, and some short-staffed newspapers are only too grateful to be stuffed full of scarcely rewritten news releases. But PR is not just about releasing information, it is also about controlling information. And controlling access. Many journalists have an ambivalent attitude to PR. On the one hand, they maintain they are too hard-bitten to listen to PR departments, yet they are also quick to moan about bullying by political spin doctors, demands for copy-approval on behalf of celebs, or the freezing out of journalists who don't comply. Perhaps an ambivalent attitude is only natural. Although many press officers have good working relationships with journalists, based on trust and even grudging respect, the fact remains that they are working to different agendas. (Harcup, 2004: 25)

While journalists working within the media remain largely committed, at least in their rhetoric if not always in their news-gathering and reporting practices, to the ideal of disinterested and rational enquiry, observation and reporting, this growing army of journalism-competent public-relations specialists and freelances increasingly subordinate such professional values to the requirements of commercial values or political persuasion. ... [P]ublic-relations and press officers have no desire to explore in-depth issues which may be in the public interest. They are not detached observers and reporters of the world but hired ... advocates and defenders of whichever sectional interest employs them. ... [T]he intention ... is to persuade, not to inform. (Franklin, 1997: 20)

Spin doctors: a turn of phrase, often employed critically, to describe people whose job it is to present a certain person ... or policy in the best possible light *vis-à-vis* the news media. To 'spin' a story is to emphasize its positive aspects at the expense of those aspects which might potentially harm certain interests if they were reported 'straight'. It is the task of the journalist to recognize 'spin' for what it is so as to avoid reproducing it as fact. (Allan, 2004: 223)

The first thing to be said about spin doctors is that in the British context they are overrated – by themselves, by political leaders who employ them and mostly by journalists who write about them. They are advisers. Their job is to help political leaders present themselves and their policies to best advantage and to underplay problems. They aim to put a spin on the ball on the news story, like the spin on a tennis ball or a cricket ball intended to make it go in the direction they desire. They have some success with advance publicity when, for instance, they influence stories about an important ministerial speech to be made or about a new policy to be announced a few days hence. When their spin works, it creates an atmosphere in which the speech or policy is favourably received or helps to concentrate the subsequent debate on the points the party wishes to emphasize. (Wilson, 1996: 204)

The celebrity interview area is increasingly problematical. Even the highest profile newspaper supplements are faced with extraordinary demands by studios, record companies, PR companies and their clients. Often they will attempt to specify the writer, the photographer, the size of the eventual piece and its prominence. You should

(Continued)

resist this, but if celebrities constitute the cornerstone of your feature coverage, you will usually have to live with it. Unfortunately, this creeping disease is spreading to other areas which have fallen in thrall to professional PR people. The word 'No' often comes in useful. (Morrish, 2003: 133)

It is helpful to draw a distinction between the functions of a public relations officer (or PR) and a press officer. What they do overlaps to some extent and varies from one organization to another. A broad distinction between the two creatures is that a PR is more likely to take what's known as a 'proactive' role towards the media, which is to say she will be expected to initiate contact with journalists and try to persuade them to give favourable mention to whatever product or line or person she is pushing. She will, of course, be on hand in case of emergency or adverse news about her client or employer seeping out into the press. ... More generally, though, PRs are the ones with expense accounts for taking journalists out to lunch to sell the ideas. They are also the ones who organize press trips to sun-soaked resorts for the test-driving of cars or the launching of new perfumes. To someone who hasn't worked in the media before, the array of inducements which flow in from businesses through PR agencies or in-house officers can be bewildering. ... More seriously, PR specialists are nowadays heavily involved in the manipulation of political and business news agendas. ...

What press officers do is usually less proactive (their words), which is to say they are more likely to react to events than to act as agents trying to get free advertising space in editorial pages. Press officers do rather less contacting the press and trying to sell a client, rather more responding to enquiries from the press. ... They send out press releases, organize press conferences and photo-opportunities, collate information and cuttings. They also try to interest the press in stories relating to their organization. ... Good press officers who tailor a story to the publication are successful because once journalists realize that the material they send is likely to be of interest they are more inclined to read it.

Most journalists, quite rightly, are sceptical, if not cynical, about both sets of people, because so often what the PRs and press officers seem to be doing is preventing journalists from getting the information they want. The ones who are good at their job are masters of manipulation. (McKay, 2000: 50)

The relationship your media outlet has with key players as sources of information is fundamental in shaping journalistic practice. ... [J]ournalists operating at the more 'quotes-driven' end of the sports market need to continually cultivate relations with a range of sources who have become professionalized in terms of media and image management. As a result, the space for uncomplicit sports journalism, free from spin, manipulation and public relations management is becoming increasingly located in distinctive areas of the contemporary sports journalism landscape. This process is taking place at a time when the audience for sports journalism is becoming increasingly aware of the range of techniques being used by various stakeholders in sport to set and control news agendas. ... There is also the growing problem for journalists of elite sports stars using the media simply as a vehicle through which to promote their brand image and the commercial interests which they endorse. (Boyle, 2006: 112–113, 118)

Exercise

- What occupational values emerge from the quotes in Box 6.3?
- What underlies tensions between PR and journalism?
- What issues arise from the quotes for you as a public relations student and how do the quotes make you feel about your chosen occupation?

Thinking back to the concepts of critical thinking presented in Chapter 1, analyze the quotes in Box 6.3 and discuss:

- What sorts of arguments are used?
- How is language used to create particular impressions?

In conclusion

This chapter has introduced some key perspectives and associated terminology from media studies which are intended to help readers be sensitive to journalists in practice and to media studies in academia. Some of the material may not have been comfortable reading and may make you feel differently about your chosen occupation.

REVIEW

Returning to the questions at the beginning of the chapter you mighe like to reflect on the following:

- is there any room for idealism in either journalism or PR?
- is the relationship between journalism and PR purely functional?

RECOMMENDED READING

I have cited standard texts on media (McQuail, 2000) and would also commend *The Media Student's Handbook* (Branston and Stafford, 2006) for public relations students. Chris Frost's *Reporting for Journalists* (2002) is an excellent readable introduction, as is Harcup's *Journalism* (2004). The latter is styled more as a workbook and has lots of useful definitions and critical insights as well as drawing on research interviews with journalists. Good insights into general magazine journalism are provided in the books by Jenny McKay (2000) and John Morrish (2003), and there is also a fascinating insight into women's magazines by Anna Gough-Yates (2003). Anyone tackling content analysis either academically or professionally would do well to consult Riffe et al. (1998), Neuendorf (2002), Bryman (2001) and Deacon et al. (1999).

Health Communication and Social Marketing

7

Key concepts

Anti-health campaign	Media advocacy
Circuit of interaction	Media panic
Circuit of mass communication	Mediating science
Community-based health promotion	Persuasion
Corporate social responsibility	Pseudo health campaign
Critical psychology	Public health campaign
Entertainment-education	Publics
Health education	Public understanding of science
Health promotion	Social marketing
Mass media fantasy	Stakeholders

Introduction

This chapter focuses on problems of communication in health and science, key issues and the limits of psychological approaches that ignore social, political and economic contexts. Thus this chapter highlights the challenges that face policy-makers and the sponsors of health communication, for whom public relations practitioners might work. It also describes social marketing and its overlaps with public relations. The chapter does not attempt to describe detailed psychological models or techniques of persuasion at the individual level, although it defines some key terminology. While psychology can help in health communication in determining to some extent quantitative opinions, it cannot help us in understanding the context of health behaviours. To gain this knowledge we need to understand politics, economics, community contexts, the role of the media, and the production and consumption of health meanings.

CHAPTER AIMS

On completion of this chapter you will be able to:

- define the field of health communication and its relevance for PR
- describe the potential role and scope of PR in various health communication sectors
- design a strategy for a health campaign
- understand media perspectives and content in relation to health
- understand the broad definition of social marketing and its relationship to PR

Why this chapter in this book?

Many readers may wonder why the subject of health and social change are given such emphasis in a text on public relations. Several reasons underpin its inclusion. First, health encompasses a range of public and private sector initiatives internationally, including pharmaceutical companies (product development and promotion, social responsibility) and world health campaigns. International organizations shape health and social agendas, which are subject to lobbying, diplomacy and cross-cultural communication. Second, the field of health promotion or health education is very well developed, with its own extensive academic and practitioner literature and, in the UK at least, its own professional body. Third, since health promotion began as a largely persuasive effort, it has also depended to some degree on psychological frameworks common to public relations. Fourth, healthy or unhealthy behaviours are a consequence of individual judgements about risk. And finally, the best reason of all is the intrinsic interest of the field and the many controversies that arise within it, from the 'obesity epidemic' (Gard and Wright, 2005) to the 'demographic time bomb of ageing populations'. This is a specialism that lives!

Public relations in health

Health is subject to governments' public policies and international standards (World Health Organization), is tied to economic decisions, is highly politicized and is often controversial in media terms. Health is subject to scientific and political flux and change is inherent: changing opportunities for health care, pharmaceutical developments (new medicines and treatments) but also threats (ageing populations, obesity crisis). All these provide stories for the media. Public relations has a key role to play in various areas: **lobbying**, **issues management**, **crisis management**, rhetorical work (spokesperson), **media relations**, **campaigning**, **fundraising** (health-related charities). It is also the case that because health is such a precious resource, threats that emerge quickly rise on the media agenda, such as SARs and Avian flu. Media coverage in this area can spiral because health risks are frightening, threaten the innocent, produce human drama and may be on an apparently apocalyptic scale (Sandman, 1999). The latter category (the *'Armageddon' cases*) may well blow a threat well out of proportion (Bennett and Calman, 1999). This is described as a **media panic**. This term seems to have developed from the *moral panic* concept in media studies, which emerged in the 1960s (Cohen, 1972). Media panics take place because detailed, clearly understood scientific facts are not available and so media speculation fills the newspapers and broadcast TV programmes (Bennett and Calman, 1999). Of course, not only is media coverage a concern to those who represent scientific or health organizations, but the media is also a major source of information and potential influence on all of us in our everyday lives.

CRITICAL REFLECTION

- Are non-scientifically trained PR practitioners credible as communicators about science?
- Can public relations practitioners working on behalf of a particular interest (government agency or department, hospital, scientific organization or university, medical charity, consumer group, etc.) claim to be presenting 'the truth'?
- Is their information really reliable? How do we know? What do we need to know to make that judgement? Can they be trusted? In any case, what do we really mean by 'the truth' in this context – science is often open to alternative explanations and interpretations.

These questions show that health communications share common problems with scientific and technical communication in relation to complexity. Accurate, trustworthy guidance is a public good.

There have been various attempts to classify different approaches to health campaigns, for example:

- Ewles and Simnett: medical, behaviour change, educational, client-centred and societal (2003: 43–46)
- French and Adams: collective action, self-empowerment and behaviour change (1986: 71–74)
- Beattie: health persuasion, community development, legislative action, and personal counselling (Beattie, 1991 cited in Katz, Peberdy and Douglas, 2002: 91)
- Downie, Tannahill and Tannahill: traditional (prevention), transitional (scare tactics), modern (holistic/participatory) reflecting different orientations: disease-orientated, risk factors orientated, health orientated
- Tones and Tilford: the preventive model (individual behavioural modification), the radical model (focus on social, economic, and political factors) and the empowerment model (encouraging personal growth and self-esteem) (1994 cited in Katz et al. (eds) 2000: 169–172).

These various frameworks overlap to some extent or give a slightly different emphasis. All highlight the difference between approaches to health promotion that vary between those that are focused on changing the individual, those that encourage and facilitate community change, and others that suggest societal change.

In the opening pages of this chapter I draw on the work of a range of established sources including Rice and Atkin (2001), Downie et al. (1996), Maibach and Parrott (1995), Salmon (1989), Sidell et al. (2003), Jones et al. (2002), Katz et al. (2000) and Ewles and Simnett (2002).

Some areas of PR work in health are controversial, for example:

> [The] marketing of drugs by pharmaceutical companies to the medical profession has long been a way of influencing medical opinion and practice, which in turn has a knock-on effect when doctors communicate their opinions to mass media organizations. Analysis of these promotional efforts is an interesting but rarely explored sub-genre of media health studies. (Seale, 2002: 57)

More obvious problematic ethical areas are those working in *anti-health* (Wallack, 1990: 147), such as the tobacco industry (unsafe products used to brand sports events), alcohol or dietetically unhealthy products such as those which include hydrogenated 'trans' fats, which are present in many processed foods, and sugary, salty and fatty products directed at children. PR practitioners in the food industry therefore also have to engage with the scientific composition and implications for the health of their products.

Misleading health-related claims (Novelli, 1990: 80) or *pseudo-health education* consists of interested parties, usually commercial, who have a product or service to sell. Examples could include producers of low-fat spreads and other low-fat products that avoid mention of the additional salt and sugar that are required to make those products palatable; 'front' organizations that purport to be independent and supply 'product information' but are in fact financed by producers; and weight-loss organizations, some of which promote healthy diets and others of which promote fatty diets or extreme diets that exclude whole food groups important for human health.

Pro-health includes government campaigns, such as those for behavioural change and modification, local government efforts to develop healthy communities, health charities promoting health awareness (e.g. self-monitoring: breasts, bladder, bowels, testicles). It can be argued that pro-health PR includes conventional and alternative medicine and therapies and luxury services, such as spas, as well as the burgeoning fitness industry – health and fitness centres, products and services.

Public health campaigns employ a range of communication techniques, including interpersonal and small-group communication focusing on opinion and community leaders (which immediately implies the importance of culture) to encourage the adoption of healthier living (Rice and Atkin, 2001). This is in addition to mass communication techniques such as public relations and advertising. These techniques are often harnessed in combination to ensure that messages are supplemented and reinforced in different contexts so that messages are repeated and filtered through multiple channels creating reciprocal reinforcement (McGuire, 2001). A definition of a **public communication campaign** is that one agency, in this context usually a government (publicly funded) or medical establishment or medically sponsored charity, seeks to change attitudes/behaviour which they believe to be damaging to the fabric of society, or to the health and welfare of citizens (e.g. drink driving, drug-taking). Government campaigns are often initiated to alert citizens to changes in legislation. Mostly, such campaigns seek to use the mass media to disseminate their message. These campaigns can usually be classified as *single-issue campaigns* or *media advocacy* and may be conducted by activist groups to try to change public policy (Wallack et al., 1993). **Health education** focuses on the body, services, policies and processes (Downie et al., 1996). Health educators use media to communicate general health messages but also need to access power elites and inform politicians and industrialists. Community work is increasingly seen as absolutely vital in facilitating individual change (Bracht, 1999).

Box 7.1   Examples of PR work in health communication

- Food safety
- Health scares
- GM foods
- Health-enhancing foods and the promotion of 'nutriceuticals' and 'cosmeceuticals'
- Legislation restricting the use of homeopathy and alternative medicine
- Anti-smoking legislation and social change
- Media publicity and nutritional labelling
- Pharmaceutical companies and corporate social responsibility

Exercise

- What are the current health issues on the media agenda?
- Review a week's media coverage of health issues in a variety of print and broadcast outlets. Note the range of topics and the way in which they are handled by the media. How many stories do you think were initiated by PR sources for health charities, universities or hospitals?

Discipline box: Psychology

The discipline of psychology aims to study and explain human behaviour and actions through studying perceptions, learning, memory, thinking, social worlds and individual differences. Psychology is useful for public relations because it presents concepts and methodologies for analyzing human attitudes, beliefs, opinions, behaviour and communications.

Psychology evolved from statistics, ethology, physics and philosophy, and has remained interdisciplinary in nature, drawing on biological sciences such as biochemistry, neurology and physiology. Social psychology has connections with sociology and anthropology. The field of persuasive communication relies heavily on social psychological theory and research in a variety of contexts, from propaganda and psyops to public relations and marketing (including consumer behaviour).

Health psychology is a growing field which tries to understand the psychological influences on how people stay healthy, why they become ill and how they respond to illness. Health psychologists help people to cope with illness, pain, accidents and also promote healthy lifestyles in community settings (Prilletensky and Nelson, 2002: 108).

Critical psychology in a health setting highlights power differentials between medical professionals and patients; the importance of understanding patient perspectives of health, illness, treatment and relationships; the existence of patriarchy; the

(Continued)

understanding that ideas about health and illness are socially constructed. It focuses on the health of disadvantaged groups (Prilletensky and Nelson, 2002: 108). Critical psychologists emphasize patient participation and empowerment. There are also political implications: research demonstrates links between poverty and health and the fact that in countries with a more egalitarian income distribution (Sweden) infant mortality is lower and life expectancy higher (Prilletensky and Nelson, 2002: 111).

CRITICAL REFLECTION

- What aspects of psychology are useful to PR and why?
- Which values have resonance for existing PR theories, and why?
- How can PR add value to a health campaign devised by health psychologists and social marketers?

Persuasion

Persuasion is the intention to achieve a particular response. It is this, according to many theorists, which distinguishes persuasive communication from communication, although some see communication and persuasive communication as synonymous (Miller, 2002). Other writers argue that the focus on the sender of persuasive communication leads to a misunderstanding of the nature of persuasive communication because it underplays the strong effect of self-persuasion. In some cases, persuasion can occur without the specific intent of the receiver – perhaps in response to other pressures, such as conforming to peer or social pressure – so clearly the social and cultural context of persuasion is at least as important as the message and the sender. Recently, the concept of *resistance to persuasion* has been highlighted in relation to health campaigns (McElroy, 2002).

Health promotion

A definition of a public health campaign is to enhance the quality of the health of the community and to do no harm. The World Health Organization's definition of health is: 'A state of complete physical, mental and social well-being and not merely the absence of disease' (Downie et al., 1997: 2). The World Health Organization (WHO) was established in 1948 as the United Nations' specialized agency for health.

Its aim was to achieve the best possible health for all peoples (www.who.int/). The notion of well-being is, however, subjective, although it has been usefully defined as:

> Personal, relational and collective needs including self-determination, participation and mutual responsibility and community structures that foster individual and shared goals, provide security and access to vital services. Well-being is not solely an intra-psychic concept but is dependent upon social and political conditions and contexts. Well-being can be affected by crises such as war and famine but also more gradual and subtle shifts such as upward distribution of income that has occurred in developed and developing countries alike. (Prilletensky and Nelson, 2002: 112)

Thus there is an important connection between the social, political and economic context and individual health, which means that **health promotion** can never be just about changing individuals; it is also about social change, for example making it difficult for people to smoke by banning smoking in public places and social spaces such as pubs. Public health campaigns aim to educate citizens on how to improve their health and well-being, and, as part of that, to change social norms that inhibit healthful behaviours. Social change is therefore implicit and sometimes explicit. Public relations is always present in social change. Such ambitious objectives imply that public health is intrinsically political. PR is always implicated in policy and politics.

CRITICAL REFLECTION

Health communication raises a number of questions relating to social justice:

- Do we all have a right to the equitable distribution of health care?
- Who is really responsible for certain forms of sickness such as alcoholism – individual responsibility or social policy?
- How responsible are the alcohol and tobacco industries for individual illness resulting from those products?

These questions demonstrate that health communication is a field that produces fundamental disagreements about policy, resource allocation, liability, responsibility and rights.

Strategies in health promotion

Here I shall review some key terminology and give examples of approaches from the literature. The medical model or traditional approach (Downie et al., 1996: 34) aims to eliminate disease through the promotion of expert medical recommendations. It can therefore be rather paternalistic (Ewles and Simnett,

2003: 43–44). The term 'medical model' 'describes the pre-eminent scientific model used by those involved with medical science for the explanation of disease' (Hanson and Easthorpe, 2007: 2) which assumes human dysfunctions are the consequence of causal mechanisms located in the human body (Turner, 1987: 9, cited in Hanson and Easthorpe, 2007: 2).

There have been various approaches to health communication.

The *educational approach* (Downie et al, 1996: 27–49) is based on *rational choice theory*. It assumes that people will make the right choices if they understand the reasons for the behaviour that is being advocated. It aims to distribute 'value-free' information. The *entertainment-education model* inserts educational information into entertainment (Montgomery, 1990; Singhal and Rogers, in Rice and Atkin, 2001: 343–356) (see also Box 7.2). This includes TV and radio but also music employed as a medium for messages about sexual abstinence and contraception in Mexico and the Philippines in the 1980s (Rogers and Singhal, 1990).

Box 7.2   Health communication sampler

- The New South Wales Multicultural Health Communication Service (MHCS), in Australia, adapted a marketing communications campaign for use with 'culturally and linguistically diverse' (CALD) groups (Noble and Camit, 2005: 1).
- Promoting fruit and vegetable consumption for improved health (survey of 8,000+ New Zealanders supported by the Cancer Society of New Zealand) (Lawson and Williams, 2005). http://praxis.massey.ac.AZ, accessed 11 December 2006.
- The Healthy Cities initiative has proved successful in helping communities develop collaborative links and interventions to stimulate media and public debate about health and involve communities in social change in many countries (Rayner, 2002; Adams and Cunning, 2002).
- Ghiras, a national project for drugs prevention in Kuwait, had to break a 'culture of silence' about the problem and used media advocacy initially. Underlying the issue are tensions between globalization and local cultural identity. Ads could not address the issue directly but focused on family values and the importance of hobbies (Al Saqur, 2007: 128–196).
- Ogilvy PR developed a number of social marketing campaigns, including those for AIDS, epilepsy, substance abuse, anthrax, reproductive health (www.ogilvypr.com/practice-groups/social-marketing.cfm).
- BBC World Service Trust obtained funding from the UK government's Department for International Development (DfID) and collaborated with the Royal Government of Cambodian and Cambodian broadcasters on a three-year project on maternal and child health (http://www.bbc.co.uk/worldservice/trust/pressreleases, accessed 30 November 2006).

(Continued)

(Continued)

- The Bahrain Women's Society launched Be-Free, an anti-child abuse campaign to develop a sense of social responsibility. The conflict between modernization and cultural identity meant that this sensitive subject needed careful handling. The primary intervention focused on good parenting. 'In the case of the Arab Gulf states, public broadcasting has reflected the conservative perspectives held by collective Arab Gulf cultural traditions ... [and] has not discussed the issue openly ... to respect the collective cultural traditions' (Al Saqur, 2007: 211).
- China's food industry is developing at a phenomenal rate and has identified functional foods and nutritional content as a priority (Global Watch seminar, 14 March 2004, www.globalwatchservice.com, accessed 20 November 2006).

Public health campaigns draw on a range of disciplines, but as persuasion has often been central, the discipline of psychology has been important to academia and practiced.

Box 7.3 Health issues covered in soaps

- *Eastenders* has covered a range of health and well-being issues, including breast cancer, domestic abuse, heroin addiction, HIV/AIDS, prostitution, rape, and adult literacy (www.bbc.co.uk/eastenders/haveyoursay).
- *Hollyoaks* has covered sexually transmitted diseases.
- Indian soaps have campaigned against female fetocide (http://news.bbc.co. uk, accessed 30 November 2006).
- In a Tanzanian radio soap, a promiscuous male truck driver not only got AIDS but went on to suffer all sorts of grim misfortunes in a tale that seemed to include punitive elements of retributive justice.
- *Coronation Street*'s story-line, in which a character died from cervical cancer, had a major impact in the North West of England on the NHS Cervical Screening Programme. Researchers found that the number of smears increased by 21.3 per cent in the 19 weeks following the story (Howe et al., 2002).

CRITICAL REFLECTION

- Watch a variety of soap operas over the course of one week noting down any health and wellness issues that are covered in relation to sexuality, substance abuse, birth control, abortion, AIDS/HIV. What conclusions do you come to?

A further approach to health promotion is what I term *reality health programmes*, which have become popular in the UK. Examples include *Celebrity Fat Club*, *Fat Club*, *You Are What You Eat*, and *Honey We're Killing the Kids*. The format usually follows a lifestyle overhaul led by either a 'health guru' or a team of dieticians and fitness experts who advise the celebrity or ordinary mortal about their eating and exercise habits. The changes required can be radical and extreme, and the subject of the programme can be submitted to various public indignities (e.g. public examination of excreta, spots and tongue).

CRITICAL REFLECTION

- What health issues arise in the media you consume?
- How are they framed and who by?
- Have you been influenced by media coverage?
- What is your personal response to reality health programmes?

Persuasive or behaviour change approaches to health promotion focus on the individual level of change and behavioural modification in relation to learning, habit formation and behavioural conditioning. While it is associated with mass campaigns, one-to-one training and reward-giving are important. The *social influence approach* or societal change (Ewles and Simnett, 2003: 44) tries to influence community norms and collective behaviour, which can be effective where community ties are strong but might not be so effective in more individualistic or atomistic cultures. Similarly, *client–community* or client-centred (Ewles and Simnett, 2003: 45) is a bottom-up, self-directed approach organized by concerned groups and facilitated by a health educator. It has been popular in women's health (Ewles and Simnett, 2003: 44). *Community-based* health promotion emphasizes the importance of community empowerment to achieving physical, mental and social well-being. While it incorporates a practical approach to solving problems and engaging with specific programmes and services, it emphasizes the complex nature of health and its biological, social and environmental determinants and the range of political, social and technical interventions necessary to protect and promote health. Community-based health promotion has included the Healthy Cities initiative (Glasgow and Sheffield are two UK examples) and Health Promoting Schools (HPS) (Bracht, 1999: 21; Denman, Moon, Parsons and Svears, 2003: 383–392).

Media advocacy is the term for PR and media relations campaigns that aim to set the news agenda and shape debate on a health issue and to change public policy particularly by linking public health and social problems to structural inequalities rather than to individual weaknesses (Wallack and Dorfman, 2001: 393–398).

Media advocacy therefore aims to achieve a broad range of media coverage on a health topic in order to *reframe* public debate. The aim is to gain the support of *public opinion* for public policy changes (such as regulation regarding alcohol and tobacco). This approach may highlight the anti-health activities of corporates and thus stimulate activist campaigns (Wallack, 1990a: 158).

Adversarial/activist communication consists of oppositional campaigns such as anti-smoking or anti-abortion. To some degree they may be seen as the consequence of successful anti-health industry framing; for example, anti-smoking groups were castigated in the 1960s and 1970s and were socially 'uncool'.

The field of health promotion has evolved from *medical model preventative programmes*, directed by epidemiologists and policy-makers, which are focused on disease or risk factors, towards health-orientated, community-based programmes that facilitate social change and *empowerment* (Downie et al., 1996: 37). This shift acknowledges that health promotion requires education, the acquisition of life skills, self-development and self-esteem. Individual and community empowerment is social action in process that enables people and groups to gain mastery over their own lives. Empowered individuals can mobilize communities (collective action) and generate norms and social support systems to activate social change (Tones, 2001).

Exercise

A health board has involved you, as PR specialist, to help analyze the local community to identify opinion formers and networks that might be important in influencing community changes in relation to health. Carry out the following tasks:

- Define the term 'community' (geographic, cultural, psychological, political, virtual).
- Define the key publics that might form part of your community analysis.
- List the information you would need about that community in order to understand their health issues and likely problems for health communicators.

International perspectives on health promotion

The rationale for international action came from concerns over public health. The Western world is facing an increase in the diseases of affluence, affecting those in middle or later life, such as degenerative diseases resulting from consumption of too many calories in the forms of fats, reduced physical exertion, tobacco and alcohol, which lead to respiratory diseases, cirrhosis and diabetes. A huge rise in coronary heart disease (CHD) is predicted in the developing world. In less developed countries, issues such as sewage disposal, water treatment and the pasteurization of milk remain problematic. Concerns over international health led to the formation of the Ottawa Charter for Health Promotion in 1986, which defined health promotion as:

- the development of ideology underpinning health promotion via community development
- the process of enabling people to take control over, and improve, their health (http://www.who.dk/policy/ottawa.htm).

Management and evaluation issues

Health education and promotion literature has recognized the importance of evaluation procedures and of qualitative and quantitative measures in assessing the processes, outcomes and impact of health promotion (Pirie, 1999: 127–134; Valente, 2001: 105–124; Atkin and Freimuth, 2001: 125–145; Rice and Foote, 2001: 146–167; Salmon and Murray-Johnson, 2001: 168–180; Snyder, 2001: 181–192; Peberdy, 2001: 85–100; Everitt and Hardiker, 2003: 194–200). Familiar to public relations professionals are the articulation of a clear aim and supporting, measurable objectives and the utilization of research methodology (Peberdy, 2000: 275–337). Rigorous methods are advocated by Springston and Lariscy (2003) in their review of PR in health communications. Problems facing health communicators will also be familiar to public relations practitioners (e.g. how to isolate the effects of one campaign in the context of mixed messages and information overload). Some impacts may take a long time to occur. Then there are the effects and side-effects of other negative and positive interventions, such as public policy initiatives to increase taxes on tobacco, alcohol or food containing hydrogenated fats or palm oil. These are just a few of the challenges facing health communicators.

Critiques of health promotion initiatives

There are a number of sociological perspectives which develop alternative readings of campaigns and campaigners. For example, it can be argued that medical and scientific knowledge is linked to certain influential social and political structures and are embedded in certain classes in society, and are therefore not neutral.

CRITICAL REFLECTION

- How are conflicts resolved between industry and local communities where, for example, unusual 'clusters' of cancers have occurred?

A *free-market approach* to persuasive campaigns takes the line that it is individuals who have a problem (with drugs or alcohol, for example) and argues that it is up to those individuals to resolve their difficulties and accept responsibility for their problems. In this way, the social context that may have contributed to the problem that triggered the individual's harmful behaviour is ignored.

There is also an inherent problem of the *mass-media fantasy* (Wallack et al., 1993), whereby the mass media are over-used as a channel of communication and are frequently unsuitable for complex health messages. Reduction to simplistic 'say no'-type campaigns are not helpful for the individual operating in a particular social context. Furthermore, mass media convey *mixed messages*. For example, what happens to a health campaign advert that is shown in the context of programming that inadvertently glamorizes cigarettes, alcohol or drugs? Lupton (1995) also criticized scientific mass communication approaches for their linearity and reductionism:

> There is a slippage between education and indoctrination in the rhetoric of much health promotion and health communication; communication is far from being a two-way process. Once health communicators and promoters have discharged their responsibility in disseminating information and promoting awareness, the emphasis is upon the individual to act upon this knowledge to prevent illness. According to mainstream health promotion models of behaviour, if members of the target audience do not respond in the appropriate manner, they have adopted defence mechanisms or maladaptive coping responses or they lack the required level of personal control and feelings of self-efficacy, or they possess an 'addiction' to unhealthy material. (Lupton, 1995: 110)

Critics of health promotion have attacked what is seen as moral superiority or even *health fascism*, defined as an attempt to impose certain lifestyles and the ideologies/beliefs that support them (Downie et al., 1996). It has been argued that health promotion can cause obsession or fanaticism, and can lead to processes more akin to indoctrination than education, for example, in schools. There is extensive coverage of childhood obesity, for example, and less on increasing eating disorders. In the calendar year 2006, there were 1,161 mentions of the term 'childhood obesity' in UK newspapers (421 in national newspapers) and 273 of 'overweight children' (94 in nationals). Only two articles (in the *Daily Express*) mentioned 'teenage anorexia', but 'teenage' and 'anorexia' (used as separate terms) were mentioned 207 times. There were 255 items mentioning 'teenagers' and 'anorexia' as separate words. Following media debates in 2006, Brazil banned models whose body mass index dropped below 18. Subsequently the Italian fashion industry has now banned size zero models and its representatives spoke in the media about the need for the industry to demonstrate its **corporate social responsibility** by educating models about healthy eating and eating disorders. Mass media have highlighted the paradox of the size zero status in the context of rapidly rising obesity.

Social marketing

Social marketing can be seen as a catalyst or change agent at local, regional, national or global levels and has been used in a wide variety of campaigns, including malnutrition, family planning, illiteracy, sexual health, sanitation, substance abuse (Kotler et al., 2002). It segments mass audiences on the basis of geography, demographics (age, gender, family size, life cycle, income and occupation, education, religion, ethnicity, nationality), psychographics (social class, lifestyle, personality), attitudes and behaviour (Kotler et al., 2002, Andreasen, 1996, 2006). Social marketing includes social advertising, social communication, social market research, social product development, social use of incentives and social facilitation (Dhoklia and Dhoklia, 2001: 487). As a specialist field of marketing, it is based on quantitative research. Social marketing objectives are, like PR objectives, measurable, quantitative, and about behaviour change (Andreasen, 2006; Kotler et al., 2002).

Social marketing evolved in the 1970s and has gained credibility through the support of many national and international programmes that have sought to change behaviour (Andreasen, 2006). However, for some, 'social marketing' has remained a rather obscure specialism. As marketing specialist, Sheth, pointed out:

> Social marketing suffered, right at its inception, from definition debate. Is it marketing of non-profit and social services (education, health care, population control) or is it the malpractices of marketing, such as the misrepresentation, deception and ecological and cultural harm that marketing practice create? ... Even public policy research could not provide a focus for this domain. Unfortunately, there was also advocacy – or evangelistic fervor – among well-known marketing scholars who braved the research in this area. This made objective scientific enquiry untenable. (Sheth, 2000: 613)

Discipline box: Social marketing

Social marketing adapts commercial marketing concepts and thinking to the field of health (Andreasen, 1996, 2006). It has become very influential in promotional societies where marketing ideology is intrinsic. Its basic philosophy is of customer/client focus.

The social marketing approach

Social marketing deals with sensitive issues and *market intangible benefits* that do not yet exist (Kotler et al., 2002). This is a particular problem in social marketing health campaigns that are aimed at youngsters who think they will live forever and have no concept of time. Similarly, fitness benefits take time and commitment, as do weight-loss programmes. Social marketing has to sell the absence of degenerative disease in the forties to those who are just in their twenties.

Social marketing, public relations and promotion

Public relations and marketing are often presented as oppositional or rival specialisms yet they clearly complement each other. Public relations is both an intervention to effect change *and* a consequence of change (due to the emergence of **publics**, or the activities and rhetoric of **stakeholders** or opponents), but social marketing is primarily an agent of intervention and behavioural change. Marketing literature tends to confine PR to promotion or publicity support, yet public relations' stakeholder and relationship approach can support the strategic development of a social marketing campaign. Communications management and a good understanding of media processes can prove an invaluable alternative to the advertising upon which social marketers often rely. In addition, the PR skills of 'messaging' are crucial in inspiring audiences to recognize that a communication is helping them to resolve an issue.

Critique of the social marketing perspective

Critics of social marketing in the 1970s and 1980s suggested that it was too limited an approach to health problems, contrasting it unfavourably with media advocacy which could help communities gain greater control over the social and political environment (Wallack, 1990b: 162). Critics argued that social marketing was overly focused on the change of individual health behaviour, as Wallack pointed out:

> Social marketing is a seductive concept. It serves as common ground for media outlets, community groups, government agencies, and advertisers to work together. Unfortunately, the condition for this co-operation is too often the avoidance of controversial issues and the definition of health in narrow disease-orientated terms. It tends to be non-controversial because it focuses on individual behaviours and the cause of disease (and presumably the cause of health) and deflects attention from products and the environment through which these products are made available. On the other hand, social marketing may do little for those most in need of change but having 'the fewest social, economic and personal resources to facilitate change. (Wallack, 1990b: 162)

Lupton argued that the notion of social marketing is inherently contradictory. While the emphasis of social marketing is overtly on understanding the consumer and fulfilling the consumer's needs, in reality it is directed towards attempting to create needs (or more commonly anxieties) where they previously did not exist; the very antithesis of meeting consumer needs. The 'consumer', as represented in the discourse of social marketing, is therefore a paradoxical figure. The discourse of meeting the consumer's needs constructs the individual as an actively choosing subject, employing the rational purchasing behaviour of *homo economicus* and highly aware of 'buyer beware' approach to consumption. The rhetoric of marketing argues that 'the customer is always right'. Yet the approach of social marketing also constructs the consumer as malleable and amenable to persuasion, requiring the health-preserving advice of health promotion professionals ... the customer, then, is not always right, but in fact is ignorant. As with other strategies of health promotion, the assumption of social markets remains unchallenged: they seek knowledge of consumers better to influence or motivate them, not to ensure that objectives of social marketing are considered by consumers are appropriate. Social marketing, therefore, is simply the old simplistic health promotion approach to persuasion dressed up in marketing jargon about products and consumers. (Lupton, 1995: 112)

Critical theorist Glenn Morgan also questioned marketing ideals that, in a free market, marketers research and then supply consumer needs and wants in relation to products and services (Morgan, 1992: 136–158). Morgan argued that the marketing world view is an instrumental one, as marketers only wish to know enough about consumers to enable them to sell products, services and ideas to them. Marketing ideology that refers piously to customer focus and the importance of understanding and listening to customers can be seen as a form of exploitation in which human relations are subordinated to the interests of material production (Morgan, 1992). According to Morgan, the rhetoric of marketing has not so much liberated more choices for the consumer but reconstructed citizens' rights and access to health care. Likewise marketing and PR critic David Miller commented:

If people were to say... 'we want a society where people look after one another, where there is social justice' – then marketers cannot supply that. [Marketers] treat everything as a commodity ... but of course there's more to human society than commodities. (Interview, 6 October 2006)

CRITICAL REFLECTION

- Who benefits from social marketing and PR health campaigns and in what way? Are benefits equally distributed?
- Who should define the aims and objectives of health campaigns and why?

Table 7.1   Complementary disciplines in health promotion

Discipline	Underpinning theory	Approaches
PR	Social psychology Management Mass communications Media studies	Communication management Relationship management Symmetrical communication Education/information Media advocacy Personal propaganda
Social marketing	Social psychology Economics Mass communications	Exchange Customer focus Relationship management Persuasion/propaganda
Health promotion	Social psychology Intercultural communications Mass communications Community theory	Empowerment Community change Education/information Promotion/persuasion

Source: adapted from Al Saqur (2007)

Table 7.1 shows how different disciplines share underpinning theory.

Exercise

Bearing in mind the various perspectives on health promotion that have been presented in this chapter, consider how you as a communications specialist would help a college or university become a 'healthy institution'.

Box 7.4   Professional health communication

There are several international bodies for health communication:
  International Union for Health Promotion and Education (IUHPE) www.iuhpc.org
  European Public Health Alliance www.epha.org
  World Federation of Public Health Associations www.wfpha.org
  The Association of Healthcare Communicators (AHC) (www.assochealth.org.uk) in the UK, is an independent network set up in 1997. It is 'committed to promoting professional, proactive communications'. It provides training and development seminars, produces a journal, offers job opportunities and provides a forum for discussion

Box 7.5   The role of the media in advocacy and social marketing – a critical view

'The mass media can be a powerful tool for promoting health around the world. There are, however, many complexities associated with optimal use of this powerful resource. Some argue that public communication campaigns can be a source of accurate health information for individuals and that mass media can inform public debate about health issues. The media are perceived to be a valuable and willing partner. Others argue that the media are a source of anti-health education presenting people with inaccurate or misleading health information through advertising, entertainment and even news content. Rather than informing public debate, the media have been accused of limiting such debate by reflecting the profit interests of the corporate world while maximizing the health needs of populations. In this case, the media are seen not as willing allies, but as a barrier to be overcome ... the debate about the role of the mass media in health promotion reflects a fundamental difference about whether the pursuit of health promotion is personal-individual or social-political. If it is personal-individual it will primarily involve being more innovative in stimulating individual behaviour change ... If ... social-political [is linked] to social change and public policy development ... because the mass media generally serve to reinforce existing arrangements and not stimulate social change, this perspective on health promotion represents a challenge to public health professionals and mass media to re-think basic assumptions' (Wallack, 1990b: 147–148).

CRITICAL REFLECTION

- Does public relations promote health or anti-health or pseudo health?
- Does public relations support individual health change or environmental socio-political level changes?

Media, health and science

A crucial part of health promotion is an understanding of media processes and the reasons for the representation of health and science. Understanding **source–media relations** requires study of the processes of production, representation, consumption and audiences.

Medical, health and scientific communities have sometimes claimed that scientists are poorly understood and badly misrepresented by the media. This perception, and indeed any evidence that supports this view, can be partly explained by the fact that scientists and journalists inhabit different cultures. Failure to understand media processes has negatively impacted on the potential success of health campaigns:

> The epidemiological accuracy, scientific objectivity and political correctness of media health have all been shown to be at fault by the health education lobby, failing to transmit health-producing information in a host of areas. Yet the 'hypodermic needle' model of health education that conceives of audiences as somewhat passive receivers – or perhaps more often 'forgetters' or 'mis-interpreters' – of media messages is a limited one, something that has been recognized in more recent health promotion initiatives that conceive of audiences and communities as more active, and that are willing to compromise the ascetic agenda of health education in recognizing the entertainment priorities of mass media. Thus community empowerment, media advocacy and edutainment initiatives have developed with a more sophisticated image of the media health audience. (Seale, 2002: 23)

Public understanding of science has been changed by technology. Many people can now access information directly through the internet, and this knowledge and awareness to some degree threaten the scientific elite, especially if the media take up the challenge. The long-held assumption of many scientists that the public was a lumpen, passive mass that ought to be educated has had to change, and scientific culture has had to change along with it. Hence the spawning of a number of organizations and many conferences to address the problem of scientific communication. To some degree this development has caused a rupture within the scientific community because some scientists have been prepared to communicate their ideas to a wider public and have risked the disapproval of their peers for popularizing, even sensationalizing, science to conform to media requirements.

The scientific community is part of a significant elite within post-industrial societies and as such can attract media attention. However, it is also the case that the strongly hierarchical, apprenticeship laboratory culture can lead to poor media relations. In some cases this is due to a reluctance to 'dumb down' scientific results, which can lead to a fear of, or dislike of, the media, and consequent avoidance. Impatience can be caused by a media focus on a newsworthy or human interest story. Scientists may see journalists as scientifically illiterate hacks who are paid to exaggerate to sell a newspaper. The media may be seen as inconsistent in that only certain scientific stories will be covered – often those of an extreme nature. Of course, it is the case that the media will focus on scientific and health stories which pose some risk to the community, especially where there is someone who can be blamed; if there seems to have been a cover-up; if it is an area of scientific dispute or competing explanations;

if there have already been some victims (preferably high profile victims); and if the story touches on a fundamental human activity linked to competing cultural and moral values, such as sexual practices (Sandman, 1999).

Scientists, in turn, can be perceived by the media as patrician, remote, aloof and caricatured as 'ivory tower boffins', to whom the human race unwisely entrusts its future. Members of the scientific community have long recognized their communication problems, and in particular what they regard as the poor reception, interpretation and transmission of their ideas via the media. Two bodies which devote time to improving public understanding of science (perceived as an intrinsically 'good thing' by scientists) are the British Association (www.the-ba.net) and COPUS (Connecting People to Science, www.copus.org.uk).

Mediating science

Media sociologist and critic of public relations, Professor David Miller, suggested that there is a flaw in the discussion of the communication of science, which is that it is often analyzed from the perspective of one group of actors. Therefore, he argued that the communication of science could be better understood by seeing it as a **circuit of interaction** between four sets of actors:

1. Social and political institutions such as government, universities, interest groups, business and scientific research institutes, and think tanks.
2. The media, including news, current affairs and documentary programmes, science programming, popular science magazines, journals and books, advice columns within popular magazines and fiction.
3. The public.
4. Decision-makers such as government, business, interest groups, universities and scientific institutes.

The **circuit of mass communication** (Figure 7.1) helps us to appreciate the dynamism among the various actors and, according to Miller, enables us to explain 'the rise and fall of scientific issues in the media and on the public and policy-making agenda' (Miller, 1999: 211). Miller highlighted the challenges facing social and political institutions 'translating' scientific advice into official reports and promotional material while maintaining accuracy and, in some cases, political advantage. Conflicting interests result in competitive media strategies often within or between governmental or scientific organizations.

In conclusion

This chapter has reflected upon key issues in health communication. It has positioned health promotion as social change, which gives added emphasis to

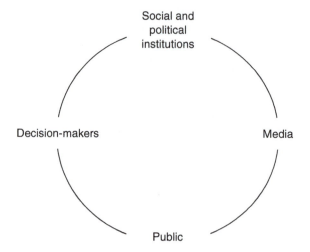

Figure 7.1 The circuit of scientific communication
Source: adapted from Miller, in Scanlon et al. (1999: 210)

communication among multiple stakeholders and community members. The role of the media has been shown to be useful in agenda setting, but also as a source of mixed messages. The chapter has argued that although psychology and strategies of persuasive communication have their place, it is vital for health communicators to take account of broader political, economic and social contexts.

REVIEW

Reflecting upon the questions raised at the beginning of this chapter, you may like to consider your ideas about the role and purpose of health communication campaigns in society. Lana Rakow, one of the first American scholars to apply critical theory to public relations, raised the following key question which can serve here as a critical exercise:

Critical Exercise

Why do we live in a world of information campaigns, and whose interests are served by them? (Rakow, 1989: 164)

RECOMMENDED READING

As this book went to press a new book on social marketing appeared in the UK. Written by the first Professor of Social Marketing, Gerard Hastings, University of Stirling, this is a must-read volume. In addition to its review of theory and many examples drawn from campaigns there is a whole series of real-life case studies written by a variety of academics and practitioners. It gives a fascinating insight into this socially important international field (Hastings, 2007).

The Open University series (Katz et al., 2000; Jones et al., 2002; Sidell et al., 2003) is an excellent source. More basic, but quite practical, is Ewles and Simnett (2003). Seale's *Media and Health* (2002) is a terrific read containing much material relevant to PR. Excellent throught-provoking sociological perspectives are contained in Lupton (1995), Nettleton (2006) and Seedhouse (2004).

Public Relations and Management

BEFORE YOU READ A SINGLE WORD...

- What is your understanding and definition of 'management'?
- Describe an archetypal manager – what do they do? How do they look? How do they dress? How do they behave towards colleagues?
- What is it like to be a manager? How do you think it feels?
- How do managers learn?
- Why do management ideas matter to PR practitioners and students?

Key concepts

Administrative management	Discourse analysis
Bureaucratic management	Excellence theory
Change agency	Human relations
Classical management	Managerialism
Circular response	Management fashion
Communication management	Management guru
Creativity	Organizational change
Creolization	Scientific management
Discourse	

Introduction

Why a chapter on management? Management ideas and the waxing and waning popularity of some ideas above others matters to PR students and practitioners because these ideas infiltrate and shape (and reshape) organizations, their climates and cultures (these terms will be discussed more fully in Chapter 9). Understanding a variety of management theory perspectives gives PR specialists an insight into assumptions that will shape professional relationships and habitats. Reflecting on management theory helps us to appreciate the contribution these ideas have made to the development of PR theory and education.

This chapter presents a brief historical review of some key traditions and approaches in management thinking, focusing on those which bear upon public relations practice. This includes some discussion of 'management gurus' and ideas that are used in training managers, thus giving insight into perspectives that may be encountered in the workplace. It thus aims to provide broader context to the operation of the working life of a PR practitioner.

Public relations work intersects with the notion of management at various different levels:

- project management
- time management
- people management
- financial management
- strategic management
- creative management
- communication management

Public relations work requires various degrees of managerial competence at all levels, so those aspiring to practice PR do need to engage with management concepts and techniques. At a deeper level it is also important to understand managerial priorities, managerial terminology and jargon, managerial mindsets and orientations, and managerial ideologies to understand those with whom they work so closely.

Public relations practitioners work with and for managers in diverse organizations (government, commerce, voluntary). PR practitioners have to relate to managers, clients and organizations that attempt to actualize managerial concepts, theories and fashions. Furthermore public relations consultancies are organizations requiring management. For example, public relations practitioners have to manage projects, budgets and time. They also have to manage creative processes and creative people (art directors, graphic designers, web designers) especially in relation to integrated marketing campaigns, advertising, promotional publications, annual reports, exhibitions, events. There are also some interesting questions to be asked of the way in which PR consultants use, adapt and sell management concepts to their clients, for example in relation to corporate culture change, corporate identity management, corporate social responsibility. This chapter therefore considers PR's relationship with management, and highlights the origins of managerial thought, focusing on a select few that have commented on the communication role of management, thus highlighting useful sources for further analysis. In this way it provides an introduction to some of the ideas that have shaped the managerial class with which PR practitioners have to engage and to some degree align.

The chapter serves two other purposes:

- it contextualizes further discussion in Chapter 2 on PR processes, strategic PR and problems with linear approaches to public relations
- it serves as a prologue to Chapter 9 by sketching some of the history of management thought which underpins Gareth Morgan's postmodern perspectives on organizational analysis which is summarized in that chapter as an important and useful framework for public relations.

CHAPTER AIMS

On completion of this chapter you will be able to:

- diagnose a range of managerial models, roles and discourses when you observe them in practice
- understand how ideology is a feature of management
- understand managerial constraints, processes and change mechanisms
- understand the concept of creativity in relation to management, with reference to public relations work
- discuss gender issues as they arise in relation to management, organizational relationships, organizational politics and power structures

Where do management ideas come from?

Management is an applied discipline that draws on psychology and sociology for many of its ideas. Yet the ideas of management practitioners have also been crucial to its development. Swedish researchers have described management knowledge as having gone through a process of **creolization** drawing on sources of knowledge from domains with blurred boundaries – practice, academia, consultancy and the media (Sakin-Andersson and Engwall, 2002: 14–28).

According to Collins English Dictionary **creole** is a term that emerged to describe a language that resulted from the inter-relations between two language communities, one usually European (and usually a colonizing power). The inter-mingling of language creates a new language. The word may have its origins in the Latin *creare* – to create. The term has also apparently been applied to those born in slavery or to those of European ancestry born in colonies or to those who are mixed race. To take a personal example, my grandfather was a mixed race Mauritian with French (presumably colonial) ancestry (and name) who spoke French, Creole (his native languages) and English (as a third language that was also part of the Mauritian colonial past).

Processes of creolization are apparent in public relations as a consequence of the fact that the first generations of academics have in many cases obtained undergraduate and postgraduate education in other disciplines and thus bring to bear a variety of insights to PR. To take another personal example, I studied American and English History for my first degree, Commonwealth History for my second degree and only later (after working in public relations) took two further Masters degrees in Public Relations (to try to understand what I'd been doing for the past five years) and Social Justice (to get a good understanding of ethics).

It seems likely that those teaching and researching public relations will become more homogenous as some PR graduates and postgraduates progress to academic careers. In the meantime, some lament the '57 varieties' academic:

Public relations faculty that lack theoretic training in public relations may read the published literature or attend conferences to partially compensate for this lack of education. This approach has an inherent bias built into it, however, and many do not avail themselves of such opportunities, resulting in some 'professors' of public relations with zero academic training in the subject area. In addition, bias results from the tendency for theory learned later to be interpreted through the theoretic lens of one's first-learned theories. As a result, some public relations faculty understand, and therefore teach their subject only from a mass communication, journalism, or organizational communication perspective, rather than as a field with its own increasingly rich body of theory. (Botan and Hazleton, 2006b: 2)

Critical exercise

- What are the advantages and disadvantages of creolization in a discipline?
- Is this book 'creole'?
- can you identify public relations practitioners who have theorized about public relations? What sorts of approaches have they taken?
- Can you identify similarities and differences between ideas generated by practice-based academics and those firmly based in academia? What value would you put on these contributions and why?

PR and managerial power

Public relations is an aspirant occupation seeking to gain acceptance societally and organizationally. Although some practitioners and academics claim it *is* a management function, others are more cautious and simply argue that is should be a management function:

> Public relations is most likely to contribute to organizational effectiveness when the senior public relations manager is a member of the dominant coalition where he or she is able to shape the organizations's goals and to help determine which external publics are most strategic. (L. Grunig, J. Grunig and Dozier, 2002: 97 cited in L. Grunig, J. Grunig and Dozier, 2006: 34)

The public relations function must be empowered as a distinctive and strategic managerial function if it is to play a role in making organizations effective. The senior public relations officer must play a role in making strategic organizational decisions, must be a member of the dominant coalition or have access to this powerful group of organizational leaders, and must have relative autonomy from excessive clearance rules to play this strategic role. (L. Grunig, J. Grunig and Dozier, 2006: 38) The distinctive managerial role which is claimed for public relations is that of **communications management**. However, this is not unproblematic since other managers are involved in communications such as marketing managers and human resource managers (employee communications).

In practice the PR role is disparate and variously positioned in terms of strategy. The extensive research into PR roles (Dozier and Broom, 2006: 139–142) which began in the USA under Professor Glen Broom concluded that it was essential for public relations to gain acceptance into 'the dominant coalition' in order to perform a strategic role managing organizational relationships rather than being restricted to publicity and crisis communications. It was also suggested that if public relations gained access to the organizational corridors of power, it could influence managerial thinking in relation to an organization's societal role and impact, its social responsibility and ability to forecast and manage issues:

> A political systems metaphor is the best way to understand relationships between public relations power and organizational power ... practitioners need to become more politically astute to serve as effective players in the organization's political infrastructure. Increased political astuteness, a strong track record of accomplishments, and especially a managerial perspective will help practitioners better serve their organizations and the public good. (Berger, summarising Spicer, 2007: 225)

According to Berger,

> Excellence theory [in PR] emphasizes the importance of an empowered public relations function that participates in the dominant coalition and other strategic decision-making arenas so that the practice can help organizations solve problems, become more socially responsible, and acquire and maintain social legitimacy. It argues that public relations professionals are more likely to be so empowered if they possess managerial skills and a managerial worldview and subsequently enact the managerial role. (Berger, 2007: 226–227)

Thus, on this account, PR practitioners are to align themselves with management.

CRITICAL REFLECTION

- In the quote above note the use of the term 'professional' – why is this useage problematic?
- What are the advantages and disadvantages of entry to the managerial class for PR's other organizational relationships?

Entry to the managerial class is articulated on the grounds of the benefits it offers organizations as shown in the two examples beneath:

> Strategic public relations management (strategic communications management) assumes public relations to be a strategic management function with a mandate to function at the strategic (macro or societal level) of an organization ... public relations thus assists an organization ... to adapt to its societal and stakeholder environment ... [and] influences organizational leaders to address reputation risks and other strategic issues identified in this process by aligning organizational goals and strategies to societal/stakeholder values and norms – serving both the organizational and the public interest. By acting socially responsible and building mutually beneficial relationships with the organization's stakeholders and other interest groups in society on whom it depends to meet its goals, an organization obtains legitimacy, garners trust, and builds a good reputation. (Steyn, 2007: 139)

> Strategic public relations benefits the organization because the members of the dominant coalition often do not see the organization's environment with an objective viewpoint ... Public relations can contribute to strategic management by helping managers and the organizations enact the environment, of which they may not be aware. (Sung, 2007: 175)

However, such interpretations somewhat underplay the power, status and financial benefits to be gained by individual members of the PR occupation.

CRITICAL REFLECTION

- How is it possible for the public relations practitioner to be 'objective' (Sung, 2007: 175) when s/he is part of the managerial class?
- Are public relations practitioners better placed than other managers and organizational members to research and 'read' the environment and, if so, why?
- How is it possible to serve the organization and the 'public interest' simultaneously?

There are a number of inter-linked barriers to PR's acceptance by organizational leaders. The rise of marketing as a discipline and its earlier path towards professionalism can be seen as having had a negative impact on the fortunes of PR. Marketing theory and practice tend to restrict PR to a communication technique and alternative to advertising. The integrated marketing communications or integrated communications 'movements' aimed to harness and to some degree unify or coalesce marketing, advertising and public relations in order to ensure consistency of messages and shared responsibility for customer focus (Heath and Coombs, 2006: 31). This has had the consequence of an ongoing jurisdictional struggle (discussion on jurisdiction See, pp. 35–41) between marketing and PR. Many in PR have been keen for apartheid and to defend the porous boundaries from 'encroachment'.

Conflicts emerge over size and control of budgets and power over definition of organizational policy with regard to the prioritization of various stakeholder groups. For example, marketing prioritizes customers and those in the supply chain.

PR practitioners have long aspired to 'Board room status' or 'the top table' that will allow public relations priorities to influence organizational direction. For example, Russell recently alluded to, 'The practitioner's need to get a seat at the management table, to speak the language of business, and to measure the impact of communications' (Russell, 2007: 590).

But the credibility of practitioners has been challenged by their lack of professional status, and a perception that public relations cannot deliver measurable results. These concerns have driven the PR industry's professional project and its efforts to evaluate its work. In the UK, there were discussions in the then Institute of Public Relations (IPR) about the value of university level education from the early 1950s (L'Etang, 2004: 189) but it was not until the 1970s that a younger generation represented by the IPR Education Committee Chair, John Cole-Morgan, began to argue for 'a more academic approach' and intellectual rigour (Interview:

L'Etang, 2004: 213–4). However, it was not until the 1980s that universities and the PR occupation began to collaborate on the development of undergraduate and postgraduate courses. It is only in the last decade that doctorates in public relations have become more common in the UK. University qualifications bestow a certain credibility on the occupation and should provide younger generations with a grounding in relevant applied and critical theory and a good understanding of how social scientific research can inform understanding and practice of public relations work, notably in relation to the formulation of aims and objectives and evaluation.

Thinking about management perspectives

Understanding how ideas about management and organizations have evolved helps us to understand our own and others' assumptions.

It is helpful to understand the topics that fall within the discipline of management. These include:

- systems theory
- boundary spanning
- motivation and work
- job design
- group dynamics
- human resource management (HRM)
- decision-making processes
- organizational culture and structure
- organizational change
- environmental analysis
- corporate social responsibility
- international communication
- globalization
- strategy
- power and leadership
- team working
- diversity
- communications
- conflict management and negotiation

Source: Rosenfeld, R. H. and Wilson, D. L. (1999) *Managing Organizations*, London: McGraw Hill.

Critical exercise

You have been called for interview for a job as a press officer. During the interview you casually mention that 'PR is a management discipline'. At this point, a member of the interview panel states, somewhat aggressively, 'I have a management degree from the University of Strathclyde, and an MBA from INSEAD – what can you tell me about management that I don't already know?'. How do you answer this question?

Box 8.1   Thinking about management and organization: the science of work, process and procedures

Classical management

Classical management emerged from the late nineteenth century and remains influential. There are three main themes which focus on worker productivity (scientific management), the functions of management (administrative management), and the overall organizational system (bureaucratic management).

Scientific management   Frederick Winslow Taylor (1856–1917) was the source of this approach. An American engineer, Taylor started his life as a labourer and then rose to foreman and later chief engineer. Subsequently, he became a consultant and published his ideas widely. Taylor's definition of managerial responsibility is to maximize the well-being of employer and employee, not only in terms of money but in terms of self-development. He tried to specify a fair day's work and performance indicators, against which employees could be evaluated. Taylor thought that each worker had their niche (employees were 'equal but different' in their talents and contributions) and that each job should be highly specified, as if it was a part in a machine.

Administrative management   French theorist Henri Fayol (1841–1925) focused first and foremost on managers. This interest reflected his own career and background since although he started work as a mining executive specializing in engineering problems, he moved on to become director of a group of pits, published a famous geological monograph and was held responsible for turning around a doomed area of mining. He began to theorize about the principles upon which he had based his decisions. Fayol's approach might now be termed 'strategic planning'. He recommended a 'survey' process, not dissimilar to what we would call today 'situation analysis', and defined management as comprising the following elements:

- to forecast and plan
- to organize
- to co-ordinate
- to control

Fayol thought that managers should have personal qualities of 'high moral character, impartiality and firmness' and be responsible for encouraging *esprit de corps*. He argued that managers should promote harmonious relations through careful and preferably face-to-face communications. This was to be achieved partly through cultivating an atmosphere of respect for others within the organization, regardless of level. He also thought it was important to maintain a consistent workforce and was opposed to a high turnover of staff, arguing somewhat controversially that: 'A mediocre manager who

(Continued)

stays is infinitely preferable to outstanding managers who merely come and go' (Fayol, 1965: 39).

Bureaucratic management   Bureaucratic management focused on the overall organizational systems and was based on the idea that firm rules, policies and procedures, and hierarchical forms of organization, were efficient and effective. It is important to bear these benefits in mind since the term 'bureaucratic' is often used pejoratively. The German sociologist, Max Weber (1864–1920), is the thinker most closely associated with concepts of bureaucratic management. Weber believed that management should be kept separate from ownership and saw the benefit of bureaucracy as being the de-personalization of the organization. In a bureaucracy, roles are circumscribed and information is carefully recorded for future reference – rules and procedures are clearly laid down. Selection for managerial office is determined by technical competence and managers should be tested to ensure they have the right skills.

Source: Pugh and Hickson, 1989

CRITICAL REFLECTION

- How does bureaucratic thinking influence public relations work and practice?
- To what extent are universities bureaucratic and how is this exemplified?

Classical thinking rationalized managerial work and organizations, but it became clear that although the approach has its uses and can explain many managerial practices and procedures, it also has its limits. Classical assumptions about organizational life suggest that it is:

- rational
- structured
- formal
- technical
- ideal
- scientifically grounded

Classical thinking is useful in contexts where there are repetitive tasks and the environment is stable, but it is limited by its lack of adaptability, potential for mindless bureaucracy and de-humanizing effects. In any case, managerial reality is experienced as:

- interrupted
- fragmented
- many short interactions
- reactive
- constrained
- a whirl of activity
- a web of complex relationships
- political
- emotional (Alvesson and Willmott, 1992: *passim*)

The mismatch between normative theory and managerial experiences led researchers to explore some of the hidden and complex sides of management and organization.

Human relations

The human relations perspective is sometimes referred to as the behavioural perspective. Its influence is contained in the common cliché (check out some annual reports) – 'our employees are our greatest asset'. Key insights from the human relations approach were that social relationships and some individual autonomy were important to productive work. The human relations movement can be seen partly as a reaction to scientific management. Some human relations thinkers have had some insightful and perspicacious things to say about communications which are relevant to PR students and practitioners. I have foregrounded these in the summaries that follow.

Box 8.2   High priestess of human relations – Mary Parker Follett

Mary Parker Follett (1868–1933)

The account that follows is drawn exclusively from Pauline Graham's edited collection of Mary Parker Follett's writings (Graham, 1995). Mary Parker Follett was a management thinker well ahead of her time. Yet although she was a leading light in American and British business circles in the 1920s, her work later became forgotten. Kanter suggested that Follett's gender was partly responsible for her neglect (Kanter, 1995: xviii), but Drucker (in Graham, 1995: 4) took a different tack, arguing instead that her ideas were seen as politically unsound since she emphasized the role of the citizen and the community rather than espousing the then current trend towards bigger government, centralization, bureaucracy and control. Some thought she had Marxist connections and saw her as subversive. Her work seems to remain outside the

---

(Continued)

mainstream and many undergraduate management texts give her little, if any, mention. The debt owed to her by later theorists, such as Chester Barnard and Douglas McGregor, is not always acknowledged.

Follett's academic background was in politics and, through her partner, a well-connected Englishwoman, Isobel Briggs, she gained entry to an intellectual circle that included politicians, writers, philosophers and the Boston aristocracy (Graham, 1995: 11–34). Follett's interests developed into decision-making and she was invited to represent the public on a wide range of public tribunals, arbitration boards and minimum wage boards, subsequently taking on the role of an arbitration consultant.

Follett focused on conflict resolution, communication co-orientation (the way in which communication contributes to inter-personal relations by enhancing the accuracy of the perceptions) and the role of the community. She generally saw management as a function and process rather than as a toolbox of tricks or techniques (Drucker, in Graham, 1995: 6). It may have been this, rather than her supposed political leanings, that is the reason for her lack of popularity. Her approach required that managers communicated openly and resolved problems jointly with each other and with the workforce. There were no quick fixes, but deep insights into relationship processes.

Follett's interests in conflict, co-operation and negotiation led her to recommend **integration** rather than compromise between parties:

> Compromise does not create, it deals with what already exists; integration creates something entirely new ... if we get only compromise, the conflict will come up again and again in some other form, for in compromise we give up part of our desire, and because we shall not be content to rest there, sometime we shall try to get the whole of our desire. ... [O]nly integration really stabilizes. (Follett, in Graham, 1995: 71–72)

Follett saw co-orientation and negotiation as dynamic processes that were interlinked with the progress and development of relationships (as depicted by Dance's model of communication, see Figure 3.3). Follett's ideas seem to have reappeared in contemporary popular management, for example in management guru Steven Covey's work. She described the problems of negotiation somewhat pithily when she wrote:

> I can never fight you. I am always fighting you plus me. ... We feed Cerberus [three-headed dog that guarded Hades in Greek mythology] raw meat and hope that when we lie between his paws, he will turn out to be vegetarian. (Follett, in Graham, 1995: 81)

(Continued)

(Continued)

Follett argued that managers should foster *power with* rather than *power over* (Graham, 1995: 23–24, 103–104). These alternate views of power were brought into PR academic literature quite recently by Berger (2005). For Follett, the role of the manager was to facilitate the power of the group by helping them to realize their potential, and that of others, in tackling tasks.

Source: Graham, P. (ed.) (1995) *Mary Parker Follett: prophet of management – a celebration of writings from the 1920s*, Boston, MA: Harvard Business School Press.

CRITICAL REFLECTION

- How might the concept of integration be useful in public relations practice?
- Which particular public relations skills might be important in trying to achieve integration?

Mary Parker Follett and public relations

Follett's approach was revolutionary, and inspired by politics and psychology. Some of her ideas appear to anticipate developments in public relations and organizational theories. For example, she spent some time analyzing the internal processes of organizational communication and likening it to that of individual *intra-communication* – the process of internal reflection that leads to self-realization and the ability to resolve internal *psychoanalytic* conflicts and puzzles through the discovery of hidden insights. In developing her ideas about organizational introspection, *constructive conflict* (Graham, 1995: 67–87) and problem resolution, Follett emphasized the importance of understanding not just another party's opinions, but their opinions about other's views, thus anticipating ideas developed in communication about *co-orientation*. Follett thought that it was vital for employees and managers to see what she termed 'the whole field of desire', by which she meant that the wishes and intentions of all parties should be brought out into the open and discussed together (Graham, 1995: 76).

Communication, for Follett, was a process of continual influence and cross-referencing between parties, in which the history and development of each relationship played a vital role in subsequent communications. Her concept of *circular response* was offered as an alternative to the then dominant classical psychological stimulus–response theories (Graham, 1995: 35–65). For Follett, communication was a process of complex interactions in which each communication was affected by the developing relationship and previous interactions. There was never a 'clean slate' because both parties would have had expectations of each other, even before they met, which would have shaped their behaviours and influenced subsequent communication – and there was no going back once the relationship had started.

To recognize and apply Follett's concept of circular response is to accept the process of change. Openness to understanding the complex composition of relationships and embracing change is hard but necessary, and individual change was vital if conflict was to be resolved, because individual change led to group change and ultimately to societal transformation. Indeed, Follett argued that circular response played a vital part in the development and transformation of human societies. She believed that the absence of circular response led to the breakdown of understanding and relationships and ultimately led to conflict.

Follett also had ideas ahead of her time in relation to the moral responsibilities of business. She thought that business had obligations to society beyond its purely economic function, which she referred to as 'reciprocal service', because she believed that business was a 'truly social agency' whose 'work itself is to be our greatest service to the community' (Graham, 1995: 290). For Follett, business was not separate from society but part of the same overall organic whole and therefore an important and powerful agency to influence and create change.

Follett's ideas are relevant to many aspects of communication strategy and techniques, but perhaps they are of particular relevance to health communication, community relations, corporate social responsibility and public and political communication.

Box 8.3   Chester Barnard – humanist co-operation and systems

Chester Barnard (1886–1961): humanist co-operation and systems

Chester Barnard was a manager who made key contributions to management through highlighting the role of *co-operation*. He was a humanist who emphasized the importance of managerial integrity, service to society and the dignity and worth of each individual in the workplace.

(Continued)

(Continued)

Barnard saw organizations as interconnected systems that were part of broader social and economic systems. They were constantly dynamic, impacting and influencing each other. Barnard is of interest to public relations students because of the emphasis he placed on communications in helping organizations to be effective. Communications between the parts and the whole of the organization should deliver co-ordination.

Barnard thought that executives should establish and maintain a communications system among their employees, and perceived the manager as a teacher who was responsible for explaining policy. He thought communication was key to facilitating the operation of the organizational systems and believed organizations were cultures that included both formal and informal communication networks through which their personal identity was constructed and their social needs met. To achieve this a process of integration between individual and organization was necessary, and in this idea we can see Barnard's debt to Follett.

Source: Wolf, 1974

Neo-human relations

Neo-human relations (NHR) is a term which describes the theories of a group of US authors from the 1950s onwards. It is based on the idea that industrial conflict would be minimized if employees were allowed to do meaningful work, because this would allow them to share managerial goals. The application of NHR was realized in the techniques of *organizational development* (OD), which gave organizational leadership the responsibility for instigating **organizational change** through the articulation of humanizing ideals that valued the individual worker and their needs. However, it has been pointed out that:

The efforts to humanize work are seen to serve an *ideological* purpose, rather than necessarily being part of management practice. They represent a body of ideas that may be called upon if management is being held open to public criticism, and that is favoured by certain sections of management (like personnel and PR) concerned with the firm's outward image yet with little real impact on work process. (Fincham and Rhodes, 1988: 169)

CRITICAL REFLECTION

Much of the standard writing in public relations emphasizes that the public relations role should be conducted at the strategic level and that it should have boardroom status.

(Continued)

- If public relations is part of the senior management team, how can it avoid being influenced by managerial perspectives that objectify employees?
- How can public relations practitioners get around this political problem and the fact that their own role may be perceived as ideologically suspect by employees?

Box 8.4   The excellence perspective in management and public relations

Japanese perspectives highlighted the importance of **culture** and drew on the highly successful enterprise management model.

The **excellence** perspective (Peters and Waterman, 1982) provided US management with a response to Japanese success and identified the key characteristics of excellent companies: activity, closeness to the customer, autonomy and entrepreneurship, productivity through people, hands-on management, value-driven, focus on core business, simple organizational structures, flat structures. This approach was adapted to PR by Professor James Grunig, whose theoretical work identified the key features of **excellent public relations**. These included: strong cultures, symmetrical communication systems, empowering leadership, decentralization of strategic planning, entrepreneurship and social responsibility (Grunig, 1992). However, the excellence **paradigm** in management was discredited, partly because five years after the concept was publicized two-thirds of the 'excellent' sample had slipped, were facing problems or had gone bust. If that were not enough, the empirical data on which the concept was based had also been discredited (Jackson, 2001: 17–18).

The use of excellence in management theory was based on research into the management practices of financially successful organizations. Peters and Waterman (1982) sought to ascertain attributes that made companies excellent. Excellence literature defined the concept of excellence variously including financial criteria, sales, innovativeness, quality of management, services and products, human resource management, social responsibility (Grunig, 1992: 222). The focus of the Excellence Study in public relations focused initially on excellence in management and its impact on effectiveness with a view to discovering the implications for the management of communication (Grunig, 1992: 223). The use of the excellence concept in public relations addressed the questions:

- for what reason does public relations contribute to organizational effectiveness?
- by what means do excellent public relations departments make organizations more effective? (Grunig, Grunig and Dozier, 2007: 26).

(Continued)

(Continued)

The research began with large quantitative surveys in the USA, Canada and the UK in order to produce 'a single index of excellence in communication management' (Grunig, Grunig and Dozier, 2007: 27).

Excellent public relations was defined as: 'The glue that holds excellent organizations together, because of the importance of symmetrical communication and collaboration in organizations that are organic, value human resources, are innovative, have leaders who inspire rather than dictate, and have strong participative cultures ... excellent public relations can help the rest of the organization be excellent' (Grunig, 1992: 246).

Critical exercise

- Write a definition of 'excellence' – how do we know something is 'excellent'?

The term 'Communication management' began to be employed because Many practitioners define communication more broadly than public relations. They see communication as the management of the organization's communication functions. They see public relations as one of several more narrow functions, especially as publicity, promotion, media relations, or marketing support ... (Grunig, 1992: 4).

'Communication management' is used as the title in some educational contexts for degree or department titles, for example at the University of Waikato, New Zealand.

In PR practice in many parts of the world, the term 'public relations' either connotes the limited role of publicity and media relations, or is discredited as 'spin doctoring', which is probably why other terms have become more popular. For example 'corporate communications', which is used as the title of some degree courses, for example at Queen Margaret University, Edinburgh. Another common term which appears to imply a more senior status is that of 'public affairs', even though strictly speaking this is quite clearly the domain of issues management and lobbying.

The excellence approach in management can be seen as one of a number of *management fashions* that have emerged with accelerating speed in the past thirty years. While the uptake of such fashions is often explained as responsiveness to environmental change, globalization, and the requirement for effectiveness and shareholder and stakeholder value, they may also be seen as competitive one-upmanship within the managerial class. The impact of fashions is almost perpetual organizational change as structures are altered and efforts are made to effect employee behavioural change, or even to change organizational culture (the inevitable superficiality of such 'change' is discussed in the next chapter). Public relations is implicated in such fashions and changes in its role to support managerial objectives.

CRITICAL REFLECTION

- Why hasn't excellent PR been discredited in the same way that excellence in management has been?

Management 'fashions' and 'gurus': management training

Management thinking has been developed by different types of contributor: theorist consultants or academics or successful managers who have formulated various approaches to leadership, management and organization. The latter group have been characterized by a number of academics as **management gurus**. They have become highly influential and have been largely responsible for **management fashions** which, in turn, have been responsible for widescale restructurings and job losses in private and public sectors, the growth of management consultancy, and the emergence of new terminology and jargon (Jackson, 2001).

Examples of management fashions include Total Quality Management (TQM), customer-focus and kaizen (continuous improvement) which emerged from Japanese management and Business Process Re-engineering (BPR), which was designed for large-scale change and Knowledge Management (KM) which focused on knowledge creation and transfer.

Management fashions have included Steven Covey's effectiveness movement (1989), Peter Senge's learning organization (1990) and Daniel Goleman's emotional intelligence (EI) (1996, 1999). Gurus package and promote books, videos and training courses. Covey's effectiveness movement focuses on personal change and growth, including a form of spiritual reflection and growth that bears some similarities to the genre of self-help books, particularly those of M. Scott Peck, author of *The Road Less Travelled: A New Psychology of Love* () and *Traditional Values and Spiritual Growth*. Covey is a Mormon and Scott Peck espouses Christian values; both are evangelists for their causes (Jackson, 2001). Senge's work includes an eclectic range of multicultural, multi-religious references, although he himself is a Buddhist (Jackson, 2001).

Box 8.5   The nature of Quality – thinking about TQM

'Quality is a characteristic of thought and statement that is recognised by a non-thinking process. Because definitions are a product of rigid formal thinking, quality cannot be defined ... But even though Quality cannot be defined, you know what Quality is ... He singled out aspects of Quality such as unity, vividness, authority, economy, sensitivity, clarity, emphasis, flow, suspense, brilliance, precision, proportion, depth and so on' (Pirsig, 1989: 210–211)

CRITICAL REFLECTION

- What do you think of the quote in the Box above?
- How would you define 'Quality'?
- Why are concepts such as 'Quality' and 'Excellence' so hard to define?
- If they are hard to define, why and how are they useful as organizational and managerial concepts?
- What might be the public relations role in implementing organizational excellence and quality?
- Why is this all so difficult?

Senge took a systems perspective on organizations to integrate personal reflection and development with group learning and vision that understands inter- and intra-systemic connections and larger processes in a way that enables adaptive and creative responses (Jackson, 2001). Senge emphasized dialogue and improvement in a way that will be familiar to public relations students.

Goleman's approach suggested that 'self-awareness, impulse control, persistence, zeal and motivation, empathy and social deftness' are prime indicators of industrial success and predictors of those who will succeed (Goleman, 1996). It emphasizes emotional awareness and sensitivity, 'not technical expertise or book learning to be what mattered most for excellence' (Goleman, 1996: 5). However, scientific tools have been developed that purport to evaluate an individual's emotional intelligence.

Critics have noted that management gurus function like 'witch doctors'; that they expound platitudes and clichés (Jackson, 2001: 2), and that they threaten proper academic analysis of complex problems. It is also clear that they have a built-in obsolescence and are open to reinterpretation and reinvention. According to Huczynski, the competitive nature of business requires this reinvention of concepts in order to appear novel and ahead of the game. The consequence of this is that 'too many modern managers are like compulsive dieters' (Huczynski, 2006: 303). Ironically, however, 'virtually all of the management ideas and techniques ... are based upon six families of management ideas' – bureaucracy, scientific management, administrative management, human relations, neo-human relations and guru theory (Huczynski, 2006: 303). The marketing and PR of business gurus could be a fascinating study.

Gurus have been criticized for superficiality, for not acknowledging academic sources from which they have drawn ideas, for making too much money and for popularizing ideas that do not work. To give a couple of examples, Argyris attacked the contradictory dualisms in guru frameworks, pointing out that:

> Gurus espouse participation empowerment, and personal initiative and responsibility. Yet ... they create programs whose successful implementation depends upon the use of hierarchy, unilateral control, and employee limited freedom. Moreover, they do so by being systematically unaware of their inconsistencies and unaware of their unawareness. Those who attend these programs often begin with an intention to be cooperative and to exhibit their sense of stewardship toward the organization. Soon, they begin to realize that they too do not know how to overcome these problems. They experience double-binds. If they do not cooperate, they maybe seen as disloyal, if they do cooperate, they do so by reinforcing what they consider to be a sham. (Argyris: 2001, x)

Magda Pieczka pointed out that '[i]f communication is crucial to modern organizations, why do gurus assume that all it takes to achieve it is to make symbolic gestures publicly and reorganize people's jobs?' (Pieczka, 1999) These criticisms point to the weaknesses of what are essentially evangelistic persuasive programmes (or is it propaganda?) aimed at behavioural change. While guru programmes may espouse ethical values, reflection, self-awareness and assertiveness, the fact is that they operate within a power system, specific cultures and climates and in the context of organizational history, myths and legacies. It is with these issues in mind that the next chapter takes up the theme of organizational culture more directly.

Business process re-engineering (BPR) is an entirely market-driven approach, even more radical than total quality management, because it is designed for large-scale change. BPR was proposed to managers as the only choice to improve organizations. It required: 'Fundamental re-thinking and radical design of business processes to achieve dramatic improvements in critical, contemporary measures of performance, such as cost, quality, service and speed' (Hammer and Champy, 1993: 32, cited in Jackson, 2001: 72). Key features of BPR include downsizing, flattening structures, multi-tasking, project teams and management coaching, and this focus on process has led some to criticize it as a reinvention of Taylorism. However,

Hammer's revision of his initial ideas emphasized other benefits for the process-centred organization besides the radical overhaul of processes. These included a focus on:

> Responsibility, autonomy, risk, and uncertainty. It may not be a gentle environment, but it is a very human one. Gone are the artificial rigidities of the conventional corporation. In its place is a world full of messiness, challenges and disappointments, that characterize the real world of real human beings. (Hammer, 1996: 14, cited in Jackson, 2001: 78)

Leadership and management

Leaders can be distinguished from managers in their visionary goal-setting function, which managers then help organizations to achieve. Leaders have ultimate power (and responsibility) and are **change agents** who, through the management of meaning, can alter the way people see things.

As Pieczka pointed out:

> To be effective, the leader must be believed; and to be believed he/she must show energy and integrity. ... A leader is one of us, and yet set apart from the rest of us mortals to breathe life, excitement and a sense of person into his organization. Presented like this, how can the leader's vision be presented or questioned? (Pieczka, 1999: 9–10)

Leadership is conceptualized as transformational, charismatic, visionary and even spiritual. Leaders are seen as those who should define organizational reality through a vision and supporting values. *Vision* explains the future direction and ambition of the organization; the *mission* defines the purpose of the organization; the *values* lay out the basic principles and business ethics of the organization. All of these were realized through detailed programmes or work carried out by organizational members (employees).

CRITICAL REFLECTION

- What is the vision of your university?
- What is its mission?
- Where do vision and mission come from? Have you contributed to their development and, if so, how?
- What are its values?
- How are all these communicated to staff and students?

Business leaders in the UK, such as Richard Branson, John Harvey Jones, Alan Sugar and Anita Roddick, have become heroes in contemporary culture and are given space by the media in programmes such as *The Apprentice* and *Dragon's Den*. The heightened political, economic and social power of business leaders gives them opportunities for personal PR and celebrity status.

Transformational and spiritual leadership

Visionary leaders are seen as vital to forming and shaping a **strong culture** to facilitate management control, partly through colonizing the minds of organizational members. As Pieczka pointed out: 'Despite the messianic vision, culture change is perhaps about finding an alternative way of motivation and control' (Pieczka, 1996: 12).

CRITICAL REFLECTION

- What PR issues arise from these definitions of leadership?

There are various aspects to the notion of spiritual leadership. Much of the language around leadership uses religious vocabulary and metaphors, for example 'vision', 'mission', 'conversion'. However, the influence of New Age management from the late 1990s (some originating from the Findhorn Community in north-east Scotland) has re-focused discussion on to relational aspects of leadership and management. The Findhorn Foundation is 'a learning community and eco-village, demonstrating the joy, the magic and the challenges of practising spiritual principles in our daily lives, affirming the interconnectedness of all life and living with the common ethics of love, service, integrity, responsibility and leadership' (Promotional brochure, 2007). In the early 1990s Findhorn held a major conference on corporate social responsibility and current courses include 'Leadership Edges' and 'The Art of Leadership – Embracing Diversity'. Some of this work encourages inner reflection (personal and professional) on issues of integrity and the way in which rather different and unconventional approaches to management have the power to influence work in a magical and dramatic way. Indeed, in some business schools in the USA students meditate, are encouraged to 'confess' organizational sins, tell stories and use dance, music and prayer as a way of coming to terms with organizational leadership as stewardship and service (the leader as servant) (Calas and Smircich, 2003).

Box 8.6   Useful sources

There is a themed section on spirituality, management and organization in *Organization*, 10 (2) 2003: 327–400.

Findhorn Community (www.findhorn.org)

CRITICAL REFLECTION

- What role could public relations play in a spiritual leadership environment?

The shift to a creative economy means that managers must learn to manage creativity and to be creative themselves. **Creativity** can now be seen as part of team and process management rather than the product of individual genius (Bilton, 2006: 1–2). According to Bilton:

> Creativity in management is used to describe alternative approaches to business processes, such as strategy formation and organizational change, and at the operational level to refer to new product development and technological innovation. ... The desire to think outside the box and challenge conventional wisdom is all very well, but can also lead to rash decisions and a fetishization of novelty at the expense of continuity. ... Behind much of the rhetoric of creativity in management is a binary opposition between 'business as usual' and 'challenge everything' with the assumption that creativity requires a radical break with tradition and convention, while any more pragmatic, grounded approaches to management are to be derided as 'uncreative'. In fact the challenge of creativity in management is to overcome these stereotypes of novelty and continuity, and to find ways of stitching together or tolerating the paradoxes and contradictions between them ... acceptance of eclecticism and paradox is to be found in the work of many management theorists, notably Charles Handy and Henry Mintzberg. (Bilton, 2006: xv)

Creative industries are occupations based on intellectual property, such as technology, arts, design and fashion, or on providing business-to-business creative services, such as advertising. Although the UK government's Department of Culture, Media and Sport (DCMS) appears to include public relations as one of the creative occupations subsumed under advertising, Pieczka argued that:

> Although in many respects the public relations industry is comparable to advertising (it employs the idea of creativity), it is not a creative industry in the sense of

being based on the creation and exploitation of intellectual property, as the official definition in the UK has it. ... Public relations consultancy is more akin to a traditional professional service – providing a diagnosis and treatment derived from a body of expert knowledge ... the kind of knowledge that lies at the core of the occupation's expertise has profound implications for the way the occupation acts and presents itself. (Pieczka, 2006b: 307).

Thus, according to Bilton's account, management is partly a creative process of facilitating and constraining activities that will produce creativity.

CRITICAL REFLECTION

- In what way or ways is public relations 'creative'?
- Is PR part of the creative industries?

Box 8.7   Useful source

UK government's Department for Culture, Media and Sport (DCMS) (www.culture.gov.uk)

Critical theory and management studies

Management studies was for a long time dominated by the assumption that the management discipline was to be instrumental, technical and practical:

...devoted to the (scientific) improvement of managerial practice and the functioning of organizations. It is assumed that questions directly and indirectly connected to efficiency and effectiveness are central; and that knowledge of management is of greatest relevance (only) to managers. In the literature on management, managers are routinely presented as carriers of rationality and initiative (for example in many versions of strategic management and corporate culture) while other actors appear as objects of managerial action. Management is considered to be a socially valuable function, normally acting in the general interest of workers, employees, customers and citizens alike. (Alvesson and Willmott, 1992: 1)

Critical management theorists are fearful of leaving management to business schools and want to explore the implications of management and **managerialism** for society, political and economic structures (exploring the influence of corporate elites and considering their impact on democracy, for instance), culture, ecology and to challenge the myth of managerial science. To sum up, critical theory in management is a counterpoint to the domination of the demands of mass production and industrialized technocracy. And it has the potential to liberate us from our prescribed roles of employee, worker, consumer.

While most of the management disciplines are devoted to the improvement of managerial practice and aim to support the successful function of organizations, critical management perspectives see management as a broader social phenomenon that affects all our lives. Such approaches draw on social theorists such as Weber, Marx, Habermas and Foucault to look at issues such as power, communication ethics, and emotional and sexual relations in the context of the organization. These ideas present alternative priorities in organizational studies to the more conventional and functional assumptions of rational management. Perspectives from the critical paradigm open the way to seeing much of organizational life as a struggle between different interests. Critical management also recognizes the stresses placed on managers. As Alvesson and Willmott pointed out:

> Caught between contradictory demands and pressures, they run the risk of dismissal, they are 'victims' as well as perpetrators of discourses and practices that unnecessarily constrain their ways of thinking and acting. Managerial ideologies – notably a belief in their prerogative to manage – tie them to ideals and identities, that, paradoxically, limit their options as they simultaneously appear to secure for them a position of relative power and influence ... critical management studies have an agenda for research, teaching and (indirectly) organizational practice that understands management as a political, cultural and ideological phenomenon, and that gives a voice to managers not only as managers but as persons and also to other social groups (subordinates, customers, clients, men and women, citizens in other capacities) whose lives are more or less directly affected by the activities and ideologies of management. (Alvesson and Willmott, 1992: 7–8)

For some, *power* is the natural right of management and an important attribute that is linked to a decision-making capability. On the other hand, one can question this right and, indeed, the decision-making faculties of management. Management can be seen as an elite class that seeks to dominate using symbolic systems of meaning (ideology) to promote their political worldview in a persuasive and convincing manner in political contests to achieve hegemony over other interest groups who might resist (non-managerial class employees).

According to some theorists there is a 'new managerial discourse' arising from fast-paced change, globalization, deregulation and information overload (Jackson, 2001). This discourse reflects those themes but emphasizes:

> [The] uncertainty of the external environment; the need for organizations continually to learn to adapt by being constantly flexible and always in action; challenges to existing knowledge forms; and the creation of organizations that are made up of willing

and willed subjects. ... This discourse [is spread] by 'agents' ... management 'gurus', consultants, business schools and the business media which form an increasingly powerful 'circuit of capital' ... responsible for the production and distribution of managerial knowledge to managers. (Jackson, 2001: 26)

Discourses are patterns of language which communicate (and may seek to persuade) a particular set of values or knowledge, such as 'feminist discourse', 'political discourse', 'public relations discourse'. **Discourse analysis** is the methodological approach, which seeks to interpret texts for the discourses which lie within (van Dijk, 1997a, 1997b; Wetherell et al., 2001a).

Gender issues

Profiles of managers tend to present heroic 'captains' of industry, who are ruthless and macho, aggressive and individualistic, and masculinity is embedded in *gendered managerial language*, such as 'penetrating markets' and 'getting into bed with suppliers/customers/competitors' (Collinson and Hearn, 1996: 3). Media coverage (i.e. news, feature and entertainment) continue to reinforce the idea that business is a male-dominated sphere. For example, in the UK, entertainment programmes have been structured around popular male businessmen, financial reporters on British TV are usually male and *The Financial Times* is dominated by male journalists demonstrating that financial journalism is a gendered practice. (It would be interesting to know whether financial PR is also gendered.) Historically, some occupations have been associated more with one gender than another, and social taboos reinforce those stereotypes. For example, in Sweden, dairying was a female task until it was technologized, and then it became a male task (Alvesson and Due Billig, 1997: 55). In the UK, typing was seen as a female task until the advent of computers. Individual attributes or personal characteristics may also be gendered, for example caring, communicative, negotiative traits may be seen as more female while aggression and entrepreneurial capacity may be seen as traditionally associated with men.

Feminist approaches have highlighted a number of problems for women in progressing as far as their talents warrant. These problems include:

- an absence of mentors
- a lack of support from superiors
- exclusion from informal networks
- double standards for assessing performance
- a lack of training opportunities
- outdated attitudes to female roles
- pay and contractual inequities
- a lack of flexitime and child care

- stress resulting from over-adaptation to male values
- sexual harassment
- bullying
- a lack of female role models
- senior women who 'pull the ladder up behind them' and who appear unsympathetic to younger, junior women – the 'queen bee' phenomenon

Exploring gender in organizations sheds light on the logic that dominates, the way power is distributed and which 'actors and groups set the agenda and how the relations between people are formed' (Alvesson and Due Billig, 1997: 5). 'Gender studies' should not, of course, mean 'women studies', so organization theory has also explored the role of men in management, exploring masculinity in the workplace through the themes of paternalism, technocracy, patriarchy, entrepreneurship and sexual orientation (Collinson and Hearn, 1996).

Within public relations literature much attention has been given to women, but little to men. PR is now feminized, meaning that PR practitioners are more likely to be women than men (Smith, 2005: 1). Smith's doctoral research in Western Australia is the first effort to discover why numbers of women have grown and why numbers of men have declined, and to understand how the development of PR has impacted on gender composition of the occupation (Smith, 2005: 3).

CRITICAL REFLECTION

- Are there PR gurus? If so, who are they and how do they promote themselves?

PR gurus?

Professor Charles Fombrun of the Stern School of Business, New York University, and Professor Cees van Riel of the Rotterdam School of Management, Erasmus University, might be on the verge of PR gurudom. Their books are read beyond academic circles, and they have established a professionally focused journal, *Corporate Reputation Review*, and a base – the Reputation Institute. From this base they sell their books and promote reputation measurement. The Institute's mission is:

> To build thought leadership about corporate reputation, corporate reputation management, corporate reputation measurement and corporate reputation valuation. (www.valuebasedmanagement.net/organizations_reputationinstitute, accessed 23 January 2007)

CRITICAL REFLECTION

- Who are the PR academic gurus and why?
- Who are the PR practitioner gurus, and why?
- Who are the main producers of PR knowledge?
- What counts as PR knowledge?
- Is PR theory 'creole'? and, finally,
- Is this book 'creole'?

REVIEW

Reflecting on the questions raised at the beginning of this chapter you may like to consider whether you realized that public relations was a managerial career and whether you can see yourself in this role. How might it affect your self-concept and notions of identity? (see chapter 3 page xx) How does the concept of managerial role influence your ideas about your own impression management? (see chapter 3 pages 51–52).

In conclusion

This chapter has sketched a few of the main concepts in managerial thinking since the evolutionary days of the management discipline. It has been argued that understanding something of the history of management ideas and current trends is essential for public relations practitioners since it not only allows them to understand the managerial class in organizations, but also because it may allow for some self-reflection and insights with regard to both the professional and personal identities of practitioners.

RECOMMENDED READING

Fascinating insights into management gurus are offered by Jackson (2001), Barley and Kunda (2004) and Huczynski (2006). The management guru literature itself (Covey, 1989; Goleman, 1996, 1999) needs to be read alongside these sources for a really rich understanding. Bilton's book on *Management and Creativity* (2006) is an excellent introduction to this topical subject.

Organizational Communication: Understanding and Researching Organizations

A spaceship has just landed outside. Friendly aliens from another planet are approaching you, seeking the answer to an important question: 'What *is* an organization?'

You cannot speak their language (but you know what they want because they have communicated to you telepathically) so you take a piece of paper and a pen and draw a picture that sums up, for you, the meaning of 'an organization'.

Do this now, drawing the first image that comes to mind.

Key concepts

Communication audit

Organizational culture

Corporate social responsibility

Organizational development

Creativity

Organizational symbolism

Organizational climate

Paradigm

Organizational communication

Introduction

It is sometimes said that wo/man is born free but that everywhere s/he is in organizations! Think of all the organizations you have experienced: playgroup, kindergarten, school, college, university, youth group, Brownies, scouts, religious groups, sports clubs, music clubs. We are all organizational veterans with diverse experiences of organizational cultures.

This chapter will give you an overview of the key concepts in organizational communication that are relevant to public relations practice, particularly in relation to employee communications and the research processes entailed in conducting communication audits. Part of the agenda here is to demonstrate that the field of organizational communication is crucial to the public relations occupation and its development. Perhaps because public relations has been struggling to achieve academic status as an independent discipline (the academic agenda) and professional status (the occupational agenda), much of what is useful to academics and practitioners may not have received sufficient attention. Indeed, Leitch and Neilson (2001: 131) noted that: 'Stronger links need to be developed between the areas of organizational communication and public relations.'

This chapter also aims to alert readers to many of the hidden and often under-acknowledged aspects of organizational life, which are important in considering relationships at work, for example the role of emotion and the practices of misbehaviour, rebellion and punishment. This chapter therefore provides much of the background necessary for understanding organizational life – a prerequisite for employee communications.

Finally, the chapter highlights some challenging questions about the nature of organizations, with a view to encouraging readers to think twice about the concept and what it might imply about ourselves and our relationships with and towards organizations.

CHAPTER AIMS

On completion of this chapter you will be able to:

- describe the field of organizational communication and identify its value for public relations discipline and practice
- define the technical term 'communication audit' and understand the implications for PR practice
- understand the use of the terms 'culture' and 'climate'
- describe the difference between functional and interpretative approaches to organizational culture, and explain why it is important for public relations practitioners to employ the interpretative approach rather than the dominant managerialist perspective
- understand the reasons for the limits on 'managing' culture – and explain these to senior managers and clients

What is organizational communication?

Organizational communication is the academic field which tries to understand the way organizational participants understand and experience organizations. Scholars from organizational communication seek to understand:

> The big issues about human conduct in organizational settings: how to understand and explain patterns and divergences in attitudes, perceptions and values; how to make sense of language and symbols; how to balance continuity and change; how to intervene in organizations to deliver cultural change, improve climates for service and innovation, influence career development, and manage mergers and acquisitions. (Pettigrew, 2000: xiii)

Organizational communication helps us to understand how people experience organizations. It is essential for PR work, bearing in mind that employees are potential ambassadors for their organizations, and this diplomatic role cannot be taken for granted.

Discipline box: Organizational communication

This historical summary is drawn from Tompkins and Wanca-Thibault (2001: xvii–xxxi).

(Continued)

The field of organizational communication originated in the USA in the 1930s and 1940s within a speciality known as 'speech communication' – a descendent of the Greek rhetorical tradition and a specialism that to this day encompasses the technical aspects of communication in terms of debating techniques, the development of the appropriate argumentative skills, and the psychological knowledge to support these in applied areas such as business communication skills. Organizational communication has always been an academic enterprise while management studies has developed from managerial experiences and has been directed towards the improvement of management practice.

Early researchers in speech communication focused on formal and informal channels of communication and superior–subordinate relations, tending to take a top-down approach. From the 1950s, interests developed in small-group communication networks. In the 1970s an important intervention was made by key theorist Redding when he introduced the notion organizational climate and took further ideas about feedback, redundancy, communication overload and serial transmission (Tompkins and Wanca-Thibault, 2001: xix–xx). Perhaps of crucial importance to public relations was Redding's argument that understanding organizational climate was more important than communication skills and techniques.

By the 1980s, organizations were no longer seen as structure and function but as systems comprising communicative individuals who created their own social reality. This opened the way into questions about how organizational reality was created and negotiated; how and where power emerged and was implemented; how discourses emerged; and the way in which rhetoric was employed. Research was re-orientated towards anthropological approaches which sought to understand how organizational cultures operated and the experiences of organizational life. Increasingly, the term 'organization' itself began to be seen as a consequence of communicative practice, hence the importance of organizational communication for public relations practitioners and theorists – and, of course, of public relations for those from organizational communication.

Public relations and organizational communication: organizations in society

Public relations books and articles often take a rather bland approach to organizations. The concept of 'organization' is not really explored or problematized. Of more interest to PR scholars have been organizational actions with an ethical dimension, such as **corporate social responsibility** or the crisis management that might follow organizational misdemeanours. Sympathetic assumptions dominate in the way that public relations is constructed as a technocratic discipline designed to help organizations to achieve their goals. Broader political, social and economic contexts and structures are usually seen as wallpaper from which PR practitioners and their organizations appropriately focus on issues relevant to the organizational mission and organizational stakeholders. Yet there are wider questions to be considered from political and relational perspectives:

- How can we study stakeholders, publics or local communities, particularly in the less developed world, without taking into account the possibly invisible influence of national bureaucracies and international firms and agencies (Wright, 1994b: 15)?
- How can democracy work if people know so little about organizations which affect their lives (Wright, 1994b: 16)?
- What is the role of PR in relation to these knowledge gaps?
- What is the obligation and duty of PR practice?

These questions point to the fact that organizations are political bodies struggling for power and influence externally, but also internally as policy is formed. These struggles are articulated and performed through language and symbols, and systems of value and meaning that are used rhetorically to persuade.

What is an organization?

Organizations are collectivities of people with a shared mission or interest. Thus an organization might be a corporate body employing thousands of people or a small voluntary group such as a baby-sitting circle, local parent group, a music society, amateur orchestra or a swimming club. Organizations all require some degree of organization and collaboration to achieve collective aims and are comprised of individuals variously motivated, in relation to the activity in question, the process of organization and the potential for organizational power and influence.

Organizations can thus be defined as bounded communities, as processes and as sites of contest or of meaning-making.

Are organizations like people?

Much public relations work focuses on efforts to make organizations seem human. In Chapter 4, attention was drawn to debates in legal philosophy in relation to corporate crime where blame (and potentially punishment) might be apportioned to the 'brains' or the 'hands' of the organization, or indeed to the organization as a whole. Legal theory endows corporations with a fictive personality. These debates lead to questions such as: Does it make sense to think about organizational intention? Do organizations think, and if so, how?

In public relations, corporate social responsibility may help to show that the organization has a 'human face' or 'a caring side'. Efforts to construct and communicate corporate and visual identity aim to create a sense of corporate personality to distinguish organizations at a strategic as well as human level. As has been pointed out: 'The anthropomorphic metaphor endows organizations with personality, needs and character or with typically human cognitive processes' (Allaire and Firsirotu, 1984: 193).

Organizations of course may 'live' longer than people, and they absorb human lives and **creativity**. They are the consequence of multiple discussions and decisions, even if they are represented as a unified whole. Are they, then, some sort of super-human? If so, what is the role of ordinary mortals and the moral universe? Are organizational members able to act effectively as intrapersonal reflectors? What is the role of public relations in the organization-as-human analogy? Does public relations work take place in the brains, the emotions, the heart or the conscience?

How do organizations think?

The anthropologist Mary Douglas suggested that:

> The very idea of a suprapersonal cognitive system stirs a deep sense of outrage.
> ... An individual that encompasses thinking humans is assumed to be of a nasty
> totalitarian sort, a highly centralized and effective dictatorship. (Douglas: 1987, x)

In Chapter 5, I referred to theories of public opinion, and these are also relevant to opinion formation and suppression in organizations. Likewise, power structures and punishment mechanisms are as relevant to organizations as they are to political regimes. Philosopher Ludwik Fleck developed the notion of an organizational 'thought collective' with a specific 'thought style' or collective frame which established conventions to produce collective knowledge and assumptions – similar to the establishment of a **paradigm** (Douglas, 1987). Social theorist Emile Durkheim tended 'to invoke a mysterious, superorganic group mind' (Douglas, 1987: 14) perhaps similar to the notion of 'the general will'. It is perhaps useful to distinguish processes of policy from organizational knowledge:

> Given that knowledgeable individuals come together, does the *organization* know?
> And what does it actually know? More or less than the individuals engaged in it
> know? ... How does it know? When does it know? Are the experiences of the
> individual similar to or different from the experience of the organization? Why? Why
> not? (Krogh and Roos, 1995: 4)

Cognitive scientists, connectionists and information scientists have all tried to engage with these rather arcane problems. Such difficult epistemological issues can be made relevant when we ask ourselves: Do organizations have memory? If so, how do they remember? Do organizations learn? If so, how do they learn?

CRITICAL REFLECTION

- Why might it be important for a PR practitioner to try to understand whether an organization has corporate or collective memory, and ways of recalling the past?
- Why might it be important for a PR practitioner to understand if and how an organization learns or can learn to learn?

Organizational culture

Organizational studies adopted the metaphor of culture from anthropology to explore organizations as mini-societies. **Organizational culture** is taken for granted by its inhabitants. Organizational culture includes values, relationships, power and politics, formal and informal behaviour and relationships. Culture is reproduced in organizational discourse, rituals and symbols. Communication is fundamental for the co-creation and reproduction of organizational culture and values. Culture operates at conscious and unconscious levels. The organization is not just a workplace and a social domain, but a space for the **psychoanalytic**. Public relations practitioners and students would do well to remember that communication can never be neutral or 'just factual' since there are always *connotative* (implied or suggested) as well as *denotative* (explicit or dictionary definition) meanings. Organizational beliefs, values and discourse may be embedded in *organizational ideology*. Where there is ideology there is room for *manufactured consent* (this term was the title of a famous book about the media and public relations by media sociologists Edward Herman and Noam Chomsky (1988)). Organizational culture has come to be seen as a powerful influence, which is why managers are keen to try to control it through communication campaigns of *culture change*. Thus culture becomes part of an overall management *rhetoric*. Such campaigns actually put PR practitioners in an awkward situation since they may be totalitarian in intention.

The use of the term 'culture' in an organizational context has two main alternative readings: the **instrumental**, in which culture is 'an objectified tool of management control' (Wright, 1994b: 4), and the **interpretative**, in which culture is the *lived experience* of the organization – the organization's life, as expressed through its members' behaviours, values, rituals and patterns in their entirety, *is* its culture. These radically different perspectives show that 'the use of the term culture itself ... [is] ideological' (Wright, 1994b: 4). The ideological perspective that informs our approach to organizations and management influences the types of research we do in an organization (top-down questionnaire or participatory and liberationary methods) as well as PR/communication management.

Managers and some academics tend to see culture as an organizational feature which can be manipulated like organizational structure and processes. In other words, they see organizational culture as a possession. This is sometimes described as the 'corporate culture' approach. In the corporate culture approach, managers seek to align culture with the strategic direction (vision and mission) of the organization through articulating managerial definitions of corporate identity, utilizing **organizational symbolism** (visual identity), plus employee education and training, to change attitudes, values and behaviour (management propaganda). The corporate culture approach suggests that cultures can be defined judgementally as 'strong' or 'weak', and it is an approach that fits comfortably within the approach to organizational strategic change known as organizational development (OD). OD is an applied and functional approach to organizational change that seeks to reinvent an organization by improving organizational effectiveness and learning and managing organizational culture. OD focuses on the personal development of individuals and teams, and its techniques include sensitivity training, team-building, improving managerial effectiveness in relation to people and production, and humanizing the workplace.

Interpretative view of organizational culture

Alternatively, those from the critical management paradigm regard an organization *as* a culture. In other words, culture emerges from all practices, values, assumptions, behaviours, struggles, dreams, successes, failures, emotions and relationships that take place within the organization, and not just from the sanitized idealistic version that managers wish to impose. This rather more anarchic view of organizational culture proposes that the organization is a place with many sub- or micro-cultures that exist in specialized areas (e.g. the Accounts Department subculture) or hierarchies (e.g. secretarial culture) concurrently and in competition with the dominant culture that managers attempt to impose. Culture reproduces and is reinforced by attitudes, behaviours, rituals and symbols. **Organizational symbolism** became a separate subfield of organizational cultural studies.

Box 9.1   Useful sources

European Group for Organizational Studies www.egosnet.org
Standing Conference on Organizational Symbolism www.scos.org
Culture and Organization www.tandf.co.uk

Organizational climate

The term organizational climate is sometimes used interchangeably with culture, but it has its own distinct definitions and research agenda.

Climate is a metaphor to understanding the 'atmospherics' and 'temperature' of an organization. Meteorological metaphors can be employed to understand the organization's ephemeral dimensions. For example, an organization's atmosphere may be described or experienced as turbulent, stormy, electric, calm, heavy, thunderous, oppressive, cool. Climate fluctuates and is a less stable phenomenon than culture.

Climate research has been largely dominated by quantitative techniques and used to measure the extent to which climate is shared by organizational members. According to organizational theorist Schein:

> Climate is embedded in the physical look of the place, the emotionality exhibited by employees, the experiences of visitors or new employees upon entry and myriad other artefacts that are seen, heard felt. ... [I] define climate as a cultural artefact resulting from espoused values and shared tacit assumptions. (Schein, 2000: xxiv)

On Schein's account, climate is a qualitative consequence or by-product of organizational culture which contrasts sharply with the specific functional approach taken by many organizational climatologists. In Chapter 5 the term 'climate' was linked to the formation of consensues and used to highlight the political nature of organizations.

Behind the scenes

In this section some ideas are presented from a critical organization studies paradigm. Critical organization studies is linked to critical management studies but focuses on the organizational context in which management takes place; issues of organizational symbolism and culture; and aspects of organization which are sometimes not addressed in standard organizational texts.

Emotions

Why are emotions important in organizational communication and PR? From a purely functional perspective:

> It is because culture operates on the emotional level that it can have a significant impact on an individual's experience of work, affecting personal development and even the degree of one's psychological health or disturbance. Organizations, therefore, through the management of their cultures, have a crucial role and responsibility in contributing to the emotional needs of employees. As such, organizations assisting employees in developing their emotional competencies may enable these employees to develop higher quality work relationships. (Hartel et al., 2004: 135–136)

It was not until the early 1990s that organizational theorists began to turn their attention to the notion of emotion in the workplace (e.g. Fineman, 1993). Prior to that, interests in emotion had been somewhat functional, related to issues such as motivation, work stress and job satisfaction, yet every day employees experience (as opposed to express) emotion at work which may or may not be related to their formal function (Fineman, 1993). Employees have feelings about new colleagues, managers or leaders, and have to cope with rivalry and jealousy. Some jobs, such as human resource/personnel and general managers, have to undertake *emotional labour* (the term was invented by the sociologist Hochschild) as part of their role and have to negotiate and try to resolve dislikes, hatreds and loves. Other examples include secretaries (analyzed by Pringle, 1988) and flight attendants (Hochschild, 1983). Organizational members also form judgements on the basis of their own emotions. There are organizational spaces which function as stages for emotional display or emotional confidences, such as toilets, smoking areas, canteens and photocopier locations. In fact, as a leading theorist in this field, Stephen Fineman, pointed out:

> Emotions are within the texture of organizing. They are intrinsic to social order and disorder, working structures, conflict, influence, conformity, posturing, gender, sexuality and politics. They are products of socialization and manipulation. They work mistily within the human psyche, as well as obviously in the daily ephemera of organizational life. (Fineman, 1993: 1)

One might expect that public relations in its 'communication management' or 'internal/employee communication' roles might engage with emotion, yet emotion is rarely indexed in public relations texts. There is only the occasional reference to the 'emotional intelligence' stream of management training or to 'emotional marketing' (experience-based values). Even in the most extensive discussion of gender and race issues in PR (Grunig et al., 2001) there is no reference to the emotional fallout that accompanies discrimination – frustration, anger, sense of injustice and so on.

Emotion matters to public relations practice (and thus is an important area for public relations research) because, '[c]ulture and politics are ... emotional. Organizational order depends on togetherness and apartness, while organizational control would be hard to conceive without the ability to feel shame, anxiety, fear, joy or embarrassment' (Fineman, 1993: 2). Organizations predicated on the principles of rationality and bureaucracy attempt to de-emotionalize organizational life, thus implying the (unhealthy?) suppression of emotions. Fineman argues that the attempted exclusionary zone of emotions is wrong-headed, because emotions are central to human relationships and, implicitly, to public relations work.

Misbehaviour and punishment

Organizational rebellion, individual misbehaviour, conflict, discipline and punishment have been studied in organizational studies (Ackroyd and Thompson, 1999) as these behaviours are important aspects of organizational relationships and culture. Berger and Reber (2006) have discussed how PR practitioners express and explain external dissent from outside the organization to management. However, is it not possible that practitioners might identify with patterns of resistance or dissent within the organization thus experiencing conflicting emotions and guilt?

CRITICAL REFLECTION

- Is organizational misbehaviour or rebellion ever appropriate for the PR practitioner?

The organizational and communicative body

Organizational theory has explored issues such as female biology (sexuality, pregnancy and menstruation), masculinity, clothing, sexuality, sexual orientation and love (Hassard et al., 2000). While public relations itself has successfully engaged with gender, there remains much to be explored. Apart from attending to the experiences of men in the PR field, the issue and relationship between clients and consultants of sexuality and sexual orientations in public relations could usefully be explored.

CRITICAL REFLECTION

- What emotional and sexual relationships between consultants and clients may follow after the initial sales 'pitch'?

(Continued)

- What does the 'beauty parade' connote about gender and sexuality?
- What social, personal and sexual relationships may develop between press officers and journalists?

Thus far I have sketched out some critical ideas about organizational life and living. These show that organizations are sites of multiple and varied experiences. It is now time to interrogate more directly the notion of 'organization'. In order to show how an organization can have many realities and be 'read' differently by each person who experiences the organization, I adopt the approach taken by Gareth Morgan.

Metaphorical approaches to organizations

As an academic and management consultant, Gareth Morgan (1989, 1990, 1992, 1993, 2006) took the notion of metaphor and, using the historical ideas about organizations and management as a basis, devised eight key metaphors which could be applied to any organization as a tool to understand multiple and co-existing realities. The concept of metaphor, and its application to organizations, shows how language use can reveal potentially hidden insights about organizational culture and practices (Grant and Oswick, 1996). A metaphor is a language tool, which, through the transfer of a concept from a familiar subject to an unfamiliar subject, helps to generate fresh thinking and perspectives (Grant and Oswick, 1996). This process happens when we are encouraged to see something in an entirely new light. The familiar is 'made strange' and that opens up our perceptual range. In other words, we are encouraged to think divergently and creatively.

Over the course of the next few of pages I summarize Morgan's framework of metaphors. The framework effectively revises some key ideas about management covered in the last chapter, though in a slightly different way. Morgan's metaphors were:

- organization as machine
- organization as psychic prison
- organization as organism
- organization as politics
- organization as social domination
- organization as flux and transformation
- organization as brains
- organization as culture

Organization as machine

This metaphor likens the organization to a machine and is a classical, mechanistic way of thinking. Machine-like thinking is evident in organizations which need to meet repetitive demands, such as production-line environments (factories and fast-food outlets are good examples). Complex organizations which have attempted to clarify and control tasks are also the consequence of such thinking, which is realized in bureaucratic organizations such as universities and the civil service. Mechanistic thinking is limited by its lack of adaptability, mindless bureaucracy and de-humanizing effects. Morgan's machine metaphor considers the social consequences of mechanization and bureaucratization of society. Box 9.1 shows how bureaucratization affects public relations practice and leads potentially to psychic prisons.

Box 9.1   Bureaucratization and PR

Public relations professionals participate in bureaucracy rationalization when they refine and dehumanize message contents in editorial reviews, systematically produce reports and analyses that rationalize views, their value, develop unit missions and visions that order and direct their work lives, allocate scarce resources in the most cost-effective manner, and carry out research to refine messages, target publics, select best channels, and evaluate outcomes – all in the interests of achieving organizational goals and needs in the most efficient and effective manner ... treat the production and distribution of information as if it were a meaningful communication in itself ... when they develop precise measures to legitimate and value their work ... when they spread this managerial and administrative ideology by taking up its vocabulary and internalizing and applying its thinking in their professional and social lives. ... In these ways ... public relations practitioners reinforce and perpetuate an iron cage of professional practice. Because they are part of this system, and in some part responsible for its construction, they find themselves trapped inside it and forced to conform to its rules for action. (Berger and Ruger, 2006: 222)

CRITICAL REFLECTION

*   How can PR practitioners liberate themselves and others from the 'iron cage' of bureaucracy?

Organization as psychic prison

This metaphor plunges into the hidden depths of an organization's psyche and tries to establish managerial practices that control and punish non-conformists. Punishment in the organizational context might include withholding information and opportunities, or exclusion from networks or promotional opportunities. The psychic prison explores organizations as a vehicle for individuals to find meaning in their lives and even as a way of overcoming fear of death since the organization has the potential to live much longer than any individual. The metaphor is psycho-analytically inspired (see Chapter 3, p. 64)

This metaphor also highlights the dangers of rigidity that can develop in management thinking, particularly in relation to difficult decision-making where group dynamics can create the *groupthink effect* (see Chapter 5).

Organization as organism

This is a biological metaphor based on systems theory which presents the organization as a process with the capacity to develop complex specialized systems and subsystems to match external environmental demands. The metaphor focuses on interdependence, survival and innovation, and values responsiveness and flexibility. As the organization is seen as essentially responsive to environmental change, there is a tendency to underplay the ability of the organization to take powerful actions and instigate change. It can therefore be described as a *determinist* approach.

Organization as politics

The political metaphor interprets the organization as a site for *power struggle*. Sources of power within an organization can be identified as control over resources (human, financial, technological, strategic or creative knowledge) and decision-making processes. Power is controlled by interest groups, coalitions, and strategic alliances. Political processes can be explored through the application of political theory and concepts (authoritarian, libertarian and communitarian theories of democracy) to try to understand how the organization functions as a political system. This powerful and intriguing metaphor explodes the idea of neutral management and can lead to an analysis of managerial ideology and associated rhetoric and discourses. It can also lead to a strong sense of paranoia!

Organization as social domination

This metaphor extends the political metaphor to see the organization as a potential instrument of *exploitation* and domination. Organizations may dominate their own employees (discrimination, unsafe procedures, workload) or external constituencies (slave labour in the cocoa trade, low wages, differential compensation globally). Public relations consultancies can be instruments of domination through cultures that facilitate workaholism. Another example is the practice of some consultancies and organizations to offer extended unpaid placements to PR students and, even worse, to qualified graduates.

Organization as flux and transformation

This metaphor is very 'broad brush' and is best understood as a way of situating an organization in the context of global and national issues and development, and in explaining broad historical environmental change. This metaphor can explain the past and capture *moments of transformation*, as well as explaining key choices and the possibility for alternative organizational endings. It can therefore help one to understand the interplay between grand-scale events (terrorism, war, economic boom or bust, political and ideological changes, environmental mega-disasters) and organizational-level policy.

Organization as brains

This metaphor focuses on organizational capacities for organizational intelligence. In practice 'organizational intelligence' may be devolved to specialized units described formally or informally as 'organizational planning', 'corporate planning', 'think tanks', 'the sixth floor', 'the top floor' and so on. This approach to organizational intelligence is reflected in legal discussions of organizational responsibility, which separate the 'hands' and the 'brains' of the organization. As discussed earlier in this chapter, this is an *anthropomorphic* approach to organizations.

Organization as culture

This metaphor is based upon the *interpretative* view of culture as opposed to the functionalist approach of 'corporate culture' discussed earlier. The interpretative approach sees culture as a feature of organizational life that exists in a complex and multifaceted way, regardless of management interventions. Researchers and consultants from the interpretative tradition look for patterns which make organization possible. They see organizations as a relational and consequently emotional realm, which has its own ceremonies, rites and dramas. It highlights the limits of managerial control and the inevitability of counter-cultures and subcultures in any organization. Exploring culture from this perspective draws our attention to organizational myths, rituals (leaving and welcome parties), punishments and dress codes.

In contrast to the interpretative approach, it is the 'corporate culture' approach which tends to dominate management and, to some degree, public relations literature and thinking. This sees culture as an organizational possession, a variable that management can tinker with and control. Indeed, the purpose of culture is seen as the means to educate members of the organization about appropriate values and norms. In other words, it is seen as an educative tool to ensure conformity.

All the metaphors described above can be used as sense-making tools. Of course, they are not the only metaphors that can be applied, for example organizations can be likened to a cathedral, a family, a plant, or an octopus – the possibilities are endless. In fact, as a management consultant, Morgan suggested to clients that they spend time thinking about metaphors for their organizations as a way of generating openness about various, hitherto hidden, perspectives and exploring, in a non-threatening fashion, deep-seated problems that could then be dealt with more openly (Morgan, 1993).

Exercise

- What do all the metaphors reveal about your university (or job or club) and why?
- What animal would you use to describe your university and why?

An important feature of Morgan's approach was that all the metaphors could be present at any one time. The application of multiple metaphors to a single organization can shed light on different, partial aspects of the organization which, when taken together, can build a more complete and holistic picture.

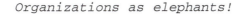

Organizations as elephants!

In an old Indian fable, six blind men were touching an elephant and describing to the others what an elephant was like using metaphors. The man touching the elephant's leg said that elephants were like tree trunks, while the one with his hands on the elephant's flank said they were like walls. Another got hold of the trunk and said that elephants were like snakes while an especially athletic man who climbed a tree to feel the ears claimed that elephants were actually like fans. One rather nervous man grasped the tusk and argued strongly that elephants were like spears while the one who held the tail said that elephants were clearly like ropes (Hofstede, 1980: 15).

The point of this little story is that when you apply this principle of multiple realities to organizations it is clear that they are necessarily many things at once. All the blind men were correct in their interpretations – but they were wrong to insist that the elephant was only and always like any one of these interpretations.

Researching organizations – into the maelstrom

The complexity and fluidity of organizational life discussed so far in this chapter makes it difficult to capture in meaningful research. Common and economical methods include staff surveys, and readership surveys, but these provide only limited 'snapshots'. A more thorough picture can be gained from a communication audit.

Communication audits

The term **communication audit** is sometimes abused in public relations practice, where it can be used very loosely to mean simply an employee survey. It is sometimes used as a term in contrast to 'PR audit', which may be limited to some informal telephone calls to journalists which are supposed to ascertain an organization's current standing or reputation. In fact, 'communication audit' emerged from two separate, but similar research efforts conducted in Finland (theorist Osmo Wiio) and the USA in the 1970s (Goldhaber and Rogers, 1979). These came together in the development of a particular communication audit tool which was complex, multi-method but highly informative. In the USA, a number of largely public sector organizations opened themselves up to academic researchers who spent around six weeks in each organization conducting research into employee opinion, perceptions, networks, opinion formation processes, beliefs about superiors and communication experiences (Goldhaber and Rogers, 1979). The findings were 'banked' for other researchers and organizations.

A communication audit explores managerial intentions and their communication philosophy. Goldhaber and Rogers (1979) and Hargie and Tourish (2000) describe the elements and process in detail but they can be summarized as:

- a review of current communication policies and needs
- the structure, flow and practice of communication
- the patterns of communication
- formal communication media and reception
- informal communication networks
- a diagnosis of communication practices and effectiveness
- an assessment of the organizational climate
- a benchmark for developing new communication practices

Research techniques include:

- Questionnaires assessing:

  — the quantity, timeliness and topic-relevance of information in relation to the amount desired
  — the extent of follow-up from official sources
  — contrasts between the use of official and unofficial sources
  — overall communication satisfaction
  — areas of communication needing employment
  — information-seeking patterns
  — the degree of trust in supervisor(s)
  — perceptions of individual influence
  — the desire for interaction with senior colleagues
  — perceptions of information accuracy of official sources
  — information overload and underload

- Employee interviews and focus groups assessing:

  — the major strengths and weaknesses of the organization
  — typical formal and informal information sources
  — the frequency of receipt of information that is *not* helpful!
  — how information flow can be improved
  — what stops information flow presently
  — how are decisions made in this organization?
  — what is the cause of conflict in this organization?
  — how is conflict resolved in this organization?
  — describe the communication relationships you have with your line manager, co-workers, middle management, top management and subordinates
  — how do you know when this organization has done a good or bad job in reaching its goals?
  — does top management admit managerial failure?

- Personal records

  — diaries – recording emotions, issues, problems, communication barriers
  — logs – recording critical incidents and important communication moments
  — network analysis – logging patterns of communication and communicative relationships (formal and informal)

The data from logs can build an overall picture of the webs of communication in an organization.

A communication audit can deliver:

- information about how an organization is perceived by employees
- the state of managerial–employee relations – do employees feel patronized?
- the state of superior–subordinate communication
- perceived quality and accuracy of downward communication
- perceived openness of the superior–subordinate relationship
- opportunities and degree of influence for upward communication
- identification of bottlenecks, barriers and misunderstandings
- identification of gatekeepers
- assessment of the quality of formal communication
- the relative importance for employees of formal and informal communication
- information underload and overload
- communication direction
- sources of anxiety
- the state of internal relationships

(*Sources*: ICA audit, http://scholar.lib.vt.edu/thesis, Goldhaber and Rogers (1979); Hargie and Tourish (2000). Accessed October 2006.

Why do managers and employees resist communication audit approaches?

Managers may resist the multi-method communication audit because they perceive it as expensive (paying for researchers, time spent by employees and managers participating in research, making changes as a consequence of the research) or because they are paranoid and think the researchers will have access to commercially sensitive information (lack of trust in research professionals) or because they fear the results. Fearing the results may well be justified because in general terms if there is a lot of investment in finding out what people really think (and the point of the research techniques adopted is that they will achieve that), then they will tell the truth! Managers may therefore be faced with a proportion of difficult responses and/or a number of complaints. This raises the expectation among employees that, as their views have been sought, changes will follow. In other words, expectations are raised that are unlikely to be met in full. Many managers choose, therefore, either not to engage with employee perspectives, or to limit and manipulate research in a way to limit possible professional damage to themselves, or even worse, to conduct some rather spurious employee survey (bear in mind that quantitative research is very limiting in this context since it only provides answers to the questions set by the employer and does not allow employees to raise their concerns), of which only limited (and positive) results are published in a staff magazine. How believable is that going to be?

Critiquing communication audits

What might be wrong with communication audits? Well what is wrong with living in Orwell's *1984* where Big Brother can observe you all the time? The audit process sounds neutral and technical but is directed to management ends. One of its underpinning tools is that of organizational psychology, which applies psychology to work settings, for example psychometric testing. If, however, we take a critical psychology approach, we can appreciate an alternative perspective that:

> Organizational psychology [and its techniques] is handmaiden to industry ... there is a history of siding with owners to enhance productivity, often at the expense of worker well-being. ... based on that history and on public relations campaigns by organizational psychologists to improve communication, alleviate industrial unrest, select and train employees, foster supportive climates and evaluate programmes. A critical psychology agenda seeks to pursue personal, relational and collective well-being, promote worker empowerment and resist oppression. ... A critical formulation requires that we go beneath the surface of a rhetoric of well-being and collective empowerment. ... Human resources and management writings call for OD (Organizational Development), a term which by itself may appear neutral or benevolent ... [but] once we start to ask questions about whose interests will be advanced and whose idea it was to initiate the intervention we can adopt a healthy degree of scepticism ... as a tool that precedes action. (Prilletensky and Nelson, 2002: 134–5)

CRITICAL REFLECTION

- What practical action could you take as a PR practitioner asked to conduct a communication audit to instigate intrinsic power balance in the situation?

REVIEW

Referring back to the opening questions at the beginning of this chapter, you now might like to consider the remarkable extent to which all adults are organizational veterans, experienced in learning how to read and interpret organizational culture. You might want to reflect on the implications of that for public relations practice. For example, formulaic managerial communication will be open to a variety of sophisticated readings. How might that affect the ability of public relations to deliver 'culture change' to top management? How should public relations practitioners handle such a request politically and functionally given the existence of multiple perspectives? The challenge for public relations is to facilitate authentic relationships. Is this possible if public relations is seen as part of the managerial class?

You might also wish to consider how, as a PR consultant, you might facilitate processes which could enable organizational members at all levels to articulate and share their varied perspectives on their organization. What might be the benefits of working through these diverse interpretations?

REVIEW

Return to your initial drawing and analyze it afresh. Have you drawn something like a standard hierarchical organization chart as shown in Figure 9.1?

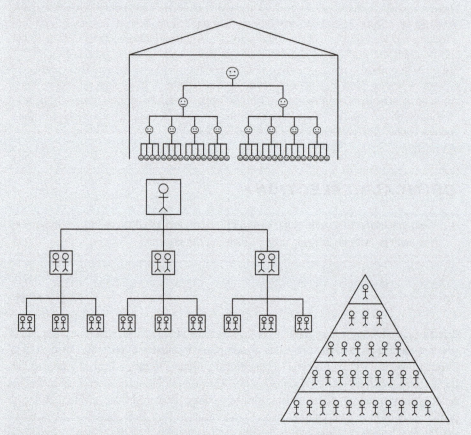

Figure 9.1 Mechanistic organizations: regulated, clear roles and functions

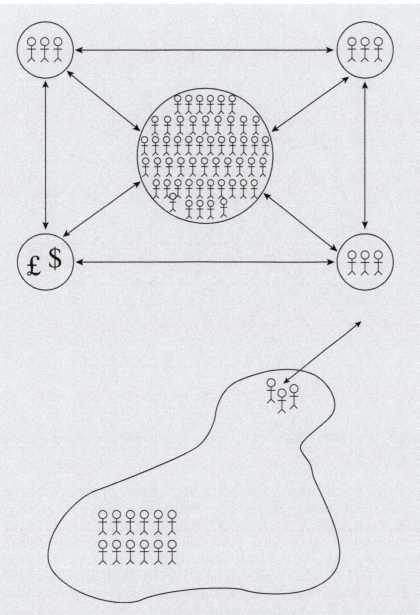

Figure 9.2   Organic organizations: responsive, adaptable, taking and seeking feedback

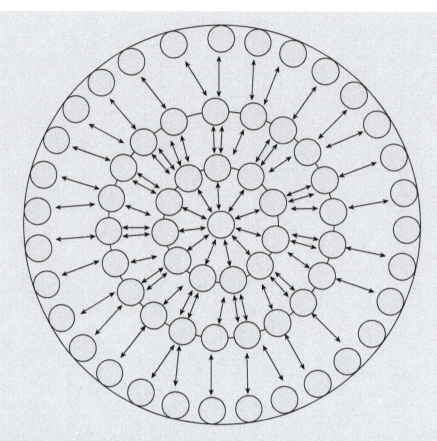

Figure 9.3 Many lines of feedback, but is this organization too introspective? Could it be a psychic prison?

If you have, this shows the influence of the mechanistic, bureaucratic paradigm on your own thinking and reveals something about your own expectations of working life. Maybe you have drawn something like the image depicted in Figure 9.2. If so, this shows the influence of the organic metaphor and also that of systems. How does your drawing show the relationship between the organization and the outside world? How porous are the boundaries? Figures 9.3, 9.4 and 9.5 include some of the limitless possibilities to demonstrate that we all see organizations differently, drawing on our intellectual frameworks, personal inclinations and values, and life experience of organizations.

I am grateful to various MSc PR classes who supplied the inspiration for the drawings on which Figures 9.1–9.5 were based.

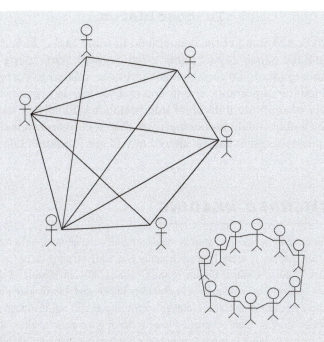

Figure 9.4 Networked organizations

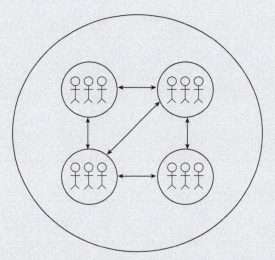

Figure 9.5 Project-based organizations – fewer levels of hierarchy, but who knows who is taking decisions? Who has authority and power?

In conclusion

This chapter indicated some of the deeper (and in some cases, darker) complexities of organizational life which impact public relations work particularly in its roles of relationship management, 'culture change' and tasks related to corporate identity. It has highlighted the importance of emotion and feelings in organizational life and the inevitability of multiple individual interpretations. Finally, it has argued that managerial and public relations perspectives that see organizational culture as a management possession that can be altered at will are fundamentally flawed.

RECOMMENDED READING

Unusual and interesting books on organizational communication abound and I have used some as sources in this chapter. A useful student-friendly text which incorporates traditional, post-modern and critical perspectives is Eisenberg and Goodall (2001). Invaluable advanced sources are available in Ashkanasy, Wilderom and Peterson (2000) and Jablin and Putnam (2001). I spent some time summarizing Gareth Morgan's approach as laid out in *Imaginization* (1993) and *Images of Organization* (2006) because I believe that it gives a useful alternative summary of many of the historical ideas in management and organizational thinking. Finally, there is an excellent source book on communication audits by Hargie and Tourish (2000).

Public Relations in 'Promotional Culture' and 'in Everyday Life'

BEFORE YOU READ A SINGLE WORD...

- What role does public relations play in your culture?
- What sort of cultural practice is public relations?
- What do you understand by the term 'promotional culture'?
- What is 'celebrity'?
- What has PR to do with celebrity?

Key concepts

Celebrity	Impression management
Circuit of culture	Lifestyle
Cultural intermediaries	Lifeworld
Cultural studies	Phenomenology
Culture	Promotional culture

Introduction

Public relations as a cultural practice can be analyzed for its role in reproducing or negotiating culture, as has been pointed out: 'Public relations has increasingly become a tool in shaping public policy and in instigating pubic debate, thereby playing an active role in shaping society, and ultimately, culture' (Banks, 1995, cited in Hodges, 2005: 83). This chapter reflects on the relationship between PR and culture in terms of the occupation's role in, and impact upon, wider society. PR as an occupational culture promotes international organizational cultures, national cultures (tourism, leisure, heritage), and government-sponsored official notions of national culture through cultural diplomacy (discussed in Chapter 11). It also, according to some theorists, plays a particular role in helping us to form our identities, promote ourselves and decode messages. Thus public relations plays a role in identity politics and our affiliations with politics, ideology, religion and ethnicity.

The chapter begins by defining the notion of 'promotional culture' and then proceeds to introduce a cultural studies framework for public relations. Public relations can be seen to have a dual relationship with promotional culture – as contributor and beneficiary. As part of this close intertwining, PR is also associated with celebrity, which is explored at the end of the chapter alongside some reflection of some possible candidates for the status of 'PR celebrity'.

CHAPTER AIMS

On completion of this chapter you will be able to:

- compare and contrast system and cultural models of public relations practice and comment on their relative strengths and weaknesses
- describe the concepts of 'promotional culture' and the implied critique of public relations
- be able to identify promotional work in various parts of contemporary culture
- identify aspects of public relations occupational culture
- define 'celebrity' and explain its connection to PR

Defining culture

The term **culture** can be used in many ways to explain particular social practices, meanings and behaviour in a variety of contexts. Culture shapes our understanding and sense-making facilities and determines what is 'taken for granted' or assumed in a particular environment. Culture produces and is produced by meanings which are consumed, reproduced, altered and co-created. As Hartley pointed out: 'culture' originated as an agricultural metaphor (cultivation) that implied managed, biological selection of refined strains (biological cultures), hence the concepts of 'high culture' as opposed to 'low' or mass or popular culture (Hartley, 1994: 68–69). 'Culture' is used to explain national, political, industrial and social groupings (e.g. Scottish culture, socialist culture, sporting culture, celebrity culture) as well as organizational values, style and practices such as Microsoft culture, university culture, bureaucratic culture. (Hartley, 1994: 69) Thus:

> The term 'culture' is *multi-discursive*, it can be mobilised in a number of different *discourses*. This means you cannot import a fixed definition into any and every context and expect it to make sense. What you have to do is identify the discursive context itself. It may be the discourse of nationalism, fashion ... Marxism, feminism or even *common sense*. (Hartley, 1994: 68–69, emphasis added)

In other words, what is common sense in one culture may not be common sense in another.

Exercise

- What other terms have you come across that are multi-discursive?
- Why is it important for public relations practitioners and students to be sensitive to such language practice?
- Try to identify some different discourses of public relations.

'Culture' and public relations

Culture in PR literature tends to be referred to in two main contexts: in international public relations and in corporate communication and organizational (employee) communication. As noted by Curtin and Gaither (2005: 105), PR literature that has engaged with cultural and intercultural communication has focused on Hofstede (1984), who identified five behavioural variables that could be used in cross-cultural comparisons, and on Hall's typology of *high-context cultures,* in which much of the communication is implicit, and *low-context cultures,* in which communications are more explicit and direct (Hall, 1976). The difficulty with such models is that they explain the designated variables but not the other ethnographic details that may be important in understanding cultural practice, such as culture members' views of their practices.

PR theorists who have engaged with **cultural studies** include Curtin and Gaither (2005, 2007); Hodges (2005, 2006) and Pieczka (2006a). Cultural studies developed from within British culture (specifically at the University of Birmingham) and is therefore a taken-for-granted feature of the academic scene in the UK.

Promotional culture

The concept of **promotional culture** was made famous by a book of that name by Andrew Wernick (1991), who developed work by the cultural theorist Mike

Featherstone (1991). In his book, Wernick explored promotion as a cultural force that alters the relationship between culture and economy. He argued that the *circuits of competitive exchange* required the *propagation* (the term comes from the same root as propaganda) and production of symbolic promotional discourses which were intertextually linked with aesthetic, educational, political and religious discourses (Wernick, 1991: 182). Economic and business requirements were made meaningful through connections and references to other areas of life. For Wernick, such developments were the consequence of a rampant and transforming capitalism and the relentless expansion of the processes of *commodification,* which led to promotion becoming a *necessary condition* of culture and communication. He argued that:

> The extension of promotion through all the circuits of social life [causes] a strategic instrumentality which degrades authenticity. ... When a piece of music, or a newspaper article ... is fashioned with an eye to how it will promote itself ... and indeed, how it will promote its author and distributor ... such goods are affected by this circumstance in every detail of their production. (Wernick, 1991: 188, 190)

This process would be similar to a student writing an essay but at the same time thinking about what cover they will use on the front of the assignment or how to impress the marker with its visual presentation. Intention to promote is thus embedded in production.

Exercise

- Identify your own self-promotional strategies in academic work, hobbies, career.
- What considerations do you take into account when preparing your CV?
- When making purchases, to what extent are you aware of branding and in what contexts does it influence your purchasing strategies?

Discipline box: Cultural studies

Cultural studies developed from the critical tradition to analyze marginalized groups (sub- or micro-cultures), such as youth cultures, gay and lesbian cultures or feminism, in relation to the broader social context. Cultural studies theorists also explored how dominant cultures maintained their economic, social and political superiority, tackling these issues from an interdisciplinary base, drawing on linguistics, sociology, anthropology and psychoanalysis (Hartley, 1994: 72). Cultural studies generally conflated PR with marketing and advertising in discussions of promotional culture and cultural

(Continued)

intermediaries. Critical work of this nature may be described as the *sociology of consumption* (Corrigan, 1997) exploring the *postmodern condition*. This prioritizes consumption in everyday life to signify to others' preferences (Featherstone, 1991), the process that Bourdieu (1979) defined as *distinction* in a famous book of that title.

Postmodernism

Postmodernism is a term applied loosely to a philosophical position that seeks to evade an overall explanatory theory or worldview. Thus, postmodernism, sometimes referred to loosely as *pomo*, has a somewhat oxymoronic nature as being defined as an approach which defies definitional efforts. Defining postmodernism is anathema to a postmodern position! The term is also utilized as an historical colligation 'postmodern' meaning 'after modernity'. According to Hartley, postmodernism is

> Committed to modes of thinking and representation which emphasize fragmentations, discontinuities and incommensurable aspects of a given object, from intellectual systems to architecture. Postmodernist analysis is often marked by forms of writing that are more literary, certainly more self-reflexive, than is common in critical writing – the critic as self-conscious creator of new meanings upon the ground of the object of study, showing that object no special respect. It prefers montage to perspective ... delights in excess, play, carnival, asymmetry, even mess, and in the emancipation of meanings from their bondage to mere lumpenreality. (Hartley, 1994: 234)

Some postmodern perspectives in PR are presented in Chapter 12.

Cultural studies and public relations

Scholars from the British cultural studies tradition have developed the concept of a **circuit of culture** in capitalist economies (du Gay, 1997; Nixon and du Gay, 2002; Nixon, 2003). The circuit explains how culture is informed by economic practice and shows how the economy can be seen as a cultural construct (Curtin and Gaither, 2005: 93, citing du Gay, 1997). The circuit, shown in Figure 10.1, shows five key moments at which meaning is produced: identity, production, consumption, regulation and representation. Identity is partly achieved through consumer purchase, consumption and symbolic display of goods as an adjunct of personal and group identities. **Cultural intermediaries** are those in PR, marketing, design and advertising businesses whose designated expertise is to:

- link identities (lifestyles) with products (market research)
- provide feedback from potential consumers to producers to help them shape products and services more appropriately

- create symbols, values and language to represent products and services which enable the producer and marketer to communicate with the consumer in the same language
- promote (Curtin and Gaither, 2005; Negus, 2002)

Public relations in its cultural intermediary role also plays a part in regulation through:

- public affairs and political lobbying
- corporate codes of ethics
- corporate culture and identity programmes
- the development of design and crisis management manuals

Public relations as a cultural practice: PR in everyday life

Thus, cultural studies theorists have tended to incorporate public relations into the general category of cultural intermediaries in their critical discussions of promotional work's negative effects on authentic communication. PR and associated actions are seen as attractive, complex and symbolic 'clutter' that appeals and entertains. Consumers have to be culturally sophisticated to read, decode and interpret signs and their multiple intertextual references.

There is another way to think about PR in culture and that is around traditional anthropological concerns. When anthropologists 'enter the field' they observe patterns of daily life and, in particular, the rituals of birth, kinship, sexual initiation, marriage, leisure and play, death, religious beliefs and practices, as well as more prosaic practices such as those relating to health, education, values of exchange (barter, money systems) and other knowledge systems (science, technology). We can take a similar approach to explore these key moments and rituals but do so through the lens of public relations. Such an approach can generate a detailed picture of everyday promotional life as it plays out in intimate and culturally situated moments. The role of PR in everyday life, in events of birth, marriage and death, reveals significant aspects of promotional culture and our individual engagement and identification in postmodern society. How does promotion affect our experience of these events and associated rituals? This approach can help us to understand the relationship between individual lifeworlds and promotional culture and values.

For example, death entails consumption for those left behind. There are important services to be undertaken (care, cleaning, housing and dressing of the body, religious or secular services to start the process of closure) and products to purchase (coffins, urns, headstones, newspaper notices), yet the promotion of these varies in different cultures. The bereaved identify themselves through such purchases but also are likely to take into account the wishes or preferences

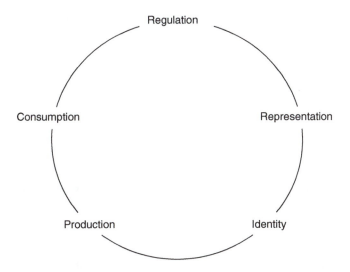

Figure 10.1   The circuit of culture

Source: adapted from Curtin and Gaither (2005: 98), citing du Gay (1997)

of the deceased. Regulation requires the death to be registered. The extent of commodification varies across cultures and according to the degree to which death is taboo.

Exercise

How are the life events of birth and marriage commodified in promotional cultures? Elaborate on the business, products and services which cluster around these events. How possible is it to experience such events without spending more than the fees for the registration of births and marriages – and why?

The concept of **lifeworld** is the concept focused on by Habermas in his later work (drawing on Durkheim, Mead and Schutz). For Schutz, the lifeworld was the world of everyday, taken-for-granted life. For Habermas, the lifeworld is 'a horizon of consciousness which includes both the public and private spheres ... the sphere of identity formation and communicative action' (which relies on co-operative interpretation) (Lechte, 1994: 188). **Lifestyle** is a term used colloquially to determine behavioural, attitudinal and stylistic patterns of an individual or group. It also defines a class of soft journalism and media output. The concept has been used instrumentally by marketers to target consumers, often as part of psychographic segmentation modelling of large populations.

Exercise

- What opportunities are available for PR work in (a) fashion, (b) music, and (c) consumer electronics?

Research your chosen area and identify how the business works. Who are the key players and what are their important relationships? How does the market work? What are the key media (news, magazines, specialist, internet, chat rooms)?

Discipline box: Anthropology and ethnography

This account is drawn from Denzin and Lincoln's excellent source book on qualitative methods (1994, 2000) and Jay Ruby's account of ethnographic film (1976). *Ethnos* means people, a race or cultural group (Denzin and Lincoln, 1994: 25). Ethnography is the formal attempt to understand a culture and recreate it in written form. Ethnography evolved as a consequence of exploration, colonization and 'civilization'. Explorers, missionaries and colonial administrators often spoke the local languages and they were partly embedded in the cultures they observed. Although they approached their 'subjects' with a particular view and relationship that framed their observations, many of these early ethnographers logged valuable detail about diverse cultural practices, religions and language.

   While ethnography sought to deliver an accurate representation of a culture, anthropologists went a step further in using such data to theorize about humanity. Description is an end in itself for the ethnographer, but the anthropologist takes a more scientific approach and so has more concerns relating to verification and the maintenance of distance between the observer and the observed. Anthropology as a discipline became professionalized in the 1920s and 1930s, following a series of groundbreaking studies that established a clear fieldwork method with its own standards and conventions.

   So ethnography developed as a tool for anthropologists and is now used in many different disciplines. *Ethnographic films* allow the viewer to observe another culture, its rhythms, practices, rituals, symbols, signs and conventions. They include the *research film*, *interpretative film* and *issue film*.

PR and 'everyday life studies'

The role of PR in political culture has been subjected to some analysis, mostly by media sociologists. Turning to patterns of leisure, one can observe that the role of PR is embedded in entertainment, sport, leisure and tourism (L'Etang, 2006a, 2006b; L'Etang et al., 2007). In fact, PR has benefited from the growth and buoyancy of such sectors. Empirical analysis in these fields is currently quite limited yet it is only by close study of these sectors and others, such as religion, that a more detailed understanding of PR in promotional culture can be established.

Social theorists and cultural studies analysts have begun to explore the zone of taken-for-granted everyday life – the terrain upon which the interplay between structure and culture takes place. This interest owes a debt to the Austrian phenomenologist Alfred Schutz, whose last work was published posthumously in 1973 (Zaner and Engelhardt, 1973) and the French academic (historian, ethnologist and Freudian psychologist) Michel de Certeau, whose book, *The Practice of Everyday Life,* was published in translation in 1984. Drawing on Foucault and Bourdieu, de Certeau sought to understand how ordinary individuals understood, interpreted and constructed meaning in a way that made sense to themselves and their sense of identity in the context of commercial capitalism. He wanted to establish how the apparently disempowered could retain a sense of autonomy and subvert dominant systems of sense-making.

Systems theorists (Durkheim, Marx) understood social interaction and commonsense as the consequence of structural forces and processes that were comparable to scientific laws, and conceived the sphere of everyday life as a space for the domination of individuals, thus ignoring the individual's capacity for agency (Bennett, 2005: 2). Critics of systems theory (Weber, Mead) pointed out that everyday life was a mediation process between structure and the individual. The construction of the individual as an active agent in determining meaning was recognized fully by phenomenologists, including Erving Goffman, the originator of impression management, whose work showed how individuals managed the process of internalizing social roles (Bennett, 2005: 3; see Chapter 3: 66). Contemporary theorists see everyday life as contested and negotiated through media consumption and leisure in a fragmented world of multiple identities. **Phenomenology** means the description of conscious experiences and was developed by Husserl. In research, the phenomenological approach is part of the qualitative paradigm that privileges the accounts of research participants.

Caroline Hodges' ethnographically inspired work sought to explore PR culture as sense-making by linking the study of occupational and societal cultures in Mexico. She defined the PR practitioner lifeworld as:

> the totality of practitioners' thoughts, concepts, values and assumptions about their occupation … and their occupational experiences and identities that guide their behaviour. These will evolve with contact with other practitioners (occupational socialization) and with wider social and cultural influences. (Hodges, 2006: 85)

Everyday life research has implications for studying public relations. PR tends to be organizationally rather than societally or culturally orientated (this point is similar to that made by Leitch and Neilson (2001) in their critique of the term 'public' referred to in Chapter 5). Therefore an everyday life focus re-orientates PR research towards a consideration of cultural impact. Everyday life may be seen potentially as a continual process of accommodation and resistances to promotional culture as individuals interpret and construct their own meanings. Fluid processes and multiple identities seem to challenge the notion of lifestyle, to which I now turn.

Lifestyle

The concept of lifestyle is important to the promotional industries (advertising, marketing, PR, design) and to cultural theorists who focus on consumption. Lifestyles are defined as: 'Features of the modern world ... patterns of action that differentiate people ... make sense of what people do ... why they do it, and what doing it means to them and others' (Chaney, 1996: 6).

Lifestyles produce and are the consequence of subtle distinctions between identities and therefore actualize social difference. Economic growth has led to consumer culture and the availability of goods, which, in the context of mass surburbanization, 'encourage private investment in the pursuit of distinction' (Chaney, 1996: 21). 'Lifestyle' may be assumed to be the consequence of individual choice and used in government rhetoric to encourage certain forms of behaviour, but, as Bell and Hollows pointed out: 'The idea of freedom of choice has been questioned ... the opposition between freedom and constraint structures many debates about the significance of lifestyle in sociology and cultural studies' (Bell and Hollows, 2005: 2).

CRITICAL REFLECTION

- How would you characterize your lifestyle?
- What actions do you take to maintain it?
- Identify some lifestyles you have observed in practice.

A key feature of promotional culture and associated 'lifestylization' is the growth of entertainment and celebrity cultures.

Celebrity

Celebrity is commonly defined as 'being known for being known', a definition that initially emerged from US political scientist Boorstin (cited in Turner, 2004: 5). Celebrity is public visibility, fame, public wonder and entertainment. Celebrity implies high visibility, the title of a book by marketers Rein et al. (2006), exceptional, sometimes mysterious qualities, charisma and a cluster of attributes that enable a 'special' person to be packaged, branded, promoted and commodified (Turner, 2004). Celebrity is achieved through talent, auspicious circumstance, connections, accident, extensive media coverage of ordinary people doing extraordinary things (Rojek, 2001). In promotional culture, according to Wernick:

> when any instance of individual self-promotion spills over from the private realm to become a topic of public communication, whether unintentionally, as a personal drama that makes the news, or deliberately, as the amplified staging of a career (sporting, political, artistic, intellectual, etc.) inter-individual competition gives rise to yet a further form of promotional practice: the construction of celebrityhood. This itself enters into the realm of public promotion, not just as self-advertising, but as an exchangeable (and promotable) promotional resource both for the individual involved and for other advertisers. (Wernick, 1991: 183)

Celebrity, while much desired in contemporary society, is not an unproblematic status. Many celebrities have failed to understand media news values. Being a major celebrity can mean the end of private/public divide and being constantly 'in role' for audiences and fans – and even stalkers. Privacy laws aim to protect the private self. Even the private self may be closely observed, as Walter Lippman, US political philosopher commented:

> Great men, seen during their lifetime, are usually known to the public only through a fictitious personality. Hence the modicum of truth in the old saying that no man is a hero to his valet. There is only a modicum of truth, for the valet and the private secretary are often immersed in the fiction themselves. Royal personages are, of course, constructed personalities, whether they themselves believe in their public character, or whether they merely permit the chamberlain to stage-manage it, there are at least two distinct selves, the public and regal self, the private and the human. (Lippman, 1991: 7)

Maintaining 'the look' may require a team of make-up artists, nutritionists, wardrobe consultants, personal trainers, plastic surgeons, website managers, promoters and agents as **impression management** is a constant task.

Rojek (2001: 17) developed a useful classification of celebrity:

- Ascribed celebrity
- Achieved celebrity
- Attributed celebrity
- Celetoid
- Celeactors

Ascribed celebrity
Celebrity acquired through blood or inheritance, whether it is royal, or as a result of political or business connections. The children of politicians, royalty and celebrities fall into this category.

Achieved celebrity

A meritocratic celebrity that is acquired through individual skills – sports stars, musicians, writers, artists, successful business people. Examples could include Paula Radcliffe (Britain's outstanding distance runner), Richard Branson (business), J.K. Rowling (author of the Harry Potter stories).

Attributed celebrity

Celebrity arising from repeated media exposure, for example newsreaders or hosts of media shows, such as Oprah Winfrey and Trisha Goddard.

Celetoid

Celebrities who command extensive media attention due to scandals, pseudo-events or participation in reality TV, such as participants in *Big Brother*. However, their celebrity status may be quite short-lived. Most *Big Brother* contestants fade into obscurity, although there are exceptions, such as Jade Goody, who is 'often held as a prime example of the growing cult of celebrity – being made arbitrarily famous by the entertainment industry and becoming a household name' (www. jadegoodyonline.com, accessed 24 January 2006). She extended her celebrity life in gossip magazines, appearing on *Celebrity Wife Swap* and *Celebrity Driving School*, starred in her own fitness video and promoted her own perfume.

Celeactors

Fictional characters who achieve media attention and become cultural reference points, such as the ogre Shrek (in the film of that name), whose celeactor also overlapped with achieved celebrity footballer Wayne Rooney, who is sometimes nicknamed 'Shrek'.

Celebrities can move from ascribed and achieved celebrity to attributed celebrity and celetoids through scandal or notoriety.

Reasons for celebrity

Celebrity has become a major cultural preoccupation, spawning its own specialized media and promoters. For Rojek, celebrity is the consequence of: 'three major interrelated processes ... the democratization of society ... a decline in organized religion ... the commodification of everyday life' (Rojek, 2001: 13).

However, celebrity culture is not a new phenomenon and its close links to consumer culture were critiqued as early as the 1930s by Marxists and cultural conservatives. Horkheimer and Adorno, in particular, criticized the 'culture industries' that produced celebrity (Marshall, 1997: 9).

CRITICAL REFLECTION

- Does celebrity celebrate democracy or does it create new elites?
- Is celebrity a different form of prostitution?

Levels of celebrity: local celebrity and celebrity subcultures

To the extent that celebrity is about 'known-ness', we may all participate in social worlds that have their own minor celebrities, for example in a sports club, a local orchestra, a youth club, a school or a university department. These might include those who appear in the local paper, are interviewed on a minor TV programme, are good amateur exponents selected for more prestigious competitions, or who have extraordinary events (pleasant and unpleasant) in their lives which bestow at least a temporary notoriety.

Exercise: defining celebrity

- Identify celebrities in your locality, college, workplace, club and social circle.
- How and why have these individuals acquired celebrity status?

The role of PR in celebrity: red tops, red carpets and red pages

Much of the PR role in celebrity circles is focused on promotion, publicity and media relations, and public relations has received some of its bad press from this association. For example, sociologist John Hartley referred to 'the smiling professions' (Cited in Turner, 2004: 16) and Rojek pointed out that: 'Celebrities are cultural fabrications ... no celebrity now gains public recognition without the assistance of cultural intermediaries who operate to stage manage celebrity presence in the eyes of the public' (Rojek, 2001: 10).

According to public relations scholarly conventions, publicity is a small part of public relations. PR practitioners in the UK from the 1930s to the 1960s tried quite hard and rather unsuccessfully to distinguish the functions and to prohibit 'publicists' and 'press agents' from membership of the professional body (L'Etang, 2004: 74–75).

According to Turner:

> public relations provided a more respectable name for the press agent as well as the rationale for change in the function of these operations ... [T]he need for positive publicity gradually became a corporate issue, not just a problem for entertainment industries. (Turner, 2004: 44)

This shift in nomenclature marked the first impression management efforts by the occupation to reinvent itself, and there have been numerous others, hence the proliferation of apparently more acceptable job titles, including 'public affairs', 'corporate communications' and 'communication management'. Some PR academics seem uncomfortable with students' interests in celebrity and its connection to public relations (both historical and contemporary). Why is this? Perhaps because celebrity is seen as hype from which academic public relations tries to distance itself. Celebrity may also be seen as trivial, as part of popular culture, as not serious. Consequently, PR texts tend to ignore publicists, 'yet publicists write press releases, organize photoshoots and personal appearances, negotiate with magazine editors, vet questions and baby-sit their clients' (Turner, 2004: 45).

According to PR author Leichty:

> Celebrity PR can be unpredictable and capricious. Publicity becomes an end in itself because it creates a celebrity premium that people are willing to pay for ... 'high visibility PR' an be a high-status, zero-sum game. The number of celebrities who can be created and maintained is rather finite and inelastic. ... The fortunes of PR promoters are driven by the fickle hand that determines who is hot and who is not. ... The practitioner also must cope with the caprices of temperamental and neurotic celebrities. Handholding is listed as one of the essential duties of the celebrity promoter. (Leichty, 2003: 282)

US academic Cynthia King also saw the PR role as being one of managing celebrities, who may be troubled people as a consequence of the celebrity experience and the burden of being a *public individual* (King, 2006: 75). She also highlighted the rising importance of 'entertainment as bait to attract audiences for other purposes' in media-cluttered environments.

Celebrity is underpinned by promotional efforts and media relations. Gossip magazines and the gossip pages of newspapers must be filled with pictures and stories. Celebrities offer branding opportunities that will connect with marketing audiences. Events (pseudo and otherwise), red carpet dos, launches, award ceremonies and parties provide the context for networking and promoting products and personalities.

Some key information tools in the UK are provided by The Profile Group, which employs 40 full-time researchers and sells a series of databases for journalists, agents, publicists. These include:

- *Foresight news* – events from arts, politics, film, broadcast, commerce, fashion and public affairs planned over the next five years.
- *Entertainment news* – forward planning diary of celebrity promotions and showbiz events.
- *Entertainment news online* – latest news on film premières, launch parties, photocalls, first nights, celebrity interview opportunities, exhibition previews, gigs, press conferences, and fundraisers.
- *Red pages* – agent, publicist and endorsement details for over 7,000 celebrities.

(*Source*: www.profilegroup.co.uk/future_events.htm, accessed 22 May 2006)

Box 10.1 Celebrity

Celebrity endorsement

Competition among retailers to capitalize on consumer spending can leave charities 'out in the cold' during the goodwill season. World Vision UK Celebrity Co-ordinator, Paula Cummings MCIPR [Member of the Chartered Institute of Public Relations] said that while Christmas was a busy time for the international aid and development charity, its fundraising and media activities constantly changed to reflect developments in social media. World Vision UK – part of a global organization comprising 22,000 employees in 100 countries – is one of many not-for-profit organizations, such as UNICEF and children's charity NSPCC, now using celebrities to endorse its work. Cummings joined World Vision three years ago to help build its celebrity programme ... [She said] 'We try to match a celebrity's interest to a problem ... if you get a person who can identify with the organization and feel passion for its work then your campaign can be successful.'
Source: Profile, 58 (November/December): 14

Celebrity skateboarder stars with celeactors

Tony Hawk, the world's best-known skater, has his own character in a video game. In an interview with Channel 4 he said that his best achievement was to appear as himself on *The Simpsons* because 'they embody popular culture' (Channel 4 Interview, 25 March 2007).

Failed film star becomes celetoid

British model Victoria Redstall went to Los Angeles aiming to become 'the next Nick Broomfield' (a British documentary filmmaker whose work included a film of a serial killer). In the highly competitive Hollywood environment, Redstall could only find short-term small film and TV roles and was forced into tacky promotional work for *Grobust*, a herbal breast enlargement product. She then commodified herself by making a self-indulgent 'documentary' about her own experiences, standing scantily dressed on the roof of her block of flats, attracting the attention of news helicopter pilots whose news station showed the footage. The helicopter noise infuriated neighbours who sued and forced her to move house. Subsequently, Redstall sought out an imprisoned serial killer who had dismembered his victims, turning up at a police station with a woman's breast in his pocket. Redstall attended his trial and attempted to speak to him daily, ultimately being banned from the prison. The case attracted massive coverage and Redstall's next move was to try to turn media interest in her 'friendship' into a film – the celetoid still hopes to acquire achieved celebrity.

Source: Harlow, J. 'Blonde from Esher and a serial killer intrigue US', *The Sunday Times*, 6 August 2006)

Media don seeks world influence

Billed as 'the world's most influential Scot', Niall Ferguson is one of the tiny group of academics whose name enters popular culture:

(Continued)

(Continued)

> a historian of the information age … no longer confined to dark libraries consulting dusty tomes … television … has made history the new soap opera. (Deveney, 2006: 8)

Ferguson hosted the TV show *Empire: How Britain Made the Modern World* as well as writing scholarly, provocative books focused on political power. Now a part-time Professor of History at Harvard (and part-time Senior Research Fellow at Jesus College Oxford) he made *Time Magazine*'s 2004 list of 100 most influential people in the world and is apparently a frequent guest at the White House discussing policy issues. The article from which this example is drawn is interesting in another aspect of celebrity-making. It sexualizes Ferguson thus:

> [History has] secrets, betrayal, power and lust … you couldn't make it up. Ferguson is the male lead. At 42 he's as young as history gets. Ladies of a certain age are torn between swooning at his conservative good looks and the size of his intellect. Ferguson, we are told, has a formidable brain. (Deveney, 2006: 7)

Celetoids seek to maintain public status

On the island of Raasay off the mainland of the Orkney Islands is a little tea-room. On the menu is a note explaining that the owners once appeared on the TV programme *Castaway*. While apparently retreating to the far outreaches of the UK to seek a rural idyll, the pair still make their claim to fame.

Celetoid pays homage to ascribed and achieved celebrity

In the small village of Helmsdale on the coast of northeast Scotland is an extraordinary restaurant, 'Le mirage', and bed and breakfast. The former owner, Nancy Sinclair, had long been an admirer of Barbara Cartland, author of light romantic fiction (achieved celebrity) and also step grandmother-in-law of Diana Princess of Wales (ascribed celebrity). Barbara Cartland holidayed in Helmsdale for many years and Nancy Sinclair modelled herself on the Barbara Cartland 'look' – bouffant hair, elaborate dress, fantastic nails. She met Barbara Cartland many times and became a celebrity in her own right. The walls of the restaurant are embellished with photos of her with many other celebrities.

Source: http://www.lamirage.org/, accessed 8 December 2006

Celebrity in the PR world

There have been and are some public relations practitioners who attain celebrity, some of a notorious or slightly scandalous nature. Typically, those who work for high-profile clients, especially existing celebrities, sports and entertainment stars and politicians, may come into public view. By so doing they break a traditional convention of public relations work, that the public relations practitioner should work behind the scenes, out of the limelight. The rationale for this convention is that public relations practitioners should be promoting others and not themselves. The erosion of this position is really the consequence of the development of the promotional culture we now inhabit, which increasingly means that everyone (even academics) require some promotional skills.

Box 10.2   PR celebrities

Max Clifford: 'the UK's best known publicist and a consummate media manipulator' (http://news.bbc.co.uk, accessed 8 December 2006)

Matthew Freud: 'the great-grandson of Sigmund Freud, son of journalist and raconteur Clement Freud and nephew of painter Lucien Freud, he is also the PR behind some of Britain's most heavily exposed names (Chris Evans, Guy Ritchie, Ali G) (http://specials.ft.com, accessed 9 December 2006)

Lynne Franks: started her own PR agency at the age of 21 and is alleged to have been the inspiration for Patsy in *Absolutely Fabulous*. She is now 'author, entrepreneur and lifestyle guru [with] a communication reach that stretches across the world' (www.growexperience.com, accessed 8 December 2006)

Julia Hobsbawm: styled 'Queen of PR', she is chief executive of her own company and coined the phrase 'integrity PR' ... the daughter of Marxist historian Professor Eric Hobsbawm. She is London's first professor of public relations ...' (www.spin-watch.org, accessed 8 December 2006)

Anne Gregory: past-President of the CIPR [Chartered Institute of Public Relations], the UK's first full-time Professor of Public Relations and Director of the Centre for Public Relations Studies at Leeds Metropolitan University, which has the largest department of public relations ... [her] specialist area of interest is pubic relations as a management discipline' (www.cipr.co.uk/news, accessed 8 December 2006). In December 2006, Professor Gregory was appointed Pro-Vice-Chancellor (www.lmu.ac.uk, accessed 24 January 2007)

Exercise

- Classify the celebrities in Box 10.2 according to Rojek's framework.
- Review a sample of PR/business professional magazines and analyze (a) the language that is used, (b) the values that emerge, and (c) any photographic presentations. What do we learn about PR professional culture and PR celebrity in particular?

REVIEW

Reflecting on the content of this chapter, you may like to re-consider the questions asked of you at the beginning of the chapter and think about conventional views of public relations expressed in textbooks and articles:

- is PR only about managing organizational relationships?

In conclusion

This chapter has aimed to broaden ideas about public relations as a cultural practice as opposed to a professional practice or area of work. The main focus has been on promotional culture and the way in which cultural studies perspectives have been taken up in PR. The chapter suggests a new line of thinking in relation to 'PR and everyday life' and the value of phenomenological research.

Attention has also been given to PR's occupational culture and its links with the rise of promotional culture and celebrity. One aspect which was briefly alluded to, but not addressed, was that of PR as cultural diplomacy, a topic to be taken up more fully in the next chapter which will explore globalization, international cultural discourse and PR's relationship to an international public sphere.

RECOMMENDED READING

Essential reading is Hodges (2005), Curtin & Gaither (2005) and Pieczka (2006a, 2006b). Curtin and Gaither's recent book (2007) promises to be a landmark text and Banks (1995), though published some time ago, remains important. Mickey (2003) received mixed reviews but is accessible for students. The field of celebrity is fast-growing within cultural, media and sports studies. A classic text, now in its third edition, is Rein et al.'s *High Visibility* (2006), which takes a marketing approach to celebrity, but also says some interesting things about public relations. Graeme Turner's *Understanding Celebrity* (2004) gives an excellent introduction because it balances production and consumption of celebrity and also refers to press agentry and public relations in more detail than is common in cultural studies.

Public Relations in a Globalized World

- What do you understand by the term 'globalization'?
- Does technology deliver a global culture, and, if so, how might this impact on public relations practice?
- Do global goods imply global values?
- What is the relationship between public relations and capitalism?

Key concepts

Anti-capitalism

Cultural diplomacy

Cultural imperialism

Global culture

Globalization

Glocalization

Intercultural communication

International communication

International public relations

Localization

McDonaldization

Multicultural communication

Subaltern studies

Technological determinism

Introduction

This chapter aims to explain the concept and practice of globalization and its relevance to public relations practice. It explains a variety of perspectives from international communications, cultural, media and public relations, including critical views regarding the role of public relations in the process of globalization. The chapter begins by defining globalization and explaining its importance to public relations students and practitioners. It reviews the debate as to whether global-ization is a positive or negative development before exploring the relationship between globalization, diplomacy and public relations. The chapter does not, however, engage with technological changes in media or ICTs, since it is more concerned with the effects of contracted time and space and the underlying pol-itics than the technical processes which are a major part of globalization accounts.

CHAPTER AIMS

On completion of this chapter you will be able to:

- define the concept of globalization
- understand and debate the critical issues of globalization in relation to public relations
- describe the field of international communication
- understand the connections between globalization, diplomacy and public relations

Discipline box: International communication

International communication is the specialist area of communications which explores the relationship between communications and culture. It has focused on international, intercultural and development communication and includes interper-sonal, mass and mediated communication (Asante and Gudykunst, 1989). Its con-cerns have been wide-ranging, including international relations, diplomacy and the New World Information and Communication Order (NWICO) which works to address imbalances of information, intercultural competencies and training, anti-racism, national development and diplomacy, and, of course, globalization (Asante and Gudykunst, 1989; Taylor, 1997).

International communication is the over-arching field which includes intercul-tural and multicultural communication diplomacy and development communica-tion. It is also a term used by public relations practitioners in the context of international PR. **Intercultural communication** is used to define communication from one cultural group to another and was a term first coined by communication scholar Edward Hall in his book *The Silent Language* (1959). Migration and diaspo-ras produce multi-cultural societies. **Multicultural communication** is a term which describes both communication which is simultaneously transmitted to many cultures and which is applied to research into the variable ways in which cultures communicate (comparative cultural research). **International public relations** describes PR that is international in focus, often carried out by consultancies which are based in many countries or which have bought out local consultancies in order to benefit from the cultural knowledge of local practitioners. The terms **localization** and **glocalization** emerged as a way of trying to explain the benefits of maintaining a dual focus, both global and local. These terms have, however, evolved into a superficial cliché which might inhibit the deeper underlying issues.

Box 11.1   Useful source

G8 Information Centre – www.g8.utoronto.ca

Globalization: definitions and concepts

Globalization has become a politicized and to some degree a controversial term. At a basic, descriptive level definitions simply describe the compression of time and space that has been facilitated by communication technology and travel.

The effect of this has been the emergence of global society, and while this if often romantically described as 'the global village' (the term originated with communications guru Marshall McLuhan) there are radical differences in wealth, opportunity, political, economic and ecological stability, many attributable to colonial histories and industrial might. Thus globalization describes the contraction of time and space for those in wealthy countries whose citizens have access to technology and travel. It also involves homogenization processes in which goods and services are available to the same standard globally and branded internationally. The brand values communicate dominant ideologies which are thought to reinforce inequities between rich and poor. Anti-globalization is a term which overlaps to some degree with anti-capitalism and includes an activist movement, some members of which take direct action, for example protests at G8 conferences.

CRITICAL REFLECTION

- What do the terms 'anti-globalization' and 'anti-capitalism' connote about the position of such groups in Western-style cultures?
- How does public relations relate to these concepts?

Exercise

- Design a project to research the media coverage of the terms anti-globalization and anti-capitalism - what insights emerge?

However, while it can be argued somewhat deterministically that the process of globalization began with early human exploration and developed through trade, imperialism, diplomacy, tourism and cross-cultural exchange, the term has come to connote capitalism and cultural imperialism of the USA or the G8. As a consequence, the term 'globalization' itself has become politicized, and may be read as: 'human progress', 'global village', 'global community', 'exploitation' or 'corporate imperialism'. Globalization may be seen as an ongoing process in which power flows through a decentred network of multicultural postmodern societies (Puchan, 2003: 7). The thesis of **cultural imperialism** suggests that globalization has promoted capitalism and consumerism. In a postcolonial world the former colonial nations still retain immense power and influence in former colonies and parts of the developing world.

Global culture may be used to imply US or Western dominant culture but, since globalization is a process, it is open to multiple reinterpretations and is a process in which the cultural influences of other parts of the globe are adapted or introduced in the Western world, for example: cuisine, alternative medicine and therapies, music, Eastern religions and *feng shui*. **McDonaldization** is a term made famous by George Ritzer in his books, *The McDonaldization of Society* (2000) and *McDonaldization: The Reader* (2002), which explore the phenomenon of globalized businesses as agents of cultural imperialism and as a psychic prison. **Technological determinism** is an argument which explains globalization as a consequence of technological changes that have facilitated instant and continuous international communication. The **global public sphere** defines a space in which national, transnational and global ties potentially can be interactively connected through 'accessible, independent, influential media' (McNair, 2006: 140). If globalization is seen as dominance by cultures that control global technology and markets, what does that tell us about the role of PR and its place in the world?

Why does globalization matter to PR students and practitioners?

Globalization is a consequence of shrinking time and connected places. Public relations makes connections. Globalization has offered new opportunities for PR, and PR has benefited from the technological and geopolitical changes that have delivered communicative opportunities with globalized stakeholders.

In its own way too, PR has stimulated the globalization process as a process that spreads ideas and values. For example, the transport and travel industries were quick to develop PR functions in the UK: Frank Pick was appointed to build a good reputation for the London Underground; Sir John Elliott (who became Chairman of London Transport in the 1960s) was appointed, in 1924, to a post at Southern Railways when they were electrifying the line; Edward Kingsley worked for the Port of London Authority from 1911 to 1948 (L'Etang, 2004: 54–55). In the same era public relations practitioners worked for British Overseas Airways Corporation (BOAC), Ford Motor Company and Brooklands Racing Track. After the technological developments of the Second World War the civilian air industry was quite literally ready for take-off. Economies needed trade to recover, and the design and promotion of British business was an important part of that process, especially at international fairs such as the Brussels Universal and International Exhibition (1958). These historic examples are instructive in showing the close connection between *international* and *intercultural* links and public relations activity.

Public relations practitioners and some academics have tended to approach the topic of globalization in a functional way, for example, focusing on how communication with those in different countries can be more effective in organizational terms or in terms of extending or replicating US models (Taylor, 2000: 630). PR practitioners and some academics may also have an agenda since the reputation of public relations as a discipline and a practice could be improved if it could be shown that PR contributes to improved diplomacy and better understanding among peoples. There is nothing wrong with such work, but there are other approaches that can be taken. It can be argued that PR is implicated in criticisms that globalization is responsible for promoting the goods, services and values of the most powerful (G8) countries. On behalf of its clients, PR may also have to respond to the consequences of anti-globalization forces. One of the critical questions that arises is whether public relations only works for the information-rich and not for the information-poor.

Thus globalization is a central issue for PR practice. Tilson and Alozie argued that the global context makes it essential for contemporary PR students to understand globalization and the networked relationships that result:

> The world has become a global village: Olympic athletes are natives of one country but represent another in the Winter Games; US football players play on teams in NFL Europe; artists, such as British rocker, Sting, play in Santiago de Compostela, Spain to packed houses of concertgoers from across Europe, and Chinese Taipei pop star A-mei performs in mainland China; Fortune 500 companies commonly earn more than 50 per cent of their earnings internationally; headquarter staffs reflect a global mix of talent; and packaged apple juice sold in the United States contains concentrate from Turkey, Poland and Argentina... (Tilson and Alozie, 2004: 1)

Globalization compresses and pressurizes time for those in the international business class and in privileged societies in which consumer opportunities are rife. Yet the dominance of Anglophone cultures has provoked resistance and nationalism appears to be on the rise. On the one hand, PR practitioners cultivate and promote global identities; on the other, they have to take account of local culture and take care of community relations. As Heath explained:

> One of the ironies of the era of globalization is the feeling that the globe is simultaneously shrinking as it expands into an enlarging kaleidoscope of people, languages, cultures, governmental structure and economic systems ... the [most] compelling issue is whether a global organization (business, non-profit, or governmental) can meet or exceed the expectations of a Babel of voices and cultures without losing its identity by trying to be everything to all markets and publics. (Heath, 2001: 625)

Finally, there is a big question mark over what all this means for us: is there really a global society? Are we all equal citizens in such a society? Can there be an **international public sphere**?

For those engaged in public relations there are also questions about how such work may take the world in one direction rather than another. How will power balances shift? Who will seek to control these processes?

To sum up, globalization affects PR work for the following key reasons:

- Globalization offers opportunities for re-packaging ideas (including politics and religion), products and services for different markets.
- Globalization increases communication opportunities and challenges.
- Globalization changes organizations, stakeholders, publics, issues and relationships.
- More organizations are becoming globalized and have international workforces and markets.
- PR is closely associated with capital (economic power) and its maintenance (seeking new markets and cheaper materials, knowledge bases and markets).
- PR is closely associated with global power (governments and international organizations such as the World Bank and the World Health Organization).
- Resistance to globalization requires diplomacy and PR for globalizing organizations.
- Anti-globalization is an issue for globalized and globalizing organizations.
- Anti-globalization campaigns need their own communicators (PR, rhetors), diplomatists and media relations experts.

Figure 11.1 demonstrates the connectivity and complexity of globalized organizational relationships.

Globalization matters to PR practice because it describes a contemporary condition and is a 'hot issue' that frames organizational relationships. Globalization structures PR practice through international organizations and international

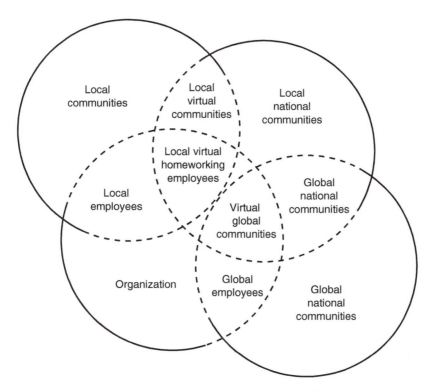

Figure 11.1 Public relations in a globalized world. Globalization changes organizations, stakeholders, publics and issues. Organizations are porous.

consultancies (usually owned by communications conglomerates). Globalization presents problems to PR in terms of cross- and intercultural communication (effectiveness) and in terms of resistance to globalization processes (e.g. 'activist' groups, terrorism). Programmes of social responsibility and community relations may be developed to counter accusations of worker exploitation in less developed countries or bad environmental practice indulged in areas of low population (where there may be no 'public' to relate to). Projects to ameliorate ethnic relations in multicultural states may be based on transnational elite views of civil society and PR may be implicated in imperially-inspired projects:

> the vision of building civil societies is used as justification for imperialist invasions of Third World nations, as witnessed in … invasions of Afghanistan and Iraq. Whereas some of these invasions are overtly implemented, others are covertly carried out through persuasive strategies such as grant programs, foreign assistance programs and democracy promotion initiatives. (Dutta-Bergman, 2005: 267–289)

PR practice is embedded in international organizations and dominant capitalist economies and therefore it is part of the process of globalization, and not simply a strategy of communication to respond to the consequences of communicative distortion that arise from global inequities. All of us who practice, teach and study PR should be sensitive to the implied responsibility PR has for globalization and its effects.

How do PR academics and practitioners view globalization?

PR practitioners are challenged to balance local (national) and global (international) expertise. The catchphrases 'think global, act local' and 'glocalization' reflect the political and economic tensions of collaborative campaigns that use culturally specific (local) PR businesses in liaison with international consultancies. However, a focus on what is essentially *the politics of consultancy practice* means that the larger picture may be ignored.

For instance, established nation-states have greater resources at their disposal to promote their vision of world order through government information services or through funded agents whose responsibility is cultural diplomacy. Public relations has long been established with nation-building activities, partly because such activities are essential at times of crisis (threats to peace or unity) when the relationship between PR and propaganda is most blurred. PR academic Mohan Dutta-Bergman has suggested the use of **subaltern studies** 'as an alternative discursive space for understanding participatory communication and marginalization practices in the Third World' (Dutta-Bergman, 2005: 268). He argues that this strategy could help acknowledge the voices of marginalized people and their resistances to an international public sphere dominated by elite, Western-style discourses of transnational capitalism and democratic imperialism. He suggested that the role of PR in development communication should be to challenge the status quo and involve subaltern voices in dialogue, so that the role of PR:

> becomes one of facilitating the articulation of subaltern voices by listening to them and documenting them in policy-oriented forums. The process of engaging in dialogue with marginalized people brings forth the critical issues as defined by subaltern participants. The approach of listening to the subaltern voices fundamentally changes the way development communication is practised; participation does not simply remain a means to achieving the ends pursued ... [it] becomes the core of the praxis, drawing on the agency of subaltern participants in choosing their own destiny. [Thus] PR ... actively participates in resistance against acts of marginalization and silencing. (Dutta-Bergman, 2005: 287)

For some, public relations can be seen to be part of the ideological apparatus of world capitalism, as suggested by Miller and Dinan in their critique of public relations:

> Public relations is increasingly a global business activity and the PR industry is intimately linked with the power of capital. It has two key inter-related functions: firstly, to protect and enhance corporate power in order that, secondly, it can promote consumerist ideology and practice. The PR industry is so intimately entwined with capital that it makes sense to argue that PR is global as a result of the globalization of capital and that PR has been instrumental in the globalization of capital. (Miller and Dinan, 2003: 193)

Public relations is thus implicated in a colonization thesis by virtue of its connection with global organizations, at least some of which may be inspired to respond to articulated needs of transnational communities threatened by the scarcity of basic requirements such as clean water, poverty, environmental catastrophe, war or the consequences of political and economic disaster.

Discipline box: Subaltern studies

Subaltern studies developed out of postcolonial studies to engender the perspectives of those who had been colonized or were from cultures that had been colonized. The area seeks to liberate 'edge' perspectives that can:

- sensitize us to the controlling power of dominant perspectives
- alert us to the importance of understanding historical developments that may have long-term impact on the collective unconscious of various cultures and ethnicities; for example Turner's 'frontier thesis' explored the long-term effects on the US psyche of the frontier in its colonial past.

Source: www.lin.virginia.edu/area-studies/subaltern

CRITICAL REFLECTION

- How might a subaltern studies perspective affect our practice of PR?

Globalization: utopia or dystopia?

There are optimistic and pessimistic accounts of globalization. Positive accounts emphasize: 'Advancement in technology, literacy, the development of a common global language ... increase in speed of travel between geographical points

... the empowerment of public opinion ... global access to information' (Sharpe and Pritchard, 2004: 17).

Marshall McLuhan is credited with having coined the phrase 'the global village', a term which might be suggestive of a friendly community. However, this extended quote from McLuhan warns us against idealism:

> The new electronic interdependence recreates the world in the image of a global village ... the world has become a computer, an electronic brain, exactly as in an infantile piece of science fiction. And as our senses have gone outside us, Big Brother goes inside. So, unless aware of this dynamic, we shall at once move into a phase of panic terrors, exactly befitting a small world of tribal drums, total inter-dependence, and superimposed co-existence. ... Terror is the normal state of any oral society, for in it everything affects everything all the time. ... The main effect of electric process ... is to re-tribalise the structure of psychic and social aware-ness. Millions of people sitting around the TV tube, CNN-style, absorbing the mod-ern equivalent of shamanistic lore from the authorized source is closely analogous to the old tribal relations of tyrannous instruction and control. ... The Global Village of corporate consumer values stimulates local peoples to retrieve who they used to be as a protection for their fading identities, for electric process makes us all nobodies desperate for identity. (McLuhan and Zingrone, 1995: 4, 127)

McLuhan's argument may have influenced contemporary media sociologist Professor Brian McNair, who recently noted that: 'Critical anxiety ... is ... focused not merely on the perceived concrete evils of globalized capitalism, but on a more amorphous, existential fear of the consequences on the human psyche of the media environment we now inhabit' (McNair, 2006: 14). McNair argued that such pes-simistic fears are based on conspiracy theories that the globalization of media and culture is one stage in the proliferation of elite power (McNair, 2006: 14).

CRITICAL REFLECTION

- To what extent are you optimistic or pessimistic about the future, and why?

Globalization and the role of PR: the art of diplomacy

Diplomacy manages a nation-state's relationships with other countries and international organizations in order to further its aims. Diplomats manage political relationships and intercourse through temporary residence in other countries and though permanent representation on international bodies such as NATO or the United Nations. There are clear practical similarities between the role of public relations and that of diplomacy:

> In fact it is possible to trace a number of related functions in public relations and diplomacy ... rhetoric, oratory, advocacy, negotiation, peacemaking, counselling, intelligence gathering. There [are] three orders of function ... representations (rhetoric, oratory, advocacy), dialogic (negotiation, peacemaking), advisory (counselling). The function of intelligence gathering describes research and environmental scanning and underpins the issues management function. (L'Etang, 1996a: 15)

In a globalized world the similarity between public relations and diplomacy becomes even more striking. PR practitioners are organizational diplomats operating internationally and negotiating a range of political machineries in multiple economic and social contexts. Some organizations are larger than small countries (L'Etang, 1996a: 18) and some organizations may take on the work of states as pointed out in Chapter 4 in discussions of corporate social responsibility (CSR).

More than a decade ago I contrasted a particular diplomatic framework to public relations models to draw out common assumptions with regard to relationship management and approaches to communication. I argued that applying the diplomatic metaphor to organizations (rather than nation-states) implied that, as corporate diplomats, organizations have 'a specific interest in power broking at an elite level ... and ... the need for representative agents' (public relations practitioners) (L'Etang (citing Mitnick), 1996a: 17). Corporate or governmental elites overlap and in a globalized world share a semi-diplomatic culture (see Box 11.2) within which there is an extended chain of agent relationships which may not be particularly transparent to the outsider. It is in an organization's interests to cast their opponents as politically and ideologically motivated, as captured in the pejorative terms 'activist groups', 'single-issue publics' and 'social activists'. The recognition that such groups exist is a rationale for the existence of PR experts.

Applying diplomatic models to PR

The assumptions that underlie diplomacy were developed by international theorist Martin Wight in the mid-twentieth century. He based his model partially on the ideas of three thinkers: Machiavelli (Realist model), the Dutch diplomat Hugo Grotius (Rationalist model), and the philosopher Immanuel Kant (Revolutionist model). Realist ideas fed into the field of Strategic Studies, Revolutionist ideas into Peace Studies. It is beyond the scope of this chapter to explain the diplomatic models – interested readers can follow up this debate elsewhere (L'Etang, 1996a; 2006c; 2008, forthcoming). Instead, here I will show how these diplomatic models might be applied to PR to demonstrate the assumptions upon which PR work may be based:

Real PR advocates a hard-nosed approach with a clear focus on environmental scanning and issues management. The interests of the organization are placed above all else. The *leit motif* of this model is 'adapt, forestall, facilitate and control' (Wight, cited in L'Etang, 1996a: 28).

Rational PR focuses on reputation and relationship-building, highlighting values of reliability, truth-telling and trustworthiness. Since trusteeship and reciprocity are important principles, corporate social responsibility seems central to this model.

Revolution PR privileges the voice of international citizens in an international public sphere. The role of public relations is to help resolve tensions that inhibit the fulfilment of human potential, so the driving motivation is to make peace.

Applying the diplomatic models to PR highlights various intentions that may underpin representational work on behalf of organizations, not just states. This little exercise also shows that it is possible to derive alternative perspectives about PR from other disciplines and that it is possible to build different typologies (though they might overlap) from those that currently dominate the field.

Exercise

- What types of public relations work seem to fit the three models?
- Why might underpinning assumptions matter?
- What are the implications of the three models for PR practitioners operating internationally in a globalized world?

The comparison between PR and diplomacy reveals possible motivations and assumptions for representative agents of collectivities (organizations or states). The peace-making intentions of 'Revolution PR' suggests that PR obligations lie partially outside the organization, perhaps based on utilitarian principles to maximize happiness. This model implies that PR is a social good. The model also suggests porous and weakened organization boundaries. Globalization has indeed reshaped organizations and knowledge-dependent work is international. Could this be regarded as devolution of power or colonization? Well that depends on who controls the rhetoric. And who is to shape international understandings of global relationships? And who is to represent, negotiate and manage reputations on behalf of those whose livelihood is determined by the corporate and political elites that comprise 'international society'?

Cultural and public diplomacy

Cultural diplomacy is directed at the populations of other countries rather than political elites using cultural means (education, sport, the arts, science and technology, language) to achieve medium- or longer-term foreign policy ends and to render opinion formers in those countries better disposed towards the principal country (L'Etang, 2006c: 374). The nation's cultural capital is offered to target countries to generate goodwill with younger generations. State diplomacy encompasses political and cultural diplomacy. Cultural diplomacy is targeted at hearts and minds of citizens from other countries. In a globalized age, diplomacy has become increasingly *intermestic* (domestic + international) (Crowe, cited in L'Etang, 1996a: 20). Therefore, states need PR to manage public opinion in foreign countries. Cultural diplomacy may also be linked to aid programmes which can be seen as a form of social responsibility – or as a way of finding new markets. Such programmes may be seen as part of globalization processes.

Box 11.2 is another type of example of PR in its diplomatic role. It displays the promotion of a PR company seeking to orchestrate a 'summit' focused on Britain's international reputation. The PR industry's alignment with elite power was exemplified by the conference organized by TMS Consulting Group Europe, in co-operation with the Management School, London. Described in diplomatic discourse as 'a summit', the brochure claimed that 'the theme will be hotly debated on TV and radio...'. The sales pitch expounded themes of global terrors, nationalism and patriotism.

Box 11.2   Promotional flyer for conference: 'Enhancing Britain's global reputation: the challenges for business and PR, 26–27 February 2007', TMS Consulting Group

[The conference is for] decision makers, chief executives, managing directors, financial directors, government officials, top public relations practitioners and all CIPR [Chartered Institute of Public Relations], PRCA [Public Relations Consultants' Association] and IPRA [International Public Relations Association] members, Chamber of Commerce, Confederation of British Industries (CBI), Institute of Directors, Chartered Institute of Marketing, media and advertising industry ... executives from the private or public sector, senior military officers and the police.

Britain is globally recognized as a financial and cultural centre that is to be commended, admired and emulated. It also has a strong reputation for tolerance,

(Continued)

(Continued)

human rights, and integrity. More recently, Britain's global reputation has been called into question. Downstream effects of this criticism have consequences that impact on commerce, industry, the government, public relations practice, and the mood and morale of citizens in all walks of life.

Success in winning the 2012 Olympics: Olympic hosting victory has, in some circles, helped to lift the pessimism and at the same time also highlighted the need to resolve the question affecting the country's reputation.

In certain parts of the world, British citizens have become the object of attacks, kidnapping, terrorism and suspicion. British military has suffered accusations of maltreatment of captives and civilians, and the role of the British military has attracted criticism.

Despite recent events, Britain remains a leading tourist destination and executives the world over view British establishments as setting and maintaining standards of excellence.

The dilemma: Recent events do raise interesting questions about the reputation of Britain. Is the reputation sinking or rising? If the reputation is sinking, what are the cause and remedies? If it is rising, what are the causes and how can they be measured and enhanced? What strategies and tactics should be used to strengthen the position of Britain? Who is in charge of maintaining or increasing the reputation of Britain?

The issue of Britain's reputation must be raised at the highest of levels and under a neutral banner on a multi-stakeholder platform that will deal sensitively and professionally with the issue. That is the purpose of this summit.

Source: www.tmssummit.co.uk

CRITICAL REFLECTION

- What discourses emerge from the text in Box 11.2?
- Which groups are privileged and which are othered?
- How should the reputation of a country be evaluated?

In conclusion

This chapter has suggested that the PR industry as a commercial enterprise has contributed to globalization through its work for powerful governments and corporate interests, as well as benefiting (in terms of commissioned work) from that process which has increased international communication activity (political/legal/diplomatic; economic/legal/commercial). Some PR has also accrued to the PR industry as a consequence of negative impacts of globalization and resistances to its effects. It has been suggested that the diplomatic metaphor of PR is appropriate and useful. It presents an alternative framework for thinking about the PR role in a globalized world. The model can be applied to explore assumptions that lie behind PR work at a range of levels, from small organization to state PR or international organizations such as the World Health Organization or corporate bodies. Finally, it has been suggested that there is more room for discussion within the public relations academy of the implications of processes of globalization. Hutchison and Pauly's challenge seems apposite:

> We are concerned about the soul of the profession. Globalization offers a moment of great opportunity for public relations practitioners. Agencies have chosen to capitalize upon that moment by emphasizing their reach and scale, mimicking the wealth and influence of the global corporations they hope to serve. But the more difficult challenges ahead will involve governance and responsibility – the worldwide demand to make the new economic order accountable to democratic politics and local need. Public relations practitioners could claim this moment as their own. After all, they have been thinking local for a long time. (Hutchison and Pauly, 2001: 245)

The question is, will you?

REVIEW

Taking account of the questions raised at the beginning of the chapter and the subsquent discussion, you may now wish to consider the following:

- How is globalization connected to world capitalism? Are they different aspects of the same phenomenon?
- Does globalization contribute to a world society? Is there an 'international public sphere'?
- What implications does globalization have for nation-states?
- In a global world are ethnic and religious affiliations more important to the formation of publics than nationality?

RECOMMENDED READING

Miller and Dinan (2003) present a powerful critique of public relations in a global context. A more favourable account can be found in Sharpe and Pritchard (2004). Sriramesh and Vercic (2004) present a framework for global public relations research and practice, highlighting what they see as important variables. Dutta-Bergman (2005) presents a subaltern interpretation of public relations' global role in supporting dominance. There are also a number of key collections which engage with international PR and globalization: Heath (2001), Sriramesh and Vercic (2003), van Ruler and Vercic (2004).

Key Thinkers and Thought in Public Relations

12

BEFORE YOU READ A SINGLE WORD...

- What are the important questions that need to be answered about public relations practice, and why?
- Who are the most important academics in public relations and why are they so important?
- What aspects of public relations make you curious? Why?

Key concepts

Meta-theory	Post-positivism
Organizational social capital	Rhetoric
Othered	Sociology of the media
Positivism	Theory of Communicative Action
Postmodernism	

Introduction

This chapter returns to themes of the first chapter: paradigms and critical thinking. Thus the book concludes with a brief description of paradigm developments in public relations, including some commentary on the politics of the field.

CHAPTER AIMS

On completion of this chapter you will be able to:

- describe how the public relations discipline has been shaped
- describe the different types of research that have been conducted in public relations
- discuss the various approaches taken in public relations research
- discuss the evolution of the critical paradigm
- write critical research questions

Evolution of the public relations discipline: a British perspective

I begin by reflecting on how the public relations academic field has evolved. In Box 12.1 quotes from a selection of British writers from the 1930s onwards are presented. The examples selected illustrate functional and critical perspectives on public relations. Public relations practice and education emerged first and most fully in the USA. College-level evening classes were already running in the 1920s. In the UK, thinking and writing about public relations took place from the 1920s in relation to government communications, advertising and propaganda (L'Etang, 2004: 20–60). Practitioners began to think about formal education and training within a couple of years of the formation of the then Institute of Public Relations in 1948 (L'Etang, 2004: 186–220). Consequently, the market for qualifications demanded books. Box 12.1 acknowledges some of the early authors from instrumental and critical perspectives in the UK.

Box 12.1   Early British work on public relations: instrumental and critical perspectives

Public relations texts: PR function and technique (instrumental approach)

Wilson, P.A. (1937) 'Public relations departments', in Plant, A. (Ed.) *Some Modern Business Problems*, London: Longmans, pp. 132–133; 149. **Key quote:** 'A public relations officer ... should because of his responsibility for the public good name and public reputation of the concern, be an official of high rank and authority ... an official diplomatist...'

(Continued)

(Continued)

Brebner, J.H. (1949) *Public Relations and Publicity*, London: Institute of Public Administration, p. 8. **Key quote:** 'The more powerful a group is, the more important it is that its public relations and publicity should be well managed and the more difficult it becomes to manage them well. Big animals move slowly, but their movements can be dangerous both to themselves and to others; they have to be careful where they put their feet. The concentration of power and responsibility may be so great that the cultivation of correct attitudes becomes an absolute condition of survival. Such groups are the great nationalized industries of Great Britain like coal mining and transport.'

Institute of Public Relations (1958) *A Guide to the Practice of Public Relations*, London: Newman Neame, p. 5. **Key quote:** 'The world's most urgent need and opportunity are for a more sensitive and penetrating system of communications at every level from the transmission of ideas between peoples to the daily exchange of information and opinion in the workshop and even across the shop counter. That new system must combine both old media or proven authority, notably the press, and new media such as films and radio and television.'

Gloag, J. (1959) *Advertising in Modern Life*, London: Heineman, Chapter IX, pp. 142–150. **Key quote:** 'Powers of persuasion, focused upon known and agreed objectives and accomplished through the use of suitable media ... the PR specialist is concerned with informing and moulding public opinion ... reputation rests on public opinion ... the initial plan in making a PR plan is to find out what people think, why they think in a particular way about an industry or body, and to attempt to change any corporate behaviour that is creating the wrong impression. ... The importance of PR is ... likely to increase still more as democracies become socially more complex and highly organized ... the people who help to make and carry through PR educational work must have first-class brains.'

Black, S. (1962) *Practical Public Relations*, London: Pitman, pp. 8, 13. **Key quote:** 'Commonsense, objectivity, logic and clear thinking are perhaps the most important assets of a successful public relations practitioner and these cannot be taught in the classroom. ... [If] the policy of the organization is contrary to law or to his conscience there can be no doubt that the public relations practitioner should resign immediately.'

Ellis, N. and Bowman, P. (1963) *The Handbook of Public Relations*, London: Harrap, Foreword. **Key quote:** 'This book is published at a time when public relations is in the limelight – a healthily critical limelight. People confuse it with propaganda and hidden persuasion; they forget that it is concerned primarily with communication, an essential ingredient in any democratic society ... there has been no British work devoted to public relations techniques. This book sets out to remedy that omission.'

(Continued)

Derriman, J. (1965) *Public Relations in Business Management*, London: University of London Press, p. 7. **Key quote:** 'This book is primarily for the manager or the director as distinct from the public relations practitioner. ... [PR] is a valuable tool of management. ... It is to make the role of public relations in British management better known that this book has been written.'

Biddlecombe, P. (ed.) (1971) *Goodwill: The Wasted Asset*, London, Business Books, p. 4. **Key quote:** 'Public relations men are forever bleating. ... They want to be loved by management. Yet PR men never bother to explain to management what PR really means. ... PR people should have to account for every single penny in proving the effect of their operations ... communications theory, semantics, cognitive dissonance ... are the passport to not only a far more stimulating and satisfying professional life but to a far more effective form of PR as well.'

Early British critiques of public relations

Pimlott, J.A.R. (1951) *Public Relations and American Democracy*, Princeton, NJ: Princeton University Press, p. 22. **Key quote:** 'Public relations is not a peculiarly American phenomenon. ... No interpretation of the role of public relations practitioners in ... society will be valid unless it is based on what they actually do rather than on what they think they ought to be doing or would like other people to think they are doing.'

West, R. (1963) *PR: The Fifth Estate*, London: Mayflower Books, p. 127. **Key quote:** 'Perhaps conscious of the attacks made on their "calling" ... many PROs use cloudy and elevated language about their trade ... [which] obscures public understanding of what they do. ... They are often preoccupied with the idea of change ... when people care so little for any cause that they leave the business or argument to the experts our society will be ripe for rule by an oligarchy of PROs; and Professor Rollo Swavely will hold the chair of Image Building at Macmillan College, Oxford.'

Kisch, R. (1964) *The Private Life of Public Relations*, London: MacGibbon and Kee, pp. 13, 14. **Key quote:** 'Public relations has suddenly come into the open as the business that has failed to do for itself what it effectively does for others; either through incompetence or because of other hidden reasons. The performance and technique of PR have given it a mystique without increasing public confidence in its value or necessity. ... The position of ... the front men and women of the back-room of big business has been consolidated by their open association with the crusading organizations of finance, industry and commerce ... the barest minimum has been done to justify its standing as a profession capable of making a positive contribution to the national welfare by performing valuable public services.'

(Continued)

Finer, S.E. (1965) *Anonymous Empire: A Study of the Lobby in Great Britain*, London: Pall Mall Press, pp. 136–137. **Key quote:** 'There is nothing intrinsically wrong in a political party ... using a PR firm to advise it in the presentation of its campaign. This represents a rational decision by the party to seek advice on how to present itself most effectively within its limited resources. ... And what is true of the political party's use of PR techniques is true of the anti-nationalization campaign mounted by the Institute of Directors, the steel companies and the like. ... But the whole point of many PR campaigns is to conceal the fact that they are campaigns. ... The Katanga government and the Central African Federation both hired British PR agencies.'

Tunstall, J. (1964) *The Advertising Man in London Advertising Agencies*, London: Chapman and Hall, pp. 155, 182. **Key quote:** 'The range of meaning given to the term "public relations" reflects ... a general vagueness (shared by public relations men themselves) as to what work in this field achieves ... status appears to be an even more nagging obsession for PR men than for advertising. ... The standard method suggested in PR textbooks for checking up on the efficiency of a campaign is to carry out opinion research ... but in the ordinary PR budget ... there is not money available ... the PR man knows that success lies not in effecting some (undemonstrable) change in public opinion about the client, but rather in gaining the client's confidence.'

CRITICAL REFLECTION

- Consider the quotes in Box 12.1. What themes emerge and how resilient have they been? What changes have taken place and why?

Formal PR education in the UK began in the late 1980s (MSc Stirling; BA Bournemouth; BA Leeds Metropolitan University; BA College of St Mark and St John, University of Exeter). More postgraduate degrees were also established in response to the *zeitgeist* of vocationalism, relevant education and the need for British universities to attract more fee-paying students (L'Etang and Pieczka, 1996, 2006). The majority of those recruited to teach on the field came from practice, with a variety of educational backgrounds that included those with and without degrees (L'Etang and Pieczka, 1996, 2006). Faced with fresh-faced students and heavy teaching loads, educators turned to the USA for undergraduate-level textbooks, especially Cutlip, Center and Broom (1985, 1994) and Grunig and Hunt (1984). Both were hugely popular, and Grunig and Hunt attained almost iconic status and has been a structuring influence in the field, even though it was not republished and never appeared as a second edition.

The consequence of this cultural borrowing had some interesting effects. It led to the proselytizing of the rather heavenly 'symmetrical communication' model, which could allow young students (and their teachers) to feel good about their occupation and side-step criticism that they were trainee propagandists. The promotion of the same mantra had some consequences in terms of the relationship between education and the practice, which was made apparent in meetings between the Public Relations Educators' Forum and the Institute of Public Relations, and in letters to *PRWeek*. Practitioners could not always recognize themselves in the theoretical mirror that was held up to them. That affected the credibility of the educational enterprise. Some practitioners expressed impatience with academic interest in defining PR and urged educators to concentrate on research that would directly help the practice. This led to debate over the research agenda and while some discussed whether academics or practitioners should control the agenda, others chose to ignore the debate either as irrelevant or because they did not wish to participate in institutionalized research under the aegis of professional bodies. In fact, the discussion had little immediate impact in the UK, as few teachers were in a position to publish.

US academics also influenced another important aspect of the architecture of the discipline in Europe: the promotion of public relations as 'science'. This presented public relations as an outgrowth of management sciences, technocratic and functional. By linking the discipline to other scientific disciplines, public relations could gain a respectable academic status that could deliver 'strategic' communicators worthy of boardroom status. In the UK, there was a discernible shift from PR's more intuitive roots, expressed variously as 'an art and a science', 'intelligence', 'public service' and also, perhaps, as one of the 'creative' industries.

A 'scientific' approach to public relations (or any other discipline) carries with it certain requirements. Scientific thinking values objectivity and sees knowledge as value-neutral. Consequently, a rigorous hard-core scientific approach uses observation, experiment and statistical methods, such as survey, to test concepts and frameworks in order to determine 'the truth'. A quantitative approach seeks to obtain useful generalizable data. However, it can only provide partial truths, as can be seen in the other half of the yin–yang diagram. Exploratory qualitative approaches provide multiple truths, alternative visions and critical perspectives.

In the UK, first-generation educators struggled to gain status among academic peers. This was partly due to the fact that late entrants to teaching had no mentors in their area and that they were constructed by their institutions solely as teachers of convenient cash-cow courses. In many institutions, even today, some educators carry very heavy teaching loads, which prohibit their ability to produce research in the field. Nonetheless, the UK hosts two PR journals, whose very titles, *Journal of Communication Management* and *Journal of Corporate Communication*, appear to have been chosen to connote functionalism. There is still no PR equivalent of the *European Journal of Communication* or *Australian Journal of Communication* (both of which have published articles on public relations). To my knowledge, no public relations academic sits on the prestigious and influential Research Assessment Exercise (RAE) panels or on the boards of the Economic and Social Research Council (ESRC) or Arts and Humanities Research Council (AHRC). This means that grant applications that could fund PhDs or post-doctoral research are not going to be reviewed by experts in the field and proposals will be subjected to scrutiny from those outside the discipline. Thus the political economy of higher education in the UK tends not to favour the discipline. It should be noted that some very large ESRC grants have been awarded to research public relations – but to teams of media sociologists.

Finally, PR educators have had a strong practice focus and been subjected to the professional body's 'recognition' process, which requires them to prove the functional benefits of teaching. Understandable though this is, it provides a context likely to discourage critical engagements. However, despite the structural disadvantages of working in a new and vocational discipline, a number of academics in a variety of cultural contexts have produced creative and original work outside the main paradigm.

Public relations thinkers

In this section, I endeavour to recount something of the story of PR scholarship. I tackle this with some trepidation since space does not permit an extended discussion and my commentary is necessarily synoptic. What follows, therefore, is offered as my personal 'take' on the field with a necessarily arbitrary selection of authors who have been or are important to the field's development as well as those who are forging new ground. I begin by sketching out the emergence of a dominant paradigm, proceed to brief summaries of some of the key approaches and conclude by highlighting the emergence of a critical paradigm and some of the contributors to that development.

A brief history of PR scholarship

Early educators and researchers were non-specialists who entered public relations education from variable backgrounds. Their hard work established the discipline which is now beginning to diversify. There is a dominant paradigm, a critical paradigm and various approaches that relate to them.

Paradigms are arbitrary and organic, operating systems of patronage. The biggest rewards in terms of status come to those who instigate and promote dominant paradigms, or who are responsible for paradigm shift. Thus academic sources need to be seen in the context of political struggles, not just arguments about ideas. Academia is no more rational than any other workplace! Paradigms are self-referential to the extent that they acknowledge sympathetic others in the paradigm's enterprise. In the early stages it may seem that all scholars are working co-operatively along similar, collegial lines. The impression of a collaborative collective may make it difficult to engage with a subject other than in the terms of those already writing about it. So a dominant paradigm can (unintentionally) stifle different approaches to a subject. Even when different work is conducted, heavy reference is usually made to the dominant paradigm even as those developing new approaches distinguish themselves through contrast and critique.

In terms of sheer bulk, the US currently dominates PR research globally. US scholarship can appear mildly introspective, making few references to European, Australian or New Zealand contributions to the field, while the reverse does not apply. For example, Toth claimed 'critical theory applied to public relations has had only a few champions' but then cited only US scholars (Toth, 2002: 243). The first edition of Sriramesh and Vercic's *Global Handbook on PR* (2004) did not include a chapter on the UK. US texts can betray cultural ignorance or insensivity, for example, referring to the UK as England (Botan and Hazelton, 2006: 5). Finally, the best known Americans, Professors James and Larissa Grunig, were invited to write the introduction to a book which explored European practice and research written by 'the best and the brightest among European professionals and scholars' (van Ruler and Vercic, 2004: xiii). Thus European research is still defined against the standards, expectations and experience of US academics.

The dominant paradigm: excellence and symmetry

I have followed Pieczka in defining 'the dominant paradigm' as comprising a group of (largely US) authors whose empirical research has been scientific and predominantly quantitative, and responsible for the development of the major theoretical framework for the field (Pieczka, 1996b: 143–144, 2006c: 349–350). This approach was the first cohesive theoretical effort to make scientific sense of public relations work and to tie it to essential research and evaluation, as illustrated by the landmark text *Using Research in Public Relations* (Broom and Dozier, 1990). The Excellence project, which began in 1985, attracted substantial funding and a number of key academics based in the USA (Dozier, Ehling, Hon, Repper, Sriramesh), led by Professors James Grunig and Larissa Grunig (who previously published under the name Schneider), and resulted in the publication of *Excellence in Public Relations and Communications Management* (Grunig, 1992). There was also one British member of the research team: Dr Jon White, a consultant, who has been a quiet influence on educational developments on the UK scene. Subsequent texts which also emerged from the same project included *A Manager's Guide to Excellence in Public Relations and Communications Management* (Dozier, Grunig and Grunig, 1995) and work from the feminist Excellence perspective, to which I shall refer later. The 'Excellence Theory' took an organizational approach to PR suggesting that excellent PR was facilitated by, and the consequence of, organic, participative cultures and structures, symmetrical communication, equality and job satisfaction (Grunig et al., 2006: 533–554). 'Excellence Theory' focused on organizational relationships and the attainment of managerial power and influence for the PR role. A key assumption of the dominant paradigm seems to be that academic work should contribute directly to practice. In addition to Excellence, the dominant paradigm has developed a strong focus on relationship-building, ethical persuasion and rhetoric, community-building (Kruckeberg and Starck, 1988; Starck and Kruckeberg, 2001) and on reputation.

The longest-running journal, *Public Relations Review*, was set up in 1974 by Professor Ray Hiebert who has edited PRR for more than 30 years and who published the definitive volume on the leading US practitioner Ivy Lee in 1967. This journal has always included a wide range of articles and subjects in the field, including qualitative and quantitative work. Between 1989 and 1991, three volumes of theoretical and empirical work were published as forerunners to the *Journal of Public Relations Research*, which at the outset was closely associated with the dominant paradigm. In 2006, Elizabeth Toth, a card-carrying member of this group, launched a new research annual, *Best Practices in Public Relations and Communications Management* to 'ensure that theory is connected to practice' (Toth, 2006: 110–111). By contrast, the online journal *PRism*, edited by Elspeth Tilley from Massey University, New Zealand, since 2002, makes a point to encourage diverse perspectives.

To sum up briefly, the dominant paradigm has been functional, applied, and initially focused on systems theory, the ideal of symmetrical communication, the four models based on US history, excellence, effectiveness, public relations roles (manager–technician dichotomy and gender), situational theory and quantitative research. This approach has been globalized by its proponents through control of some publication outlets, conferences and travel. Initially, the approach had high acceptance within Europe (from the UK to Slovenia to Scandinavia) and was welcomed as offering clear frameworks, interesting ideas and ethics. The driving force behind the Excellence paradigm, Professor James Grunig, quite recently stated that, 'we do not believe that different polycentric theories are necessary for each country, region or country of the world' (Grunig, 2006: 56–57). However, Anglophone dominance has inhibited some intellectual exchange, as was made clear in Heike Puchan's analysis of historical and intellectual developments in Germany (2006). In the UK, strategic management influenced some authors (Moss et al., 2000) and marketing, others (Kitchen, 1997).

Resistance to the dominant paradigm emerged in the mid-1990s (Elwood, 1995; L'Etang and Pieczka, 1996; Motion and Leitch, 1996). As Pieczka (1996) pointed out, the dominant paradigm is 'a discourse – not just a tentative proposition about relationships between phenomena, but a way of thinking'. Pieczka (1996) was the one of the first to refer to 'paradigm struggle' in the PR context but more recently the concept has received further attention by Botan and Hazleton (2006). Although various approaches to analyzing PR have now emerged, much of this work is still framed by systems and symmetrical communication and shares the underlying assumptions of the dominant paradigm. Only the critical perspective is truly independent, and even then (and I include myself in this category), reference may be made to the dominant paradigm. In effect, the dominant paradigm has incorporated some perspectives (feminist, rhetorical, relational) and rejected or ignored other critical perspectives. It is quite clear that what counts as 'good theory' and critical theory evidently does not cut the mustard:

> Critics of the symmetrical/excellence approach have spoken up but either the field has failed to see enough merit in what they have said to develop their work into alternative paradigms, or they have limited their remarks to critiques and failed to conduct affirmative research, share their data, and sufficiently open up their own theories to critical discourse. (Botan and Hazleton, 2006b: 9)

Thus, to some extent, critical scholars are **othered** by the dominant paradigm. The fracture in the field partly follows philosophical faultlines in beliefs about the nature of knowledge between those who believe in objective science and those who believe that reality is socially constructed. The objective group draw their perspective from positivism and are likely to value applied, quantitative and statistical research. Those who embrace critical and cultural perspectives (**post-positivism**) value qualitative approaches that facilitate richly patterned and detailed analysis of research participants.

The feminist approach

In the 1990s Professors Larissa Grunig, Elizabeth Toth and Linda Childers Hon followed up the 'roles research' conducted by Professors Glen Broom and David Dozier which showed discrepancies in career progression, salaries and roles between women and men in public relations. Extensive research was conducted in the USA, mostly quantitative and operating on the assumptions of liberal feminism (Grunig et al., 2001; Toth and Aldoory, 2001). Liberal feminism argues that through argument and lobbying women can achieve equal status in society. Radical feminists, on the other hand, believe either that societal structures must be changed (Marxist feminism) or that women should live separately (separatist feminism). Feminist research was largely conducted within the dominant paradigm, for example exploring how women in public relations in the US contributed to excellence and symmetrical communication.

The relational approach

The relational approach 'suggests that balancing the interests of organizations and publics is achieved through management of organization–public relationships' (Ledingham, 2006: 465).

The key concepts include degrees of co-orientation and transparency drawing on social psychology, interpersonal and organizational communication and conflict resolution and mutuality. The main authors of this approach have been Professors Ledingham (2001) and Bruning. Their edited volume (Ledingham and Bruning, 2000) included contributions by Professors Glen Broom, James Grunig and Elizabeth Toth. The quality of relationships and the loyalty of stakeholders is important (Ledingham, 2006: 4571) as is the management of expectations and the public.

The communitarian approach

Professors Kruckeberg and Starck extended dialogic and relational concepts to argue that PR relations served society best when it focused on community building. They suggested that:

> 'a fundamental reason why public relations practices exist today is the loss of community resulting from the new means of communication and transportation ... especially the escalating development of ... technology, multiculturalism and globalism' (Kruckeberg, Starck and Vujinovic, 2006: 487–88).

On this account, it is PR's responsibility to overcome alienation and facilitate the general public's identification with consumer communities.

Communitarianism is a philosophical tradition which emerged from Aristotle, through Cicero, St Augustine, Thomas Aquinas, Edmund Burke, Rousseau and Hegel, and has developed more recently as a critique of individualism put forward by the US philosopher Rawls (Avineri and de-Shalit, 1992: 1–2). Communitarian concepts have particular relevance to PR in relation to internal PR, organizational culture and corporate social responsibility.

The rhetorical approach

Early discussions of **rhetoric** tended to focus on exploring the legitimacy of rhetoric as persuasion. American Professors Elizabeth Toth and Robert Heath teamed up in 1992 to edit an important volume *Rhetorical and Critical Approaches to Public Relations*. This book opened up a number of themes and included the work of critical US scholar Ron Pearson, whose work encompassed PR history and discourse ethics. He was the first person to bring Habermas's framework of the **Theory of Communicative Action** into public relations to highlight discourse ethics and the way in which power could distort communication (Pearson, 1988, 1990; L'Etang, 1996c, 1997, 2006d). Pearson's premature death deprived the PR field of a good scholar and someone who could possibly have established a critical paradigm rather earlier than has turned out to be the case. Subsequently, Professor Heath wrote a number of books exploring issues management and the role of rhetoric to solve PR's 'legitimacy gap' based on the framework of argumentation to achieve consensus and permitting advocacy and persuasion for change within the context of dialogue (Heath, 1994, 1997b; Heath and Coombs, 2006). My own engagement with rhetoric (1996c, 1997, 2006d) was intended to unpack the concept and provide some historical and political context, as well as providing a link to debates in the 1980s and 1990s about postmodernism and 'new rhetorics'. A subsequent exchange between myself and Heath was the consequence of my articulation of the view that a rhetorical position (advocacy/persuasion) was only workable outside the dominant paradigm and that the effort to incorporate the rhetorical approach within systems and symmetrical frameworks was an attempt to reconcile the irreconcilable (Heath, 1997; L'Etang, 1997). Heath has argued that the challenge for PR is to make society more fully functional through the development of mutually beneficial relationships which may, in some circumstances, be comprised of static relationships of minimal disagreement. Elwood's edited collection of essays on rhetoric (1995) included Kathleen German's useful intervention, which explains how the critical world can uncover otherwise taken-for-granted motivations:

> PR is based on a will to power. PR messages reflect the interests of the dominant powers, which in our society are entrenched in political and financial gain. Whatever the aims the goal remains relatively constant. PR messages are grounded in the economic values of the corporation. Critical theory recognizes the

existence of powerful motivations that support the vested interests of capitalism. (German, 1995: 293)

CRITICAL REFLECTION

- Why might it be important for PR practitioners to be aware of the insights of critical theory?
- Should critical thinkers promote CT to practitioners? If so, how and why?

Critical paradigm: power, culture and ethics – towards a sociology of PR?

The critical paradigm is very clearly outside the dominant paradigm. It points out the limitations of systems by asking hard questions about the possession and use of power, the nature of authority, morality and political economy. Critical academics explore questions about propaganda, corporate power, the public sphere, culture and commodification. They might also ask questions about class, race and exploitation. Sociologists of PR might write critiques which they hope will change practice and the assumptions that underpin it. To some degree, work in this paradigm overlaps with that of the **sociology of the media**, and authors in this area have drawn on frameworks and insights from sociology and cultural studies, such as Bourdieu, Weber, Marx, Foucault and Habermas. Critical theory (CT) is firmly entrenched in the qualitative paradigm and often theorizes about theory (**metatheory**). For example, US scholar Greg Leichty applied a theory of cultural rhetoric to explore different discourses about PR (Leichty, 2003). He identified several world views of PR which offer a helpful framework for understanding the field in practice:

- fatalism (low expectations for PR, indifferent to debates about social obligations)
- egalitarianism (critiques the establishment and accuses PR of distorting communication; feminist critiques)
- hierarchy (dominant paradigm aiming to improve PR's status)
- competitive individualist (charismatic)
- freedom (avoids coercive relationships, especially those that demand 'right thinking').

CRITICAL REFLECTION

- Which of the discourses above can you discern in this chapter?

Critical work challenges assumptions of the dominant paradigm so the 'myth of symmetry' was explored by US scholar Robert Brown (2006) who argued that public relations history has been distorted by symmetrical concepts which 'confuses the science of evolution with a belief in evolution'. He also defined different styles of public relations: activism, oratory, narrative and performance. Similarly Stefan Wehmeier from Leipzig challenged discipline conventions when he examined 'the myth of rationality in public relations' to argue that attempts to control and measure public relations were misguided in a complex and dynamic public sphere (Wehmeier, 2006: 213–220).

Until recently the critical paradigm was rather marginalized and in some cases on the geographic periphery. Early critical scholars from the USA were Pearson (1988, 1989), Rakow (1989) and Kersten (1994). There is what might quite reasonably be described as 'The New Zealand School'[1] notably Professors Kay Weaver, Judy Motion, Juliet Roper, Shirley Leitch, David McKie and Debashish Munschi (the last two named edited a significant collection of critical essays in *Public Relations Review* in 2005) and Margalit Toledano. In Europe, some of the earliest critical contributions were from Professors Ronneberger, Manfred Ruhl, Henrik Rebel and Gunther Benetele. Professor Inger Jensen from Roskilde (a university with a strong critical tradition) produced original work on legitimacy. Other important names are Roslyn Petelyn, who has edited the *Australian Journal of Communication* for many years, Professor Betteke van Ruler, Astrid Kersten, Susanne Holstrom, Oyvind Ihlen and, more recently, Rebecca Harris, Lisa Tyler, Tiffany Derville, Priya Kurian, Elizabeth Dougall, Ashli Quesinberry Stokes, Chris Galloway, Mohammed Sidky, Michele Schoenberger-Orgad, Caroline Hodge and Lee Edwards (McKie and Munshi, 2005).

Much work has been done on reconceptualizing publics. Key work has been done on inactive publics (Hallahan, 2000), and Leitch and Neilson (2001) and others have explored the notion of publics in the context of a risk society (Jones, 2002; Demetrious, 2006). In the UK, Kevin Moloney has written on spin doctoring and propaganda (2000). Barry Richards, from the University of Bouremouth, contrasted terrorism and PR as forms of public communication highlighting the spectacular and performative aspects of power-driven (military-driven) communication and the challenges these present democratic regimes (Richards, 2004). Dutta-Bergman (2005) has produced radical work on development and participatory communication issues in relation to subaltern theory. New and exciting work on power, which employs Bourdieu as a framework, has been written by Oyvind Ihlen from the University of Oslo (Ihlen, 2002, 2004a, 2004b, 2005) and Lee Edwards from Leeds Business School (2006, 2007). Ihlen's work connects interestingly with the relational approach as he likens relationships to **organizational social capital**, a concept he has adopted from Bourdieu's framework of capital employed by individuals.

- economic capital (money, property)
- cultural capital (knowledge, skills, qualifications)
- social capital (connections and membership of groups)

Ihlen argued that analysis of the combination of various types of organizational capital helps us to understand 'relative power distributions and how public relations contribute to them' (Ihlen, 2005: 496).

Lee Edwards (2007) also used Bourdieu and similarly argued that 'adopting a relational view of PR as a profession defined by its relationships will help explicate power more effectively' (Edwards, 2006: 22). Edwards' approach highlights the deceit involved in PR work that disguises organizational intent and consequently distorts relationships: 'PR practitioners, for whom language is at the heart of their work, as symbolic producers, transforming or disguising interests into distorted meanings and legitimising arbitrary power relations...' (Edwards, 2006: 230). But she also pointed out that PR is not entirely responsible because the occupation is dependent upon, and beholden to, organizational interests. She also argued *contra* Ihlen, that organizational power is embedded, requiring critical review.

Thomas Mickey's books introduced the notion of deconstruction to PR to try to show that PR plays a role in social construction. His work marked an invaluable, if controversial, turn in the field towards cultural studies, ideology and consumption (Mickey, 2003; see also Derville, 2003; McKie, 2003). A linguistic approach to rhetoric was taken by Anne Surma from Murdoch University, Australia, who took a critical discourse analytic approach to examining organizational texts to explore themes such as ethics and power (Surma, 2005, 2006b).

As noted in Chapter 10, Americans Curtin and Gaither have drawn on cultural studies to develop a new approach to thinking about PR and, from the UK, Caroline Hodges has produced exceptionally interesting empirical work exploring practitioner culture (Hodges, 2005, 2006), as has Magda Pieczka in her ethnographic research into public relations expertise and the concept of 'chemistry' (Pieczka, 2006b). And mention should also be made of Derina Holtzhausen (2000, 2002a, 2002b) based in the US, whose work is based on **postmodernism**, and aims to free PR from its narrow definition as organizational communication management to argue that symmetry can be seen as manipulation and management control. Holtzhausen argued that the 'postmodern PR practitioner' would 'serve as the conscience and change agent of the organization' (Holtzhausen, 2000: 105), thus apparently using postmodernism to support a core myth in public relations (L'Etang, 2003).

According to Holtzhausen, it is the responsibility of PR practitioners to democratize organizations internally and externally (Holtzhausen, 2000). She argued very interestingly that it is not the role of public relations 'to strive for consensus' (as in the dominant paradigm), but to identify 'tensors between the organization and internal and external publics' in order to expose and acknowledge differences, a position which seems quite similar to the ideas of Mary Parker Follett (discussed in Chapter 8). A somewhat functionalist response to Holtzhausen emerged, suggested that 'postmodern theorists must have a "cash value" for modern public relations practitioners to use their ideas' (Toth, 2002: 243).

However, one could argue that Holtzhausen's project is distorted by instrumental objectives to find ethical justification to the PR role. (This drive remains a consistent theme in the field, for example Tilson and Alozie (2004) chose to title their edited collection *Towards the Common Good*). Furthermore, one might question whether Holtzhausen's project is truly postmodern in the sense of evading an over-arching theoretical framework rather than a critical project concerned with liberation from power control. (You might wish to refer back to Chapter 10 and the section on postmodernism.

Critical thinkers 'do different' (the motto of the University of East Anglia which I had the good fortune to attend in the mid-1970s) and 'make strange' the taken-for-granted aspects of PR. Critical work in public relations has developed considerably in the last decade and its proponents now publish in the main journals. At some point in the not too distant future, those who research in the critical tradition will surely have their own journal. While this will doubtless enhance the status of critical PR, it is to be hoped that this will not result in the balkanization of the field.

Box 12.2   Postmodernism and PR – a perspective shared by Professor David McKie, University of Waikato, New Zealand

'(Un)Disciplining Postmodernism

I call myself a partial postmodernist for a number of reasons. I am partial, firstly, in the sense of being less than completely committed and this is not just because it is hard to commit totally to a term that defies definition. Although the failure to define the postmodern has been characterised as intellectual sloppiness, or proof that the concept is so vague as to be worthless, I see the struggles to define its meaning as struggles about the nature of contemporary reality. If postmodern versions of reality are accepted as contemporary realities, then material consequences

(Continued)

follow. Arguments over what is real, and, therefore, what is politically realistic, are not likely to be resolved semantically because they concern struggles for power. In those struggles, I am also partial, in the other sense of being interested (or baised) in favour of an open, egalitarian, and inclusive social order that respects the environment and promotes sustainable enterprise (see McKie and Munshi, 2007). In fact, much public relations practice that I admire has been generated by activist groups. While, traditionally, activism is not seen as part of the field or discipline, I favour "undisciplining" it in order that activist practices (and academic consideration of them) are acknowledged as innovative and socially important public relations.

I am also partial to, in the sense of fond of, postmodernism because its concerns contextualize key concerns of contemporary knowledge in general and public relations in particular. I particularly value the postmodern emphasis on the importance of the following three postmodern Rs in understanding the present: 1) an end to ethnocentrism by *relativising* the single truth pf the western male as the apex of human achievement; 2) an attack on modernism's in-depth map of reality by showing that *referencing*, or adequately representing, the world requires multiple maps and different levels of cartography; and 3) a demand for *reflexivity* by asking all questioners to reflect back on how their own position influences the construction and credibility of different truths and multiple realities.

I see these three Rs as essential to present-day public relations education and practice. The first R, *relativising*, works to check tendencies to see US public relations – or any single national or continental public relations body of work – as the prototype for the rest of the world. As the growth of other national histories and research (see, for example, L'Etang, 2004; Toledano, 2005) has established, it is not, and should not be. There is much to deplore as well as admire in the North American field and so it needs to be drawn from selectively, especially as it can be significantly inept in dealing with nations whose commerce, culture and politics differ dramatically (see, for example, Holtzhausen, Petersen and Tindall's 2003 account of the inapplicability of symmetry to South African conditions). The US has much to learn from, as well as to teach to, other nations and continents. The second R, *referencing*, applies a similarly useful corrective to spread of questionable assumptions. Action to avert global warming, for example, has been held back because a climate change denial industry was allowed to peddle false representations into the mainstream media. The third R, *reflexivity*, asks that the discipline as a whole, and individual practitioners, reflect on their actions and impacts in the light of changing circumstances. Such reflection forms the foundation for acting to avoid unethical behaviours or for working proactively to generate life-enhancing outcomes for the natural and social environment. And I am very partial to that happening for the good of the profession and the planet'.
Professor David McKie, University of Waikato, New Zealand

Summary

My synoptic review has shown that while there is healthier variety in the field of PR, the dominant paradigm is still alive and well. The dominant paradigm is uneven in its acknowledgement of new developments; for example, while many perspectives were included in the mammoth Sage *Handbook of Public Relations*, edited by Professor Heath (2001) (a very useful starting point for dissertation students). Professors Botan and Hazleton's new edition of *Public Relations Theory* (1989), *Public Relations Theory II* (2006a), excludes 'edge' perspectives (McKie and Munshie, 2004: 243) and is, alongside Toth (2007), probably the most recent summing up of the dominant paradigm:

> More people have done more research using [the symmetrical/excellence approach] than any other ... having one clearly dominant theory raises its own questions ... scholarly research moves forward by competition between differing perspectives, not by the domination of any one perspective ... the lack of a paradigm struggle is a characteristic, not of having found the 'truth' but of having given up the search. ... The lack of a dynamic, changing and challenging theoretic landscape in public relations is not a criticism of the dominant paradigm, or its adherents. Rather it is a criticism of the rest of the field for failing to develop, test and defend other strong ideas. (Botan and Hazleton, 2006b: 16–17)

The quote above neatly illustrates how a paradigm works in practice in shaping assumptions and world views of what is important, what counts as good research and what is therefore worthy of attention.

As for the future of critique, the signs seem very promising. Whether or not the dominant paradigm cares to notice or not, there is evidence for claiming that a *sociology of public relations* is emergent, if not yet recognized as such (Pieczka, 2006: 328–329).

In conclusion

This chapter has given a brief outline of some of the main research themes in the field and an indication of the politics of the field. It has defined two main paradigms and explained something of their approach. Where public relations now goes as a discipline and a practice is now largely up to you.

RECOMMENDED READING

Without doubt essential reading is Heath's mammoth volume *Handbook of Public Relations* (2001) and Botan and Hazleton's *Public Relations Theory II* (2006a). For contrast and a selection of some critical perspectives see *Public Relations: Critical Debates and Contemporary Practice* (L'Etang and Pieczka, 2006). There are also important contributions by Merten, Homstrom, Raupp, Burkhart and Bentele in van Ruler and Vercic (2004). Those who wish to track back European developments could usefully explore Benetele, Rebel, Jensen and van Ruler in Moss, MacManus and Vercic (1997).

Finally it would be remiss of me not to mention McKie and Munshi's *Reconfiguring Public Relations: ecology, equity and enterprise* which has the ambitious aim to reshape the field academically and in practice arguing that,

> conversations constitute realities and reconfiguring public relations means changing its conversations. For that reason we frequently challenge the content, ideas and thinkers of the discussion currently framing the field, and introduce fresh subject matter, different theories, and previously unheard voices ... words from Waikato might also perturb PR across the other side of the world. (2007: 2)

However, despite the wealth of non-PR references, McKie and Munshi focus strongly on the dominant paradigm and also seek to find an acceptable role for PR, for example citing the sociologist Giddens because his work seems to present a clear agenda where PR might act to broaden democracy and foster more inclusive social cohesion both inside of and outside of national boundaries (McKie and Munshi, 2007: 58).

Note

Kay Weaver obtained her doctorate at the University of Stirling, which houses the Stirling Media Research Institute, the base for several years of a number of academics producing critical work about public relations (Professor Philip Schlesinger, Professor Brian McNair, Professor David Miller and also Magda Pieczka and Jacquie L'Etang – only L'Etang remains located in Scotland).

Bibliography

Ackroyd, S. and Thompson, P. (1999) *Organizational Misbehaviour*, London: Sage.

Adam, B., Beck, U. and van Loon, J. (2000) *The Risk Society and Beyond: Critical Issues for Social Theory*, London: Sage.

Adams, L., Amos, M. and Munro, J. (eds) (2002) *Promoting Health: Politics and Practice*, London: Sage.

Allaire, Y. and Firsirotu, M. (1984) 'Theories of organizational culture', *Organization Studies*, 5(3): 193–226.

Allan, S. (2004) *News Culture* (2nd edition), Maidenhead: Open University Press.

Alvesson, M. and Berg, P.O. (1992) *Corporate Culture and Organizational Symbolism*, Berlin: de Gruyter.

Alvesson, M. and Due Billig, Y. (1997) *Understanding Gender and Organizations*, London: Sage.

Alvesson, M. and Willmott, H. (1992) *Critical Management Studies*, London: Sage.

Alvesson, M. and Willmott, H. (1996) *Making Sense of Management: A Critical Introduction*, London: Sage.

Amnesty International (2003) The Human Rights Responsibilities of Companies: New Draft UN Norms Provide Guidelines for Business, Business and Human Rights Resource Centre. Available at: www.business-humanrights.org (accessed August 2006).

Andreasen, A. (1995) *Marketing Social Change: Changing Behaviour to Promote Health, Social Development and the Environment*, San Francisco: Jossey-Bass.

Andreasen, A. (2006) *Social Marketing in the 21st Century*, London: Sage.

Andrews, K. (1968) 'Introduction', in Barnard, C. *The Functions of the Executive*, Cambridge, MA: Harvard University Press, pp. vii–xxi.

Argyris, C. (2001) 'Foreword', in Jackson, B. *Management Gurus and Management Fashions*, London: Routledge, pp. ix–xii.

Al Saqur, L.H. (2007) 'Promoting social change in the Arab Gulf: two case studies of communication programmes in Kuwait and Bahrain'. Unpublished thesis, University of Stirling, Scotland.

Asante, M.K. and Gudykunst, W.B. (1989) *Handbook of International and Intercultural Communication*, Newbury Park, CA: Sage.

Ashkanasy, N., Wilderom, C. and Peterson, M. (eds) (2000) *Handbook of Organizational Culture and Climate*, London: Sage.

Avinieri, S. and de-Shalit, A. (1992) *Communitarianism and individualism*, Oxford: Oxford University Press.

Balmer, J.T. and Greyser, S. (eds) (2003) *Revealing the Corporation: Perspectives on Identity, Image, Reputation, Corporate Branding and Corporate-Level Marketing*, London: Routledge.

Banks, S.P. (1995) *Multicultural Public Relations: A Social Interpretive Approach*, London: Sage.

Barker, P. (1998) *Michel Foucault: An Introduction*, Edinburgh: Edinburgh University Press.

Barley, S.R. and Kunda, G. (2004) *Gurus, Hired Guns and Warm Bodies*, Princeton, NJ: Princeton University Press.

Barnard, C. (1968) *The Functions of the Executive*, Cambridge, MA: Harvard University Press.

Bate, R. (ed.) (1999) *What risk? Science, politics and public health*, Butterworth Heinnemann.

Beattie, A. (1991) 'Knowledge and control in health promotion: a test case for social policy and social theory' in Gabe, J., Calnan M. and Bury M. (eds), *The sociology of the health service*, London: Routledge.

Beck, U. (1992) *Risk Society: Towards a New Modernity*, London: Sage.

Bell, D. and Hollows, J. (2005) *Ordinary Lifestyles: Popular Media, Consumption and Taste*, Maidenhead: Open University Press.

Bennett, A. (2005) *Culture and Everyday Life*, London: Sage.

Bennett, P. and Calman, K. (eds) (1999) *Risk Communication and Public Health*, Oxford: Oxford University Press.

Bentele, G. (2005) 'The theory of public trust as a PR theory'. Conference paper presented at International Communication Association, 26–30 May, New York.

Berger, B. (2005) 'Power over, power with, and power to relations: critical reflections on public relations, the dominant coalition and activism' *Journal of Public Relations Research* 17(1): 5–28

Berger, B. (2007) 'Public relations and organizational power' in Toth, E. (ed.), *The future of excellence and communication management: challenges for the next generation*, Festschrift. Mahwah, NJ, Lawrence Erlbaum Associates: 221–234.

Berger, B. and Reber, B. (2006) *Gaining Influence in Public Relations: The Role of Resistance in Practice*, Mahwah, NJ: Lawrence Erlbaum Associates.

Bernstein, D. (1984) *Company Image and Reality: A Critique of Corporate Communications*, Eastbourne: Holt, Rinehart and Winston Ltd.

Bettinghaus, E.P. and Cody, M.J. (1994) *Persuasive Communication*, Fort Worth, TX: Harcourt Brace.

Biddlecombe, P. (1968) *International Public Relations Encyclopaedia*, London: Grant Helm.

Biddlecombe, P. (ed.) (1971) *Goodwill: The Wasted Asset*, London: Business Books.

Bilton, C. (2006) *Management and Creativity*, Oxford: Blackwell.

Black, A. (2006) 'Dignity in dying calls in Brocklehurst for top job', *PRWeek*, 20 October: 10.

Black, S. (1962) *Practical Public Relations*, London: Pitman.

Blumer, H. (1948) 'Public opinion and public opinion polls', *American Sociological Review*, 13: 542–554.

Blumer, H. (1966) 'the man, the public and public opinion' in Berelson, B. and Janowitz, M. (eds), *Reader in public opinion and communication*, New York, Free Press: 43–53.

Borghetti, G. (2003) 'The history of Italian PR: from prehistory to innovation'. Dissertation submitted as part fulfilment of the MSc in Public Relations, University of Stirling, Scotland.

Botan, C.H. and Hazleton, V. (eds) (1989) *Public Relations Theory*, Mahwah, NJ: Lawrence Erlbaum Associates.

Botan, C.H. and Hazleton, V. (eds) (2006a) *Public Relations Theory II*, Mahwah, NJ: Lawrence Erlbaum Associates.

Botan, C.H. and Hazleton, V. (2006b) 'Public relations in a new age', in Botan, C.H. and Hazleton, V. (eds), *Public Relations Theory II*, Mahwah, NJ: Lawrence Erlbaum Associates, pp. 1–20.

Bourdieu, P. (1973) 'Les Temps Moderne' in Mattelart, A. and Sieqelaub, S. (eds), *Communication and class struggle*. New York, International General.

Bourdieu, P. (1979) *Distinction: A Social Critique of the Judgement of Taste*, London: Routledge.

Bowie, N. (1990) 'Empowering people as an end for business', in Enderle, G., Almond, B. and Argandona, A. (eds), *People in Corporations: Ethical Responsibilities and Corporate Effectiveness*, Dordrecht and London: Kluwer Academic Publishers.

Bowen, S. (2003) '"I thought it would be more glamorous": preconceptions and misconceptions among students in the public relations principles course', *Public Relations Review*, 29: 199–214.

Boyle, R. (2006) *Sports Journalism: Contexts and Issues*, London: Sage.

Boyne, R. (2003) *Risk*, Buckingham: Open University Press.

Bracht, N. (ed.) (1999) *Health Promotion at the Community Level*, London: Sage.

Brebner, J.H. (1949) *Public Relations and Publicity*, London: Institute of Public Administration.

Bromley, D.B. (1993) *Reputation, Image and Impression Management*, Chichester: John Wiley and Sons.

Broom, G. and Dozier, D. (1990) *Using Research in Public Relations*, Harlow: Prentice Hall.

Brown, J.A.C. (1963) *Techniques of Persuasion: From Propaganda to Brainwashing*, Harmondsworth: Penguin.

Brown, R.E. (2006) 'Myth of symmetry: public relations as cultural styles', *Public Relations Review*, 32(3): 206–212.

Bryman, A. (2001) *Social Research Methods*, Oxford: Oxford University Press.

Calas, M. and Smircich, L. (eds) (2003) 'Introduction: spirituality, management and organization', *Organization*, 10(2): 327–328.

Campbell, F.E., Herman, R.A. and Noble, D. (2006) 'Contradictions in "reputation management"', *Journal of Communication Management*, 10(2): 191–196.

Cornegre, D. (1936) *How to Win Friends and Influence People*, New York: Simon and Schuster.

Chandiramani, R. (2006) 'Full Sunday trading will be tricky sell' *PRWeek*, 16 June: 19.

Chandiramani, R. (2006) 'The next generation: 29 under 29' *PRWeek,* 30 June: 19–23.

Chandiramani, R. (2006) 'Full Sunday trading will be tricky sell' *PRWeek,* 16 June: 19.

Chaney, D. (1996) *Lifestyles*, London: Routledge.

Citigroup Giving in Asia Pacific: 2005 Community (Annual Report), Citigroup.

Clampitt, P. (2000) 'The questionnaire approach' in Hargie, O. and Tourish, D. (eds), *Handbook of Communication Audits for Organizations*, London: Routledge. pp. 45–65.

Clarkson Centre for Business Ethics (1999) *Principles of Stakeholder Management*, Toronto: University of Toronto, Canada.

Cline, C., Smith, H., Johnson, N., Toth, E. and Turk, J. (1986) *The Velvet Ghetto: Summary Report.* Available at: http://www.iabc.com/fdtnweb/pdf/velvetghetto (accessed 20 October 2006).

Coalter, F. (2006) *Sport in development: a monitoring and evaluation manual*, London: UK Sport.

Cohen, S. (1972) *Folk devils and moral panics: the creation of the mods and rockers*, London: McGibbon and Kee.

Collinson, D. and Hearn, J. (1996) *Men as Managers, Managers as Men: Critical Perspectives on Men, Masculinities and Managements*, London: Sage.

Cooper, B.H. (1982) 'Accentuating the positive', in McLaurin, R. (ed.), *Military Propaganda: Psychological Warfare and Operations*, New York: Praegar, pp. 310–312.

Corneissen, J. (2004) *Corporate Communication: Theory and Practice*, London: Sage.

Corrigan, P. (1997) *The Sociology of Consumption*, London: Sage.

Cottrell, S. (2005) *Critical Thinking Skills*, Basingstoke: Palgrave Macmillan.

Covey, S.R. (1989) *The 7 habits of Highly Effective People: Powerful Lessons in Personal Change*, London: Simon & Schuster.

Cowlett, M. (2006a) 'London's youth games piggyback 2012 fever', *PRWeek*, 10 February: 21.

Cowlett, M. (2006b) 'Science museum puts Brunel snaps on show', *PRWeek*, 15 September: 21.

Cowlett, M. (2006c) 'Campaigns to the Common Good' *PRWeek,* 6 October: 22.

Curran, J. (ed.) (2000) *Media Organisations in Society*, London: Arnold.

Curran, J. and Gurevich, M. (eds) (2005) *Mass Media and Society* (4th edition), London: Hodder Arnold.

Curtin, P. and Gaither, T.K. (2005) 'Privileging identity, difference and power: the circuit of culture as a basis for public relations theory', *Journal of Public Relations Research*, 17(2): 91–115.

Curtin, P. and Gaither, T.K. (2007) *International Public Relations: Negotiating Culture, Identity and Power*, London: Sage.

Curtis, M. (1991) 'Introduction', in Lippman, W., *Public Opinion*, New Brunswick, NJ: Transaction Publishers, pp. xi–xxxvi.

Cutlip, S.M., Center, A. and Broom, G.M. (1994) *Effective Public Relations* (7th edition), Harlow: Prentice Hall.

Daugherty, E. (2001) 'Public relations and social responsibility', in Heath, R. (ed.), *Handbook of Public Relations*, London: Sage, pp. 389–402.

Davis, A. (2002) *Public relations democracy: public relations, politics and the mass media in Britain*, Manchester: Manchester University Press.

Davis, A. (2004) *Mastering Public Relations*, Basingstoke: Palgrave Macmillan.

de Certeau, M. (1984) *The Practice of Everyday Life*, Berkeley: University of California.

Deacon, D., Pickering, M., Golding, P. and Murdock, G. (1999) *Researching Communications*, London: Arnold.

Demers, D. (ed.) (2003) *Terrorism, Globalization and Mass Communication*, Washington, DC: Marquette Books.

Demetrious, K. (2006) 'Active voices', in L'Etang, J. and Pieczka, M. (eds), *Public Relations: Critical Debates and Contemporary Practice*, Mahwah, NJ: Lawrence Erlbaum Associates, pp. 93–110.

Denman, S., Moon, A., Parsons, C. and Stears, D. (2003) 'The future of the health promoting movement' in Sidell, M., Jones, L., Katz, J., Peberdy, A. and Douglas, J. (eds), *Debates and dilemmas in promoting health: a reader*, (2nd edition) Basingstoke: Palgrave Macmillan: 383–392.

Derriman, J. (1965) *Public Relations in Business Management*, London: University of London Press.

Derville, T. (2003) 'LEA: liberating expressive authorship or licensing editorial abdication? Another view', *Public Relations Review* 29(2): 219–221.

Deveney, C. (2006) 'Man of the world', *Scotland on Sunday* 6 August: 7–13.

Dhoklia, R. and Dhoklia, N. (2001) 'Social marketing and development', in Bloom, P. and Gundlach, G. (eds), *Handbook of Marketing and Society*, London: Sage, pp. 486–505.

DiFonzo, N. and Bordia, P. (2000) 'How top PR professionals handle hearsay: corporate rumours, their effects and strategies to manage them', *Public Relations Review*, 26(2): 173–190.

Dillard, J.P. and Pfau, M. (eds) (2002) *The Persuasion Handbook: Developments in Theory and Practice*, London: Sage.

Douglas, M. (1987) *How Institutions Think*, London: Routledge.

Downie, R.S., Tannahill, C. and Tannahill, A. (1996) *Health Promotion Models and Values*, Oxford: Oxford University Press.

Downing, J., with McQuail, D., Schlesinger, P. and Wartella, E. (eds) (2004) *The Sage Handbook of Media Studies*, London: Sage.

Dozier, D. and Broom, G. (2006) 'The centrality of practitioner roles to public relations theory' in Botan, C. and Hazleton, V. (eds), *Public relations theory II*, Mahwah, New Jersey: Lawrence Erlbaum Associates, pp. 137–170.

Dozier, D., with Grunig, J. and Grunig, L. (1995) *A Manager's Guide to Excellence in Public Relations and Communication Management*, Mahwah, NJ: Lawrence Erlbaum Associates.

Drucker, P. (1995) 'Introduction', in Graham, P. (ed.), *Mary Parker Follett: Prophet of Management: A Celebration of Writings from the 1920s*, Boston, MA: Harvard Business School Press, pp. 1–10.

du Gay, P. (ed.) (1997) *Production of Culture/Cultures of Production*, London: Sage.

du Gay, P. (2000) 'Markets and meanings: re-imagining organizational life', in Schultz, M., Hatch, M.J. and Larsen, M.H. (eds), *The Expressive Organization*, Oxford: Oxford University Press, pp. 66–76.

Duherich, J. and Carter, S. (2000) 'Distorted images as reputation repair', in Schultz, M., Hatch, M.J. and Larsen, M.H. (eds), *The Expressive Organization*, Oxford: Oxford University Press, pp. 97–114.

Duncan, M., Cahill, F. and Heighway, P. (2006) *Health and Safety at Work Essentials*, London: Lawpack.

Dutta-Bergman, M.J. (2005) 'Civil society and public relations: not so civil after all', *Journal of Public Relations Research,* 17(3): 267–289.

Edelstein, A. (1997) *Total Propaganda: From Mass Culture to Popular Culture*, Mahwah, NJ: Lawrence Erlbaum Associates.

Edwards, L. (2006) 'Rethinking power in public relations', *Public Relations Review*, 32(3): 229–231.

Edwards, L. (2007) Exploring power in public relations: a Bourdieusian perspective'. Unpublished thesis. Leeds Metropolitan University.

Egan, J. (2007) *Marketing communications*, London: Thomson.

Eisenberg, E.M. and Goodall, H.L. (2001) *Organizational Communication: Balancing Creativity and Constraint*, Boston/New York: Bedford/St. Martin's Press.

Eisenegger, M. (2005) 'Reputation nurturing as a core function of PR'. Conference paper delivered to International Communication Association, 26–30 May, New York.

Ellis, N. and Bowman, P. (1963) *The Handbook of Public Relations*, London: Harrap.

Elwood, W.N. (ed.) (1995) *Public Relations Inquiry as Rhetorical Criticism*, Westport, CT: Praegar.

Everitt, A. and Hardiker, P., 'Towards a critical approach to evaluation' in Sidell, M., Jones, L., Katz, J., Peberdy, A. and Douglas, J. (eds), *Debates and dilemmas in promoting health: a reader*, (2nd edition), Basingstoke: Palgrave Macmillan, pp. 194–200.

Ewen, S. (1996) *PR! A Social History of Spin*, New York: Basic Books.

Ewles, L. and Simnett, I. (2003) *Promoting Health: A Practical Guide to Health Education*, London: John Wiley and Sons.

Falkheimer, J. and Hiede, M. (2006) 'Multicultural crisis communication: towards a social constructionist perspective'. Conference Paper presented to Eighth Annual EUPRERA Congress, Strategic Communications in a Multi-Cultural Context, University of Central Lancashire, 6–9 September 2006, Carlisle, UK.

Fawkes, J. (2006) 'Public relations, propaganda and the psychology of persuasion', in Tench, R. and Yeomans, L. (eds), *Exploring Public Relations*, Harlow: Prentice Hall, pp. 266–287.

Featherstone, M. (1991) *Consumer Culture and Postmodernism*, London: Sage.

Ferguson, M. (1984) 'Building theory in public relations: interorganizational relationships.' Paper presented at the annual convention of the Association for Education in Journalism and Mass Communication, Gainesville, Florida.

Fineman, S. (ed.) (1993) *Emotion in Organizations*, London: Sage.

Finer, S.E. (1965) *Anonymous Empire: A Study of the Lobby in Great Britain*, London: Pall Mall Press.

Fombrun, C. (1996) *Reputation: Realizing Value from Corporate Image*, Boston, MA: Harvard Business School Press.

Fombrun, C. and van Riel, C. (2003) 'The reputational landscape', in Balmer, J.T. and Greyser, S. (eds), *Revealing the Corporation: Perspectives on Identity, Image, Reputation, Corporate Branding and Corporate-Level Marketing*, London: Routledge, pp. 223–233.

Foucault, M. (1977) *Discipline and Punish*, London: Penguin.

Franklin, B. (1997) *Newszak and News Media*, London: Arnold.

Friedman, M. (1970) 'The social responsibility of business is to increase its profits', *The New York Times Magazine*, September 13.

Frost, C. (2002) *Reporting for Journalists*, London: Routledge.

Gandy, O. (1992) 'Public relations and public polities: the structuration of dominance in the information age', in Toth, E. and Heath, R. (eds), *Rhetorical and Critical Approaches to Public Relations*, Mahwah, NJ: Lawrence Erlbaum Associates, pp. 131–164.

Gard, M. and Wright, J. (2005) *The Obesity epidemic: science, morality and ideology*, London: Routledge.

Garnham, N. (1986) 'The media and the public sphere', in Golding, P., Murdoch, G. and Schlesinger, P. (eds), *Communicating Politics: Mass Communications and the Political Process*, Leicester: Leicester University Press, pp. 37–54.

German, K. (1995) 'Critical theory in public relations enquiry', in Elwood, W.N. (ed.), *Public Relations Inquiry as Rhetorical Criticism*, Westport, CT: Praeger, pp. 279–294.

Giacalone, R. and Rosenfeld, P. (eds) (1989) *Impression Management in the Organization*, Mahwah, NJ: Lawrence Erlbaum Associates.

Giacalone, R. and Rosenfeld, P. (eds) (1991) *Applied Impression Management*, London: Sage.

Giddens, A. (1989) *Sociology*, Cambridge: Polity Press.

Gloag, J. (1959) *Advertising in Modern Life*, London: Heineman.

Goffman, I. (1959) *The Presentation of Self of Everyday Life*, London: Penguin.

Goldhaber, G.M. and Rogers, D. P. (1979) *Auditing organizational communications: the ICA audit*, Dubuque, USA: Kendall.

Goleman, D. (1996) *Emotional Intelligence: Why it Can Matter More than IQ*, London: Bloomsbury.

Goleman, D. (1999) *Working with Emotional Intelligence*, London: Bloomsbury.

Gough-Yates, A. (2003) *Understanding Women's Magazines*, London: Routledge.

Graham, P. (ed.) (1995) *Mary Parker Follett: Prophet of Management: A Celebration of Writings from the 1920s*, Boston, MA: Harvard Business School Press.

Grant, D. and Oswick, C. (eds) (1996) *Metaphor and Organizations*, London: Sage.

Gregory, A. (2000) *Planning and Managing Public Relations Campaigns*, London: Kogan Page.

Grunig, J. (1992) 'Communication, public relations and effective organizations', in Grunig, J. (ed.), *Excellence in public relations and communication management*, Hillsdale New Jersey: pp. 1–30.

Grunig, J. (ed.) (1992) *Excellence in Public Relations and Communication Management*, Mahwah, NJ: Lawrence Erlbaum Associates.

Grunig, J. (2001) 'Two-way symmetrical public relations: past, present and future', in Heath, R. (ed.), *Handbook of Public Relations*, London: Sage, pp. 11–30.

Grunig, J. and Grunig, L. (1992) 'Models of public relations and communication' in Grunig, J. (ed.), *Excellence in public relations and communication management*, Hillsdale New Jersey: 285–326.

Grunig, J. and Grunig, L. (1989) *Public Relations Research Annual* (Vol. 1), Mahwah, NJ: Lawrence Erlbaum Associates.

Grunig, J. and Grunig, L. (1990) *Public Relations Research Annual* (Vol. 2), Mahwah, NJ: Lawrence Erlbaum Associates.

Grunig, J. and Grunig, L. (1991) *Public Relations Research Annual* (Vol. 3), Mahwah, NJ: Lawrence Erlbaum Associates.

Grunig, J. and Grunig, L. (2004) 'Foreword', in van Ruler, B. and Vercic, D. (eds) (2004) *Public Relations and Communication Management in Europe*, Berlin: de Gruyter.

Grunig, J., Grunig, L. and Dozier, D. (2006) 'The Excellence Theory' in Botan, C. and Hazleton, V. (eds), *Public relations theory II*, Mahwah, New Jersey: Lawrence Erlbaum Associates. pp. 21–62.

Grunig, J. and Hunt, T. (1984) *Managing Public Relations*, New York: Holt, Rinehart & Winston.

Grunig, L. (1992) 'Towards a philosophy of public relations' in Toth, E. and Heath, R. (eds), '*Rhetorical and critical perspectives of public relations*, Mahwah, New Jersey: Lawrence Erlbaum Associates: 65–92.

Grunig, L.A., Toth, E.L. and Hon, L.C. (2001) *Women in Public Relations: How Gender Influences Practice*, New York: Guilford Press.

Gwyn, R. (2002) *Communicating health and illness*, London: Sage.

Habermas, J. (1989) *The Structural Transformation of the Public Sphere: An Inquiry into the Category of Bourgeois Society*, Cambridge: Polity Press.

Hall, E.T. (1959) *The Silent Language*, New York: Doubleday.

Hall, E.T. (1976) *Beyond Culture*, New York: Doubleday.

Hallahan, K. (2000) 'Inactive publics: the forgotten public in public relations', *Public Relations Review*, 26(4): 499–515.

Hammer, M. and Champy, J. (1993) *Reengineering the corporation: a manifesto for business*, New York: HarperBusines.

Hammer, M. (1996) *Beyond reengineering: how the process-orientated organization is changing work and lives*, New York: HarperBusines.

Hanson, E. and Eastthorpe, G. (2007) *Lifestyle in medicine*, London: Routledge.

Harcup, T. (2004) *Journalism: Principles and Practice*, London: Sage.

Hargie, O. and Tourish, D. (eds) (2000) *Handbook of Communication Audits for Organizations*, London: Routledge.

Harlow, J. (2006) 'blonde from Esher in a serial killer intrigue' *The Sunday Times*.

Harris, P. (2005) 'The management of public affairs in the UK', in Harris, P. and Fleisher, C. (eds), *The Handbook of Public Affairs*, London: Sage, pp. 86–104.

Harris, P. and Fleisher, C. (eds) (2005) *The Handbook of Public Affairs*, London: Sage.

Harris, P. and Harris, I. (2005) 'Lobbying in the United Kingdom' in Harris, P. and Fleisher, C. (eds), *The Handbook of Public Affairs*, London: Sage, pp. 224–246.

Hart, S. (2003) *Marketing changes*, London: Thomson.

Hartel, C., Kibby, L. and Pizer, M. (2004) 'Intelligent emotions management', in Tourish, D. and Hargie, O. (eds), *Key Issues in Organizational Communication*, London: Routledge, pp. 130–143.

Hartley, J. (1994) 'Culture', in O'Sullivan, T., Hartley, J., Saunders, D., Montgomery, M. and Fiske, J. (eds), *Key Concepts in Communications and Cultural Studies*, London: Routledge, pp. 68–71.

Hartley, J. (1994) 'Postmodernism' in O'Sullivan, T., Hartley, J., Saunders, D., Montgomery, M. and Fiske, J. (eds), *Key Concepts in Communication and Cultural Studies,* London: Routledge.

Hassard, J., Holliday, R. and Willmott, H. (eds) (2000) *Body and Organization*, London: Sage.

Hastings, G. (2007) *Social marketing: why should the devil have al the best tunes?* Butterworth Heinemann Elsevier.

Hazan, B.A. (1976) *Soviet Propaganda: A Case Study of the Middle East Conflict*, New York: John Wiley and Sons.

Hearit, K. (2001) 'Corporate apologia: when an organization speaks in defence of itself', in Heath, R. (ed.), *Handbook of Public Relations*, London: Sage, pp. 501–512.

Heath, R. (1994) *Management of Corporate Communication*, London: Sage.

Heath, R. (1997a) *Strategic Issues Management*, London: Sage.

Heath, R. (1997b) '(Rejoinder) Legitimate "perspectives" in public relations practice: a rhetorical solution', *Australian Journal of Communication*, 24(2): 55–64.

Heath, R. (ed.) (2001) *Handbook of Public Relations*, London: Sage.

Heath, R. and Coombs, T. (2006) *Today's Public Relations*, London: Sage.

Heath, R. and Toth, E. (eds) (1992) *Rhetorical and Critical Approaches to Public Relations*, Mahwah, NJ: Lawrence Erlbaum Associates.

Herbst, S. (1998) *Reading Public Opinion: How Political Actors View the Democratic Process*, Chicago: Chicago University Press.

Herman, E.S. and Chomsky, N. (1988) *Manufacturing Consent: The Political Economy of the Mass Media*, New York: Pantheon Books.

Hiebert, R. (2005) 'Commentary: new technologies, public relations, and democracy', *Public Relations Review*, 31(1): 1–9.

Hinrischen, C. (2001) 'Best practices in the public relations agency business', in Heath, R. (ed.), *Handbook of Public Relations*, London: Sage, pp. 451–460.

Hodges, C. (2005) 'Relaciones humanas: the potential for PR practitioners as cultural intermediaries in Mexico city'. Unpublished PhD thesis, University of Bournemouth, Bournemouth, UK.

Hodges, C. (2006) '"PRP culture": a framework for exploring public relations practitioners as cultural intermediaries', *Journal of Communication Management*, 10(1): 80–93.

Hofstede, G. (1984) *Culture's Consequences: International Differences in Work-Related Values*, London: Sage.

Holtzhausen, D. (2000) 'Postmodern values in PPR', *Journal of Public Relations Research*, 12(1): 93–114.

Holtzhausen, D. (2002a) 'Towards a postmodern research agenda for PR', *Public Relations Review*, 28(3): 251–264.

Holtzhausen, D. (2002b) 'Resistance from the margins: the postmodern PR practitioner as organizational activist', *Journal of Public Relations Research*, 14(1): 57–84.

Holtzhausen, D., Petersen, B., and Tindall, N. (2003) 'Exploding the myth of the symmetrical/asymmetrical dichotomy: public relations models in the New South Africa', *Journal of Public Relations Research*, 15(4): 305–341.

Hornik, R. (ed.) (2002) *Public Health Communication: Evidence for Behaviour Change*, Mahwah, NJ: Lawrence Erlbaum Associates.

Hochschild, A. K. (1983) *The managerial heart*, California: University of California Press.

Howe, A., Owen-Smith, V. and Richardson, J. (2002) 'The impact of a television soap on the NHS Cervical Screening Programme in the north-west of England', *Journal of Public Health Medicine*, 24(4): 299–304.

Huczynski, A. (2004) *Influencing within Organizations* (2nd edition), London: Routledge.

Huczynski, A. (2006) *Management Gurus*, London: Routledge.

Hughes, E. (1958) *Men and their work*, New York: The Free Press.

Hume, D. (1980) *A Treatise of Human Nature*, Oxford: Oxford University Press.

Hutton, J., Goodman, M., Alexander, J. and Genest, C. (2001) 'Reputation management: the new face of corporate PR?', *Public Relations Review*, 27(3): 247–261.

Ihlen, O. (2002) 'Rhetoric and resources: notes for a new approach to public relations and issues management', *Journal of Public Affairs*, 2(4): 259–269.

Ihlen, O. (2004a) 'Norwegian hydroelectric power: testing a heuristic for analyzing symbolic strategies and resources', *Public Relations Review*, 30(2): 217–223.

Ihlen, O. (2004b) 'Rhetoric and resources in public relations strategies: a rhetorical and sociological analysis of two conflicts over energy and the environment', Oslo, Norway: Unipub forlag.

Ihlen, O. (2005) 'The power of social capital: adapting Bourdieu to the study of public relations', *Public Relations Review*, 31(4): 492–496.

Institute of Public Relations (1958) *A Guide to the Practice of Public Relations*, London: Newman Neame.

Ismail, H. (2007) 'From managing ethnic conflict to nation-building: public relations strategies in Malaysian history'. Doctoral work in progress, University of Stirling, Scotland.

Jablin, F. and Putnam, L. (eds) (2001) *The New Handbook of Organizational Communication: Advances in Theory, Research and Methods*, London: Sage.

Jackall, R. (ed.) (1995) *Propaganda*, Basingstoke: Macmillan.

Jackson, B. (2001) *Management Gurus and Management Fashions*, London: Routledge.

Jahansoozi. J. (2006) 'Relationships, transparency and evaluation: the implications for public relations', in L'Etang, J. and Pieczka, M. (eds), *Public Relations: Critical Debates and Contemporary Practice*, Mahwah, NJ: Lawrence Erlbaum Associates, pp. 61–92.

Janis, I. (1972) *Victims of Groupthink: A Psychological Study of Foreign Policy Decisions and Fiascos*, Boston, MA: Houghton Mifflin.

Janis, I. and Mann, L. (1977) *Decision Making*, New York: Free Press.

Jefkins, F. (1977) *Planned Press and Public Relations*, London: Blackie.

Johnson, G. and Scholes, K. (2002) *Exploring Corporate Strategy*, Harlow: Prentice Hall.

Jones, L., Sidell, M. and Douglas, J. (eds) (2002) *The Challenge of Promoting Health*, Basingstoke: Macmillan (Open University).

Jones, R. (2002) 'Challenges to the notion of publics in public relations: implications of the risk society for the discipline', *Public Relations Review*, 28(1): 49–62.

Jowett, G. and O'Donnell, V. (1986) *Propaganda and Persuasion*, London: Sage.

Kanter, R. (1995) 'Preface', in Graham, P. (ed.), *Mary Parker Follett: Prophet of Management: A Celebration of Writings from the 1920s*, Boston, MA: Harvard Business School Press, pp. xiii–xix.

Katz, J., Peberdy, A. and Douglas, J. (2000) *Promoting Health: Knowledge and Practice*, Basingstoke: Macmillan.

Katz, P. (1982) 'Intelligence for psychological operations', in McLaurin, R, (ed.), *Military Propaganda: Psychological Warfare and Operations*, New York: Praegar, pp. 121–154.

Kersten, A. (1994) The ethics and ideology of public relations: a critical examination of American theory and practice in Armbrecht, W. and Zabel, V. (eds), Normative Aspekte der public relations, Opladen Germany, Westdeutcher, Verlag: 109–130.

Kimmel, A.J. (2004) *Rumors and Rumor Control: A Manager's Guide to Understanding and Combating Rumors*, Mahwah, NJ: Lawrence Erlbaum Associates.

King, C. (2006) 'Making the case for an entertainment approach to public relations', *Public Relations Review*, 32(1): 74–76.

Kisch, R. (1964) *The Private Life of Public Relations*, London: MacGibbon and Kee.

Kitchen, P. (1997) *Public Relations Principles and Practice*, London: International Thomson Business Press.

Knight, G. and Greenberg, J. (2003) 'Events, issues and social responsibility: the expanding terrain of corporate public relations', in Demers, D. (ed.), *Terrorism, Globalization and Mass Communication*, Washington, DC: Marquette Books.

Kotler, P., Roberto, N. and Lee, N. (2002) *Social Marketing*, London: Sage.

Krogh, G. and Roos, J. (1995) *Organizational Epistemology*, Basingstoke: Macmillan.

Kruckeberg, D. and Starck, K. (1988) *Public Relations and Community: A Reconstructed Theory*, New York: Praegar.

Lacey, A.R. (1976) *A Dictionary of Philosophy*, London: Routledge.

Laing, R.D. (1974) *Self and Others*, Harmondsworth: Penguin.

Larsson, L. (2006) 'Public relations and democracy – a Swedish perspective', in L'Etang, J. and Pieczka, M. (eds), *Public Relations: Critical Debates and Contemporary Practice*, Mahwah, NJ: Lawrence Erlbaum Associates, pp. 123–143.

Lasswell, H. (1934/1995) 'Propaganda', in Jackall, R. (ed.), (1995) *Propaganda*, Basingstoke: Macmillan.

Lawson, R. and William, J. (2005) 'Promoting fruit and vegetable consumption for improved heath', Web journal *PRism*, Social Marketing Special Issue http://praxis.massey.ac.nz/354 (accessed 15 December 2006).

Lechte, J. (1994) *Fifty Key Contemporary Thinkers: From Structuralism to Postmodernity*, London: Routledge.

Ledingham, J.A. (2000) 'Guidelines to building and maintaining strong organization–public relationships', *Public Relations Quarterly*, 45(3): 44–47.

Ledingham, J.A. (2001) 'Government–community relationships: extending the relational theory of public relations', *Public Relations Review*, 27( ): 285–295.

Ledingham, J.A. (2006) Relationship management: a general theory of public relations' in Botan, C.H, and Hazleton, V. (eds), *Public Relations Theory II*, Mahwah, NJ: Lawrence Erlbaum Associates: 465–484.

Ledingham, J.A. and Bruning, S.D. (eds) (2000) *Public Relations as Relationship Management*, Mahwah, NJ: Lawrence Erlbaum Associates.

Ledingham, J.A., Bruning, S.D. and Wilson, L.J. (1999) 'Time as an indicator of the perceptions and behaviour of members of a key public: monitoring and predicting organization–public relationships', *Journal of Public Relations Research*, 11(2): 167–183.

Leichty, G. (2003) 'The cultural tribes of public relations', *Journal of Public Relations Research*, 15(4): 277–304.

Leitch, S. and Neilson, D. (2001) 'Bringing publics into public relations: new theoretical frameworks for practice', in Heath, R. (ed.), *Handbook of Public Relations*, London: Sage, pp. 127–138.

L'Etang, J. (1988) 'Being good, doing good and looking good: aspects of corporate social responsibility and public relations', dissertation completed in partial fulfillment of the requirements for MSc in Public Relations.

L'Etang, J. (1989) 'Doing good or looking good', *New Consumer*, Summer: 12–13.

L'Etang, J. (1992) 'A Kantian approach to codes of ethics', *Journal of Business Ethics*, 11: 737–744.

L'Etang, J. (1994) 'Public relations and corporate social responsibility: some issues arising', *Journal of Business Ethics*, 13: 111–123.

L'Etang, J. (1996a) 'Public relations as diplomacy' in L'Etang, J. and Pieczka, M. (eds), *Critical Perspectives in Public Relations*, London: International Thomson Business Press, pp. 14–34.

L'Etang, J. (1996b) 'Corporate responsibility and public relations ethics', in L'Etang, J. and Pieczka, M. (eds), *Critical Perspectives in Public Relations*, London: International Thomson Business Press, pp. 82–105.

L'Etang, J. (1996c) 'Public relations and rhetoric' in L'Etang, J. and Pieczka, M. (eds), *Critical perspectives in public relations*', London: International Thomson Business Press, 106–123.

L'Etang, J. (1997) 'Public relations and the rhetorical dilemma: legitimate "perspectives", persuasion, or pandering?', *Australian Journal of Communication*, 24(2): 33–53.

L'Etang, J. (2003) 'The myth of the "ethical guardian": an examination of its origins, potency and illusions', *Journal of Communication Management*, 8(1): 53–67.

L'Etang, J. (2004) *Public Relations in Britain: A History of Professional Practice in the 20th Century*, Mahwah, NJ: Lawrence Erlbaum Associates.

L'Etang, J. (2005) 'Critical public relations: some reflections', *Public Relations Review*, 31(4): 521–526.

L'Etang, J. (2006a) 'Public relations and propaganda: conceptual issues and methodological problems', in L'Etang, J. and Pieczka, M. (eds), *Public Relations: Critical Debates and Contemporary Practice*, Mahwah, NJ: Lawrence Erlbaum Associates, pp. 23–40.

L'Etang, J. (2006b) 'Public relations as theatre: key players in the evolution of British public relations', in L'Etang, J. and Pieczka, M. (eds), *Public Relations: Critical Debates and Contemporary Practice*, Mahwah, NJ: Lawrence Erlbaum Associates, pp. 143–166.

L'Etang, J. (2006C) 'Public relations as diplomacy', in L'Etang, J. and Pieczka, M. (eds), *Public Relations: Critical Debates and Contemporary Practice*, Mahwah, NJ: Lawrence Erlbaum Associates, pp. 373–358.

L'Etang, J, (2006d) 'Public relations and rhetoric', in L'Etang, J. and Pieczka, M. (eds), *Public relations*: *Critical Debates and Contemporary Practice*, New Jersey: Lawrence Erlbaum Associates, 359–372.

L'Etang, J. (2006e) 'Corporate social responsibility and public relations ethics', in L'Etang, J. and Pieczka, M. (eds), *Public Relations: Critical Debates and Contemporary Practice*, Mahwah, NJ: Lawrence Erlbaum Associates, pp. 405–421.

L'Etang, J., Falkheimer, J. and Lugo, J. (2007) 'Public relations and tourism: critical reflections and a research agenda', *Public Relations Review*, 33(1): 68–76.

L'Etang, J. and Muruli, G. (2004) 'Public relations, decolonization and democracy: the case of Kenya', in Tilson, D. and Alozie, E. (eds), *Towards the Common Good: Perspectives in International Public Relations*, London: Pearson, pp. 215–238.

L'Etang, J. and Pieczka, M. (eds) (1996) *Critical Perspectives in Public Relations*, London: International Thomson Business Press.

L'Etang, J. and Pieczka, M. (eds) (2006) *Public Relations: Critical Debates and Contemporary Practice*, Mahwah, NJ: Lawrence Erlbaum Associates.

Lippman, W. (1991) *Public Opinion*, New Brunswick, NJ: Transaction Publishers.

Livingstone, C. (1997) *Promoting the health of the nation*, New York: Pearson Professional Ltd.

Lloyd, H. (1963) *Teach Yourself Public Relations*, London: Hodder and Stoughton.

Lupton, D. (1995) *The Imperative of Health: Public Health and the Regulated Body*, London: Sage.

MacCormack, M.H. (1984) *What They Don't Teach You at Harvard Business School*, London: Collins.

Mackey, S. (2006) 'Misuse of the term "stakeholder" in public relations', web journal *PRism*, 4(1), http://praxis.massey.ac.nz/prism_on-line_journ.html (accessed 7 December 2006).

Maclagen, P. (1998) *Management and Morality*, London: Sage.

Marriott, H. (2006) 'Dress sense' *PRWeek*, 15 September: 17.

McCormack, M. (1984) What They Don't Teach You at Harvard Business School, London:

McElroy, M. (2002) *Resistance to Exercise: A Social Analysis of Inactivity*, Champaign, IL: Human Kinetics.

McGuire, W.J. (1989) 'Theoretical foundations of campaigns', in Rice, R.E. and Atkin, C.K. (eds), *Public Communication Campaigns* (2nd edition), London: Sage, pp. 43–66.

McGuire, W.J. (2001) 'Input and output variables currently promising for constructing persuasive communications', in Rice, R.E. and Atkin, C.K. (eds), *Public Communication Campaigns* (3rd edition), London: Sage, pp. 22–48.

McKay, J. (2000) *The Magazines Handbook*, London: Routledge.

McKie, D. (2003) 'LEA = liberating expansive authorship or licensing editorial abdication?', *Public Relations Review*, 29(2): 215–219.

McKie, D. and Munshi, D. (2005) 'Global public relations: a different perspective', Special issue. *Public Relations Review*, 30(4).

McKie, D. and Munshi, D. (2007) *Reconfiguring public relations: ecology, equity and enterprise,* London: Routledge.

McLaurin, R. (ed.) (1982a) *Military Propaganda: Psychological Warfare and Operations,* New York: Praegar.

McLaurin, R. (1982b) 'Psychological operations and national security', in McLaurin, R. (ed.), *Military Propaganda: Psychological Warfare and Operations,* New York: Praegar, pp. 1–6.

McLuhan, E. and Zingrone, F. (eds) (1995) *Essential McLuhan,* London: Routledge.

McNair, B. (2006) *Cultural Chaos: Journalism, News and Power in a Globalized World,* London: Routledge.

McNally, T. (2005) 'Foreword', in Harris, P. and Fleisher, C. (eds), *The Handbook of Public Affairs,* London: Sage, pp. xx–xx.

McQuail, D. (2000) *McQuail's Mass Communication Theory* (4th edition), London: Sage.

McQuail, D. and Windahl, S. (1981) *Communication Models for the Study of Mass Communication,* London: Longman.

McQuail, D. and Windahl, S. (1993) *Communication models,* (2nd edition) London: Longman.

Maibach, E. and Parrott, R. (eds) (1995) *Designing Health Messages: Approaches from Communication Theory and Public Health Practice,* London: Sage.

Manghani, S., Piper, A. and Simons, J. (2006) *Images: A Reader,* London: Sage.

Marchand, R. (1998) *Creating the Corporate Soul: The Rise of PR and Corporate Imagery in American Big Business,* Berkeley: University of California Press.

Marshall, P.D. (1997) *Celebrity and Power: Fame in Contemporary Culture,* Minneapolis: University of Minnesota Press.

Marriott, M. (2006) 'Dress sense', *PRWeek,* 16 June: 19.

Mattelart A. and Siegelaub, S. (1979) (eds), *Communication and Class Struggle,* New York: International General.

Meech, P. (1996) 'Corporate identity and corporate image', in L'Etang, J. and Pieczka, M. (eds), *Critical Perspectives in Public Relations,* London: International Thomson Business Press, pp. 65–81.

Meech, P. (2006) 'Corporate identity and corporate image', in L'Etang, J. and Pieczka, M. (eds), *Public Relations: Critical Debates and Contemporary Practice,* Mahwah, NJ: Lawrence Erlbaum Associates, pp. 389–404.

Mickey, T. (2003) *Deconstructing Public Relations: Public Relations Criticism,* Mahwah, NJ: Lawrence Erlbaum Assciates.

Miller, D. (1999) 'Mediating science: promotional strategies, media coverage, public being and decision making', in Scanlon, E., Whitelegg, E. and Yates, S. (eds), *Communicating Science Contents and Channels Reader 3,* London and New York: Routledge (in association with Open University), pp. 206–226.

Miller, D. and Dinan, W. (2000) 'The rise of the PR industry in Britain 1979–1998', *European Journal of Communication* 15(1): 5–35.

Miller, D. and Dinan, W. (2003) 'Global public relations and global capitalism', in Demers, D. (ed.), *Terrorism, Globalization and Mass Communication,* Washington, DC: Marquette Books, pp. 199–214.

Miller, D,; Kitzinger, J., William, K. and Beharrell, P. (1998) *The circuit of mass communication: media strategies, representation and audience reception in the AIDS crisis,* Glasgow Media Group, London: Sage.

Miller, G. (2002) 'On being persuaded: some basic distinctions', in Dillard, J.P. and Pfau, M. (eds), *The Persuasion Handbook: Development in Theory and Practice,* London: Sage, pp. 3–16.

Millerson, G. (1964) *The qualifying association: a study in professionalisation,* London: Routledge and Kegan Paul.

Moingeon, B. and Soenen, G. (eds) (2002) *Corporate and Organizational Identities: Integrating Strategy, Communication and Organizational Perspectives*, London: Routledge.

Moloney, K. (2006) *Rethinking Public Relations? the spin and the substance* (2nd edition), London: Routledge.

Morgan, G. (1989) *Creative organization theory*, London: Sage.

Morgan, G. (1990) *Organizations in society*, London: Macmillan.

Morgan, G. (1992) *Imaginization*, London: Sage.

Morgan, G. (1992) 'Marketing discourse and practice towards a critical analysis', in Alvesson, M. and Willmott, H. (eds), *Critical Management Studies*, London: Sage, pp. 136–158.

Morgan, G. (1993) *Imaginization: The Art of Creative Management*, London: Sage.

Morgan, G. (2006) *Images of Organization*, London: Sage.

Morrish, J. (2003) *Magazine Editing: How to Develop and Manage a Successful Publication* (2nd edition), London: Routledge.

Moss, D., MacManus, T. and Vercic, D. (eds) (1997) *Public Relations Research: An International Perspective*, London: International Thomson Business Press.

Moss, D., Warnaby, G. and Newman, A. (2000) 'Public relations practitioner role enactment at the senior management level within UK companies', *Journal of Public Relations Research*, 12(4): 277–307.

Motion, J. and Leitch, S. (1996) 'A discursive perspective from New Zealand: another world view', *Public Relations Review*, 22: 297–309.

Murcott, A. (ed.) (1998) *The Nation's Diet: The Social Science of Food Choice*, London: Longman.

Murphy, A. (2003) 'A study of the growth of the public relations industry in Ireland, with a focus on ethics 1900–2003'. Dissertation submitted as part fulfilment of the MSc in Public Relations, University of Stirling, Scotland.

Murray, K. and White, J. (2005) 'CEOs' views on reputation management', *Journal of Communication Management*, 9(4): 348–358.

Muruli, G.M. (2001) 'Public relations in Kenya: the missing link 1939–71'. Dissertation submitted as part fulfilment of the MSc in Public Relations, University of Stirling, Scotland.

Myer, B. and Moors, A. (eds) (2006) *Religion, media and the public sphere*, Bloomington and Indianapolis: Indiana University Press.

Nettleton, S. (2006) *The Sociology of Health and Illness*, Cambridge: Polity Press.

Neuendorf, K. (2002) *The Content Analysis Guidebook*, Thousand Oaks, CA: Sage.

Nixon, S. (2003) *Advertising Cultures*, London: Sage.

Nixon, S. and du Gay, P. (2002) 'Who needs cultural intermediaries?', *Cultural Studies*, 16(4): 495–500.

Noble, G. and Camit, M. (2005) 'Social marketing communication is a multicultural environment: practical issues and theoretical contributions form cross-cultural marketing', web journal *PRism*, 3(2), http://praxis.massey.ac.uk (accessed 15 December 2006).

Noelle-Neumann, E. (1993) *The Spiral of Silence* (2nd edition), Chicago: University of Chicago Press.

Oeckle, A. (1964) *Handbuch der PR: theorie und praxis der offentlichkeitsarbeit in Deutschland und der Welt*, Munchen: Suddeentscher Verlag.

Olsen, B. (2001) 'Media effects for public relations practice', in Heath, R. (ed.), *Handbook of Public Relations*, London: Sage, pp. 269–278.

O'Sullivan, T. (1994) 'Functionalism/structural functionalism' In O'Sullivan T., Hartley, J., Saunders, D., Montgomery, M. and Fiske, J. (eds), *Key Concepts in Communication and Cultural Studies*, London: Routledge.

O'Sullivan, T. (1994) 'Profession', in O'Sullivan, T., Hartley, J., Saunders, D., Montgomery, M. and Fiske, J. (eds), *Key Concepts in Communication and Cultural Studies*, London: Routledge, pp. 244–246.

Park, R.E. (1972) *The Crowd, the Public and Other Essays*, Chicago: University of Chicago Press.

Parsons, P. (2004) *Ethics in Public Relations: A Guide to Best Practice*, London: Kogan Page, with Chartered Institute of Public Relations.

Parvatiyar, A. and Sheth, J. (2000) 'The domain and conceptual foundations of relationship marketing', in Sheth, J. and Parvatiyar, A. (eds), *Handbook of Relationship Marketing*, London: Sage, pp. 3–38.

Paul, R. and Elder, L. (2004) *The Miniature Guide to Critical Thinking: Concepts and Tools*, Foundation for Critical Thinking.

Pearson, R. (1998, May) 'Beyond ethical relativism in public relations: co-orientation, rules and the idea of communication symmetry'. Paper presented to the annual conference of the International Communication Association.

Pearson, R. (1990) 'Ethical values or strategic values? Two faces of systems theory in public relations', in Grunig, J. and Grunig, L. (eds), *Public Relations Research Annual* (Vol. 2), Mahwah, NJ: Lawrence Erlbaum Associates, pp. 219–235.

Peberdy, A. (2000) 'Evaluating health promotion' in Katz, J., Peberdy, A., Douglas, J. (eds), *Promoting health, knowledge and practice*, (2nd edition) Basingstoke: Palgrave Macmillan: 275–325.

Peberdy, A. (2002) 'Evaluating community action' in Jones, L., Sidell, M., and Douglas, J. (eds), *The challenge of promoting health exploration and action*, Basingstoke: Macmillan: 85–100.

Peck, S. (1978) *The Road Less Travelled*, New York: Simon and Schuster.

Peters, T. and Waterman, R. (1982) *In search of excellence: lessons from America's best run companies*, New York: Harper and Rowe.

Pettigrew, A. (2000) 'Foreword', in Ashkanasy, N., Wilderom, C. and Peterson, M. (eds), *Handbook of Organizational Culture and Climate*, London: Sage, pp. xiii–xvi.

Pettigrew, A., Thomas, H. and Whittington, R. (eds) (2002a) *Handbook of Strategy and Management*, London: Sage.

Pettigrew, A., Thomas, H. and Whittington, R. (2002) 'Strategic management: the strengths and limitations of a field', in Pettigrew, A., Thomas, H. and Whittington, R. (eds), *Handbook of Strategy and Management*, London: Sage. pp. 3–30.

Pieczka, M. (1996a) 'Public opinion and public relations', in L'Etang, J. and Pieczka, M. (eds), *Critical Perspectives on Public Relations*, London: International Thomson Business Press, pp. 54–65.

Pieczka, M. (1996b) 'Paradigms systems theory and public relations', in L'Etang, J. and Pieczka, M. (eds), *Critical Perspectives in Public Relations*, London: International Thomson Business Press, pp. 124–156.

Pieczka, M. (1996) 'Organizational culture, pop management and communication'. Conference paper presented at the 1st International Conference on Marketing and Corporate Communication, University of Keele, April.

Pieczka, M. (2006a) 'Public relations expertise in practice', in L'Etang, J. and Pieczka, M. (eds), *Public Relations: Critical Debates and Contemporary Practice*, Mahwah, NJ: Lawrence Erlbaum Associates, pp. 279–302.

Pieczka, M. (2006b) '"Chemistry" and the public relations industry: an exploration of the concept of jurisdiction and issues arising', in L'Etang, J. and Pieczka, M. (eds), *Public Relations: Critical Debates and Contemporary Practice*, Mahwah, NJ: Lawrence Erlbaum Associates, pp. 303–330.

Pieczka, M. (2006c) 'Paradigms, systems theory and public relations', in L'Etang, J. and Pieczka, M. (eds), *Public Relations: Critical Debates and Contemporary Practice*, Mahwah, NJ: Lawrence Erlbaum Associates, pp. 331–358.

Pieczka, M. (2006c) 'Editorial', *Journal of Communication Management*, 10(4): 328–329.

Pieczka, M. (2006d) 'Public opinion and public relations', in L'Etang, J. and Pieczka, M. (eds), *Public Relations: Critical Debates and Contemporary Practice*, Mahwah, NJ: Lawrence Erlbaum Associates, pp. 423–433.

Pieczka, M. and L'Etang, J. (2001) 'Public relations and the question of professionalism', in Heath, R. (ed.), *Handbook of Public Relations*, London: Sage, pp. 223–236.

Pimlott, J.A.R. (1951) *Public Relations and American Democracy*, Princeton, NJ: Princeton University Press.

Pirie, P. (1999) 'Evaluating community health promotion programmes: basic questions and approaches', in Bracht, N. (ed.), *Health promotion at the community level*, Thousand Oaks, Sage: 127–135.

Pirsig, R.M. (1989) *Zen and the art of motorcycle maintenance: an enquiry into values*, Vintage: Black Swan.

Prilletensky, I. and Nelson, G. (2002) *Doing Psychology Critically: Making a Difference in Diverse Settings*, Basingstoke: Palgrave Macmillan.

Pringle, R. (1988) *Secretaries Talk: Sexuality, Power and Work*, London: Verso.

Puchan, H. (2003) 'Theorising globalization and tourism', *International Communications and Media*, module 5.2. MSc. Public Relations, University of Stirling.

Puchan, H. (2006) 'An intellectual history of German public relations', in L'Etang, J. and Pieczka, M. (eds), *Public Relations: Critical Debates and Contemporary Practice*, Mahwah, NJ: Lawrence Erlbaum Associates, pp. 111–122.

Pugh, D. and Hickson, D. (1989) *Writers on Organizations*, London: Penguin.

Quainton, D. (2006) 'The Barmy Army seeks PR advice' *PRWeek*, 21 July: 1.

Rabinow, P. (ed.) (1984) *The Foucault Reader: An Introduction to Foucault's Thought*, London: Penguin.

Rakow, L. (1989) 'Information on power toward a critical theory of information campaigns', in Salmon, C. (ed.), *Information campaigns balancing social values and social change*, Newbury Park: Sage: 164–184.

Rayner, G. (2002) 'Building a UK public health movement: a phoenix from the ashes?', in Adams, L., Amos, M., Munro, J. (eds), *Promoting health politics and practice*, London: Sage, 20–25.

Rein, I., Kotler, P., Hasskin, M. and Stoller, M. (2006) *High visibility: transforming your personal and professional brand*, (3rd edition), New York: McGraw-Hill.

Rice, R.E. and Atkin, C.K. (eds) (1989) *Public Communication Campaigns* (2nd edition), London: Sage.

Rice, R.E. and Foote, D.R. (2001) 'A systems-based evaluation planning model for health communication campaigns in developing countries', in Rice, R.E. and Atkin, C. K. (eds).

Rice, R.E. and Atkin, C.K. (eds) (2001) *Public Communication Campaigns* (3rd edition), London: Sage.

Richards, B. (2004) 'Terrorism and public relations' *Public Relations Review*, 30(2): 169–176.

Riffe, D., Lacy, S. and Fico, F. (1998) *Analyzing Media Messages: Using Quantitative Content Analysis in Research*, Mahwah, NJ: Lawrence Erlbaum Associates.

Ritzer, G. (2000) *The McDonaldization of Society*, Thousand Oaks, CA: Pine Forge Press.

Ritzer, G. (2002) *McDonaldization: The Reader,* Thousand Oaks, CA: Pine Forge Press.

Robbins, J.R. (1958) 'The public affairs officer', in Daugherty, W. with Janowitz, M. (eds), *A Psychological Warfare Casebook*, Baltimore, MD: Johns Hopkins University Press.

Robertson, S. (2006) 'Nesta poaches Salt to champion sciences', *PRWeek*, 9 June: 6.

Rogers, D. (2007) 'Chelsea FC listens to its brand advisers', *PRWeek*, 19 January: 19.

Rogers, E. and Singhal, A. (1990) 'The academic perspective'. Afterword in Atkin, C. and Wallack, L. (eds), *Mass Communications and Public Health*, Newbury park: Sage.

Rojek, C. (2001) *Celebrity*, London: Reaktion.

Rosenfeld, P., Giacalone, R. and Riordan, C. (1995) *Impression Management in Organizations: Theory, Measurement, Practice*, London: Routledge.

Rosenfeld, R.H. and Wilson, D.L. (1999) *Managing Organizations*, London: McGraw Hill.

Rosenfeld, P., Giacalone, R. and Riordan, C. (2002) *Impression Management: Building and Enhancing Reputations at Work*, London: Thomson Learning.

Roth, I. (ed.) (1990) *Introduction to Psychology*, Mahwah, NJ: Lawrence Erlbaum Associates with the Open University.

Ruby, J. (1976) 'Anthropology and film', *Quarterly Review of Film Studies*, 1(4): 436–445.

Ruggiero, V.R. (1996a) *A Guide to Sociological Thinking*, London: Sage.

Ruggiero, V.R. (1996b) *Becoming a Critical Thinker*, Boston, MA: Houghton.

Russell, M. (2007) 'An education model to prepare for excellence in public relations: A case study of the Syracuse University Limited Residency/Distance Learning Master's Program in Communication Management', in Toth, E. (ed.), *The future of excellence in public relations and communications management: challenges for the next generation*, Mahwah: New Jersey, Lawrence Erlbaum Associates: 601–616.

Rycroft, C. (1972) *A Critical Dictionary of Psychoanalysis*, London: Penguin.

Sahlin-Andersson, K. and Engwall L. (eds) (2002) *The Expansion of Management Knowledge*, Stanford: Stanford, CA: University Press.

Salancik, G.R. and Meindle, J. (1984) 'Corporate attribution as strategic illusions of management control', *Administrative Science Quarterly*, 29: 238–254 (also cited in Fombrun, C. and Rindova, (2000) 'The road to transparency: reputation management at Royal Dutch/Shell', in Schultz, M., Hatch, M.J. and Larsen, M.H. (eds), *The Expressive Organization*, Oxford: Oxford University Press, pp. 77–96).

Salmon, C.T. (ed.) (1989) *Information Campaigns: Balancing Social Values and Social Change*, London: Sage.

Salmon, C.T. and Murray-Johnson, L. (2003) 'Communication campaigns, effectiveness: critical distinctions', in Rice, R.E. and Atking, C.K. (eds), *Public communication campaigns*, Thousand Oaks: Sage: 168–180.

Sandman, P. (1999) 'Mass Media and environmental risk – seven principles', in Bate, R. *What risk? Science, politics and public health*, Butterworth Heinemann.

Scanlon, E., Whitelegg, E. and Yates, S. (eds) (1999) *Communicating Science Contents and Channels Reader 3*, London and New York: Routledge (with Open University).

Schein, E. (2000) 'Sense and nonsense about culture and climate', in Ashkanasy, N., Wilderom, C. and Peterson, M. (eds), *Handbook of Organizational Culture and Climate*, London: Sage, pp. xxii–xxx.

Schlesinger, P. (1992) 'From production to propaganda?', in Scannell, P., Schlesinger, P. and Sparks, C. (eds), *Culture and Power: A Media, Culture and Society Reader*, London: Sage, pp. 293–316.

Schlesinger, P. (2006) 'Is there a crisis in British journalism?', *Media, Culture and Society*, 28(2): 299–307.

Schlesinger, P., Miller, D. and Dinan, W. (2001) *Open Scotland? Journalists, Spin Doctors and Lobbyists*, Edinburgh: Polygon.

Schultz, M., Hatch, M.J. and Larsen, M.H. (eds) (2000) *The Expressive Organization*, Oxford: Oxford: University Press.

Scriven, A. and Orme, J. (eds) (2001) *Health Promotion: Professional Perspectives* (2nd edition), Basingstoke: Palgrave.

Seale, C. (2002) *Media and Health*, London: Sage.

Seedhouse, D. (2004) *Health Promotion: Philosophy, Prejudice and Practice* (2nd edition), Chichester: John Wiley and Sons.

Senge, P. (1990) *The Fifth Discipline: The Art and Practice of the Learning Organization*, New York: Doubleday.

Sharpe, M. and Pritchard, B. (2004) 'The historical empowerment of public opinion and its relationship to the emergence of public relations as a profession', in Tilson, D.J. and Alozie, E.C. (eds), *Toward the Common Good: Perspectives in International Public Relations*, Boston, MA: Pearson, pp. 14–36.

Sheth, J. (2000) 'Relationship marketing: paradigm shift or shaft?', in Sheth, J. and Parvatiyar, A. (eds), *Handbook of Relationship Marketing*, London: Sage, pp. 609–620.

Sheth, J. and Parvatiyar, A. (eds) (2000) *Handbook of Relationship Marketing*, London: Sage.

Shoemaker, P.J. (1991) *Gatekeeping: Communication Concepts 3*, Newbury Park, CA: Sage.

Showalter, A. and Fleisher, C. (2005) 'The tools and techniques of public affairs', in Harris, P. and Fleisher, C. (eds), *The Handbook of Public Affairs*, London: Sage, pp. 109–122.

Sidell, M., Jones, L., Katz, J., Peberdy, A. and Douglas, J. (eds) (2003) *Debates and Dilemmas in Promoting Health: A Reader*, Basingstoke: Macmillan.

Signitzer, B.H. and Coombs, T. (1992) 'Public relations and public diplomacy: conceptual convergences', *Public Relations Review*, 18(2): 137–149.

Signitzer, B.H. and Wamswer, C. (2006) 'Public diplomacy: a specific governmental public relations function', in Botan, C.H. and Hazleton, V. (eds), *Public Relations Theory II*, Mahwah, NJ: Lawrence Erlbaum Associates, pp. 435–464.

Smith, D. (2006) 'Crisis management – practice in search of a paradigm', in Smith, D. and Elliott, D. (eds), *Key Readings in Crisis Management: Systems and Structures for Prevention and Recovery*, London: Routledge, pp. 1–14.

Smith, G. (2005) 'A few good men: gender balance in the Western Australian public relations industry', web journal *PRism* http://praxis.massey.ac.nz (accessed 15 December 2006).

Smith, M. and Ferguson, D. (2001) 'Activism', in Heath, R. (ed.), *Handbook of Public Relations*, London: Sage, pp. 291–310.

Snyder, L.B. (2003) 'How effective are mediated health campaigns?' In Rice, R.E. and Atkin, C.K. (eds), *Public communication campaigns*, Thousand Oaks: Sage: 181–192.

Solomon, R. (1994) *Above the Bottom Line: An Introduction to Business Ethics*, Fort Worth, TX: Harcourt Brace.

Somerville, I. (2001) 'Business ethics, public relations and corporate social responsibility', in Theaker, A. (ed.), *The Public Relations Handbook*, London: Routledge, pp. 131–144.

Springston, J. and Lariscy, R.A. (2003) 'Health as profit: public relations in health communications', in Thompson, T., Dorsey, A., Miller, K. and Parrott, R. (eds), *Handbook of Health Communication*, Mahwah, NJ: Lawrence Erlbaum Associates, pp. 537–556.

Sriramesh, K. and Vercic, D. (2004) *The Global Public Relations Handbook: Theory, Research, and Practice*, Mahwah, NJ: Lawrence Erlbaum Associates.

Starck, K., and Kruckeberg, D. (2001) 'Public relations and community a reconstructed theory revisited', in Heath, R. (ed.), *Handbook of Public Relations*, Mahwah, New Jersey: Sage.

Stewart, L. (1988) 'Women in foundation and corporate PR', *Public Relations Review*, 14(3): 20–23.

Steyn, B. (2007) 'Contributions of public relations to organizational strategy formulation' in Toth, E. (ed.), *The future of excellence and communication management challenges for the next generation Festschrift*. Mahwah New Jersey: Lawrence Erlbaum Associates: 137–172.

Stroh, U. (2007) 'An alternative postmodern approach to corporate communication strategy' in Toth, E. (ed.), *The future of excellence and communication management: challenges for the next generation, Festschrift*. Mahwah, New Jersey: Lawrence Erlbaum Associates: 199–220.

Sung, M. (2007) 'Toward a model of scenario building from a public relations perspective' in Toth, E. (ed.), *The future of excellence and communication management challenges for the next generation, Festschrift*. Mahwah, New Jersey: Lawrence Erlbaum Associates: 173–198.

Sullivan, A. (1965) 'Toward a philosophy of public relations images', in Lerbinger, O. and Sullivan, A. (eds), *Information influence and communication: a reader in public relations*, New York: Basic Books: 240–249.

Surma, A. (2005) *Public and Professional Writing: Ethics, Imagination and Rhetoric*, Basingstoke: Palgrave Macmillan.

Surma, A. (2006a) 'The rhetoric of reputation: vision not visibility', web journal *PRism*, 4(1), http://praxis.massey.ac.nz/prism_on_line_journ.html (accessed 18 December 2006).

Surma, A. (2006b) 'Challenging unreliable narrators: writing and public relations', in L'Etang, J. and Pieczka, M. (eds), *Public Relations: Critical Debates and Contemporary Practice*, Mahwah, NJ: Lawrence Erlbaum Associates, pp. 41–60.

Szyszka, P. (2005) 'Social trust and functional transparency as key terms of an organizational PR approach'. Conference paper presented to International Communication Association, 26–30 May, New York.

Taylor, M. (2000) 'Towards a public relations approach to nation building', *Journal of Public Relations Research*, 12(2): 179–210.

Taylor, P.M. (1997) *Global Communications, International Affairs and the Media since 1945*, London: Routledge.

Tench, R. and Yeomans, L. (eds) (2006) *Exploring Public Relations*, Harlow: Prentice Hall.

Thompson, J. with Martin, F. (2005) *Strategic management awareness and change*, (5th edition), London: Thomson.

Tilley, E. (2005) 'What's in a name? Everything. The appropriateness of "public relations" needs further debate', web journal *PRism*, http://praxis.massey.ac.nz (accessed 12 December 2006).

Tilson, D.J. and Alozie, E.C. (eds) (2004) *Towards the Common Good: Perspectives in International Public Relations*, Boston, MA: Pearson.

Toledano, M. (2005) 'Public relations in Israel: the evolution of public relations as a profession in Israel's changing political, socio-cultural and economic environment'. Unpublished thesis, University of Paris 8, France.

Toledano, M. (2005) 'Challenging accounts: public relations and a tale of two revolutions', *Public Relations Review*, 31: 463–470.

Tompkins, P. and Wanca-Thibault, M. (2001) 'Organizational communication: prelude and prospects', in Jablin, F. and Putnam, L. (eds), *The New Handbook of Organizational Communication: Advances in Theory, Research and Methods*, London: Sage, pp. xvii–3.

Tones, K. (2001) 'Health promotion: the empowerment imperative', in Scriven, A. and Orme, J. (eds), *Health Promotion: Professional Perspectives* (2nd edition), Basingstoke: Palgrave Macmillan.

Toth, E. (2002) 'Postmodernism for modernist PR: the cash value and application of critical research in PR', *Public Relations Review*, 28(3): 243–250.

Toth, E. (2006) 'On the challenge of practice informed by theory', *Journal of Communication Management*, 10(1): 110–111.

Toth, E. and Aldoory, L. (2001) *The Gender Challenge to Media*, Cresshill, NJ: Hampton Press.

Toth, E. and Heath, R. (eds) (1992) *Rhetorical and Critical Approaches to Public Relations*, Mahwah, NJ: Lawrence Erlbaum Associates.

Tourish, D. and Hargie, O. (2004) *Key Issues in Organizational Communication*, London: Routledge.

Traverse-Healy, T. (1994) 'Public relations: rationale and methodology', Lecture No. 3:10 given to the MSc. in Public Relations while Visiting Professor.

Tulloch, J. and Lupton, D. (2003) *Risk and Everyday Life*, London: Sage.

Tunstall, J. (1964) *The Advertising Man in London Advertising Agencies*, London: Chapman and Hall.

Tunstall, J. (1983) *The Media in Britain*, London: Constable.

Turner, B.S. (1987) *Medical power and social knowledge*, London: Sage.

Turner, G. (2004) *Understanding Celebrity*, London: Sage.

Tye, L. (1998) *The Father of Spin: Edward L. Bernays and the Birth of Public Relations*, New York: Crown.

van Dijk, T. (ed.) (1997a) *Discourse as Social Interaction*, London: Sage.

van Dijk, T. (ed.) (1997b) *Discourse as Structure and Process*, London: Sage.

van Riel, C.B.M. and Fombrun, C.J. (2007) *Essentials of corporate communication*, Abingdon: Routledge.

van Ruler, B. (2005) 'Commentary: professionals are from Venus, scholars are from Mars', *Public Relations Review*, 31(2): 159–173.

van Ruler, B. and Vercic, D. (eds) (2004) *Public Relations and Communications Management in Europe*, Berlin: de Gruyter.

van Ruler, B., Vercic, D., Butschi, G. and Flodin, B. (2004) 'A first look for parameters of public relations in Europe', *Journal of Public Relations Research*, 16(1): 35–63.

van Slyke Turk, J. and Wright, D. (2007) 'Public relations knowledge and professionalism: challenges to educators and practitioners' in Toth, E. (ed.), *The future of excellence and communication management: challenges for the next generation*, Festschrift. Mahwah, New Jersey: Lawrence Erlbaum Associates: 571–588.

Vasquez, G. and Taylor, M. (2001) 'Research perspectives on "The public"', in Heath, R. (ed.), *Handbook of Public Relations*, London: Sage, pp. 139–154.

Vollmer, H.M. and Mills, D.L. (1996) *Professionalisation*, Englewood Cliffs: Prentice Hall.

Wallack, L. (1990a) 'Improving health communication: media advocacy and social marketing approaches' in Atkin, C. and Wallack, L. (eds), *Mass communications and public health*, Newbury park: Sage: 41–51.

Wallack, L. (1990b) 'Improving health promotion: media advocacy and social marketing approaches', in Atkin, C. and Wallack, L. (eds), *Mass communications and public health*, Newbury park: Sage: 147–163.

Wallack, L., Darfman, L., Jernigan, D. and Themba, M. (1993) *Media Advocacy and Public Health*, London: Sage.

Wallack, L, and Dorfman, L. (2001) 'Putting policy into health communication: the role of media advocacy' in Rice, R.E. and Atkin, C.K. (eds), *Public communication campaigns*, (3rd edition) Thousand Oaks: Sage: 389–402.

Wallop, H. (2006) 'Reputation gives high-glow finish', *The Daily Telegraph*, p.8.

Watson, P. (1978) *War on the Mind: The Military Uses and Abuses of Psychology*, London: Hutchinsons.

Weaver, K., Motion, J. and Roper, J. (2006) 'From propaganda to discourse (and back again): truth, power and public relations', in L'Etang, J. and Pieczka, M. (eds), *Public Relations: Critical Debates and Contemporary Practice*, Mahwah, NJ: Lawrence Erlbaum Associates, pp. 7–22.

Webster, F.E. (2002) 'The role of marketing and the firm', in Weitz, B.A. and Wensley, R. (eds), *Handbook of Marketing*, London: Sage, pp. 66–84.

Wehmeier, S. (2006) 'Dancers in the dark: the myth of rationality in pubic relations', *Public Relations Review*, 32(3): 213–220.

Weitz, B.A. and Wensley, R. (eds) (2002) *Handbook of Marketing*, London: Sage.

Werbner, D. (2006) 'Camden urges locals to utilise their vote' *PRWeek*, 30 June: 21.

Wernick, A. (1991) *Promotional Culture: Advertising Ideology and Symbolic Expression*, London: Sage.

West, R. (1963) *PR: The Fifth Estate*, London: Mayflower Books.

Wetherell, M., Taylor, S. and Yates, S. (2001a) *Discourse Theory and Practice*, London: Sage.

Wetherell, M., Taylor, S. and Yates, S. (2001b) *Discourse as Data*, London: Sage.

Wilson, J. (1996) *Understanding Journalism: A Guide to Issues*, London: Routledge.

Wilson, P.A. (1937) 'Public relations departments', in Plant, A. (ed.) *Some Modern Business Problems*, London: Longmans, pp. 132–133.

Windahl, S. and Signitzer, B., with Olsen, J.T. (1992) *Using Communication Theory: An Introduction to Planned Communication*, London: Sage.

W.M. Kellogg Foundation (2005) *From Ideas to Action*, Peoria, IL: W.M. Kellogg Foundation.

Wolf, W.R. (1974) *The Basic Barnard: An Introduction to Chester I. Barnard and His Theories of Organization and Management*, Ithaca, NY: Cornell University Press.

Woodall, T. and Constantine, S. (2003) *What Not to Wear for Every Occasion*, London: Weidenfeld & Nicolson.

Woodward, K. (ed.) (1997) *Identity and Difference*, London: Sage (with Open University).

Wright, J. (1991) *Terrorist Propaganda: The Red Army Faction and the Provisional IRA 1968–86*, Basingstoke: Macmillan.

Wright, S. (ed.) (1994a) *Anthropology of Organizations*, London: Routledge.

Wright, S. (1994b) '"Culture" in anthropology and organizational studies', in Wright, S. (ed.), *Anthropology of Organizations*, London: Routledge. pp. 1–34.

Zaner, R. and Engelhardt, H. (1973) *The Structures of the Lifeworld*, Evanston, IL: North Western University Press.

Zelitzer, B. (2005) 'The culture of journalism', in Curran, J. and Gurevich, M. (eds), *Mass Media and Society* (4th edition), London: Hodder Arnold, pp. 198–214.

Index